THE CHURCH AS SALT AND LIGHT

African Christian Studies Series (AFRICS)

This series will make available significant works in the field of African Christian studies, taking into account the many forms of Christianity across the whole continent of Africa. African Christian studies is defined here as any scholarship that relates to themes and issues on the history, nature, identity, character, and place of African Christianity in world Christianity. It also refers to topics that address the continuing search for abundant life for Africans through multiple appeals to African religions and African Christianity in a challenging social context. The books in this series are expected to make significant contributions in historicizing trends in African Christian studies, while shifting the contemporary discourse in these areas from narrow theological concerns to a broader inter-disciplinary engagement with African religio-cultural traditions and Africa's challenging social context.

The series will cater to scholarly and educational texts in the areas of religious studies, theology, mission studies, biblical studies, philosophy, social justice, and other diverse issues current in African Christianity. We define these studies broadly and specifically as primarily focused on new voices, fresh perspectives, new approaches, and historical and cultural analyses that are emerging because of the significant place of African Christianity and African religio-cultural traditions in world Christianity. The series intends to continually fill a gap in African scholarship, especially in the areas of social analysis in African Christian studies, African philosophies, new biblical and narrative hermeneutical approaches to African theologies, and the challenges facing African women in today's Africa and within African Christianity. Other diverse themes in African Traditional Religions; African ecology; African ecclesiology; inter-cultural, inter-ethnic, and inter-religious dialogue; ecumenism; creative inculturation; African theologies of development, reconciliation, globalization, and poverty reduction will also be covered in this series.

SERIES EDITORS

Dr Stan Chu Ilo (St Michael's College, University of Toronto)
Dr Philomena Njeri Mwaura (Kenyatta University, Nairobi, Kenya)
Dr Afe Adogame (University of Edinburgh)

"The authors provide us with a biblical, theological, and integrated social analysis and some concrete pastoral proposals for a post-synodal African Church. This is a prophetic work with depth, and a refreshing attempt at a constructive and creative transformational praxis for a Church that truly and fully offers abundant life to all Africans in their very challenging social context. These young African scholars have offered the African continent and the universal church an important contribution to reimaging the African church for today and for tomorrow."
—Bishop John Okoye, STD
 Professor of Biblical Theology
 Spiritan International School of Theology, Enugu, Nigeria

"This book serves as a poignant reminder that the mission and identity of the church in Africa or the African Church remain open to a rich variety of theological interpretations, imaginations, and applications. The Church as Salt and Light initiates an African theology of the Church that successfully connects ecclesiology with Christology to produce a rich flourish of possibilities for the Church in Africa. No longer will the Church imagined in this book be considered a merely abstract theological construct; it is a Church of the people, by the people, and for the people. Poised between the historic Des prêtres noirs s'interrogent and the Second African Synod, The Church as Salt and Light recalls and applies Vatican II's maxim Ecclesia semper reformanda in ways that are challenging, stimulating, and refreshing. With this book, we can confidently affirm that postcolonial theology has come of age-a new world-Church is possible!"
—Agbonkhianmeghe E. Orobator, SJ
 Professor of Contextual Theology and Ecclesiology
 Hekima College, Nairobi, Kenya

"This book comes at a very crucial moment in the life of all Africans. Africa is summoned to reposition herself in the New World Order and there is no way this can be done than for African Scholars to help reflect on this reality and identify obstacles that hinder the fullness of life in Africa and how they can be overcome. This work is a bold demonstration of the resilience of Africans to define themselves and to swim above the tide. The authors succinctly post signposts of renewal and transformation for God's people in Africa in the midst of the present prophets of doom. This book is, therefore, a must-read for all who wish Africa well and all Africans who wish to work within the church for a better and a hopeful Africa."

—Benedict Ssettuuma Jr.
  Dean of Studies
  National Major Seminary Ggaba, Kampala, Uganda

The Church as Salt and Light

Path to an African Ecclesiology
of Abundant Life

∽

EDITED BY
Stan Chu Ilo
Joseph Ogbonnaya
Alex Ojacor

☙PICKWICK *Publications* · Eugene, Oregon

THE CHURCH AS SALT AND LIGHT
Path to an African Ecclesiology of Abandant Life

African Christian Studies Series 1

Copyright © 2011 Wipf and Stock. All rights reserved. Except for brief quotations in critical publications or reviews, no part of this book may be reproduced in any manner without prior written permission from the publisher. Write: Permissions, Wipf and Stock Publishers, 199 W. 8th Ave., Suite 3, Eugene, OR 97401.

Pickwick Publications
A Division of Wipf and Stock Publishers
199 W. 8th Ave., Suite 3
Eugene, OR 97401

www.wipfandstock.com

ISBN 13: 978-1-61097-100-3

Cataloging-in-Publication data:

The church as salt and light : path to an African ecclesiology of abundant life / edited by Stan Chu Ilo, Joseph Ogbonnaya, and Alex Ojacor.

African Christian Studies Series 1.

xxii + 170 p. ; 23 cm. Includes bibliographical references.

ISBN 13: 978-1-61097-100-3

1. Social problems—Africa. 2. Church and social problems—Africa. I. Ilo, Stan Chu. II. Title. III. Series.

BL2462.5 I46 2011

Manufactured in the U.S.A.

This work is dedicated to the following African Theologians whose pioneering works have continued to inspire creativity in African Christianity: Vincent Mulago (Gwa Cikala Musharhamina); Charles Nyamiti; Mercy Amba Oduyoye; Ogbu U. Kalu (1942–2009); Kwame Bediako (1945–2008); Engelbert Mveng (1930–1995).

Contents

Foreword by Agbonkhianmeghe E. Orobator, SJ · xi

Introduction · xiii

1. Beginning Afresh with Christ in the Search for Abundant Life in Africa—*Stan Chu Ilo* · 1

2. The Church in Africa and the Search for Integral and Sustainable Development of Africa: Toward a Socio-Economic and Politically Responsive Church—*Emeka Xris Obiezu* · 34

3. The Church in Africa: Salt of the Earth?—*Joseph Ogbonnaya* · 65

4. The Church in Africa and the Search for Abundant Life: Signposts for Renewal and Transformation of God's People in Africa —*Alex Ojacor* · 88

5. Globalization and the African Woman: A Socio-Cultural Analysis of the Effect of the Information and Communication Technology (ICT) on Women— *Bosco Ebere Amakwe* · 99

6. New Evangelization in Africa: Learning from the Culture of Love in the Early Church—*Bekeh Ukelina Utietiang* · 130

Conclusion · 149

Bibliography · 157

Contributors · 169

Foreword

I HAVE READ THE TEXT with keen interest and, I must admit, with a good deal of pleasure as well. In my work in theological scholarship, only rarely do texts produced by ecclesio-centric scholars from our part of the world generate sustained interest and pleasure *at the same time.*

The audacity with which the contributors take up the task of reflecting on the theological self-understanding of the Church is quite remarkable. This book serves as a poignant reminder that the mission and identity of the church in Africa or the African Church remain open to a rich variety of theological interpretations, imaginations, and applications. *The church as Salt and Light* initiates an African theology of the Church that successfully connects ecclesiology with Christology to produce a rich flourish of possibilities for the church in Africa. No longer will the church imagined in this book be considered a merely abstract theological construct; it is a Church *of* the people, *by* the people, and *for* the people. Poised between the historic *Des prêtres noirs s'interrogent* and the Second African Synod, *The Church as Salt and Light* recalls and applies Vatican II's maxim *Ecclesia semper reformanda* in ways that are challenging, stimulating, and refreshing. With this book, we can confidently affirm that postcolonial theology has come of age—a new world-Church is possible!

A personal comment will be in order. In an age where the laity is rightly recognized as critical to the theological self-understanding of the church, and gender balance recalls the Church to its identity and mission of wholeness, the predominance of clergy-contributors is something to be addressed—and, perhaps, corrected—in subsequent editions.

Foreword

I offer my sincere congratulations to the editors and authors on the publication of *The church as Salt and Light*.

—Agbonkhianmeghe E. Orobator, SJ

Author of *Theology Brewed in an African Pot*,[1] and *From Crisis to Kairos: The Mission of the church in the Time of HIV/AIDS, Refugees and Poverty*.[2]

---

1. Maryknoll, NY: Orbis, 2008.
2. Nairobi: Paulines Africa, 2005.

Introduction

IN 1956, A GROUP OF priests from Africa and the Caribbean studying in France published a book, *Des Prêtres Noirs S'Interrogent* (*Black Priests Question Themselves*), in which they raised important questions and made suggestions on how the Christian faith could address the African agenda and be at home with African culture. This work is often regarded by many as the beginning of systematic theology in the Catholic Church in Africa. While many will argue that systematic theology has been going on in Africa going back to the first hundred years of the Christian faith (see for instance, Thomas C. Oden's work, *How Africa Shaped the Christian Mind: Rediscovering the African Seedbed of Western Christianity*), one cannot ignore the pioneering work of these priests. They offered in this collection of essays some strong arguments that African cultural values possess a character of their own, and offered a valid basis for constructing vigorous Christian communities in Africa.

These ancestors of ours saw the continent in trouble and became, as Adrian Hastings commented, the "young Turks" with a new manifesto for African renaissance. At the time of their writing this book, most of the churches in Africa were run by expatriates; the "*prêtres noirs*" thus felt that the problems of the churches of Africa would be better handled when the indigenous clergy and religious took over from their Western compatriots. The "*prêtres noirs*" had argued that the "White" missionaries were westernizing the African churches without sensitivity to cultural pluralism and local social context. They were convinced that the rediscovery of the agency of the Africans in the Christian mission would re-image and re-contextualize the content, form, and goals of theology and impact significantly on the directions of the churches in Africa.

Introduction

We do not know what the judgment of the "*prêtres noirs*" would be if they saw the situation of the churches in Africa and the condition of African Christians and Africans in general under Africans' watch. These brave priests were like the brave nationalists of the 1950s who fought for independence for African countries, firm in the belief that Africans are best suited to lead Africa. The judgment on how Africans have led Africa in both political and Christian institutions is part of the conversation we introduce in this work.

Every generation of Christians must reach into their cultural and historical conditions, inner resources, and the inexhaustible gift of the Christian faith, in order to discover for themselves what the Spirit is saying for the re-creation of the human spirit of that generation. Every generation must be accountable to the Lord and to the men and women of their times, as well as the generations to come, about what fruits and gifts they have brought through the Christian faith and into the Christian faith (*Chaque generation puissant reçevoir sa proprie impulsion et sa kinesis de creation*—Chinua Achebe).

In his preface to the 50th anniversary revised and updated edition of this pioneering work, Leonard Santedi Kinkupu pointed out that it was significant because it called African theologians and Christians to a more historically minded interpretation of the Christian movement. It was a work that was contextual in the sense that it showed that the locus of divine revelation was the social context of the people and that an analysis of culture must be an essential part of African theology. It was, above all, a work that was relevant to the people because it addressed the African condition and invited Africans—especially priests, religious, and Christian leaders—to a more critical self-understanding in the light of the condition of African Christians. Thus, this work set an agenda for African theology that continues to evolve even in our times. However, it was an agenda that was expected not to be dominated by the dogmatic debates, denominational battles, and questions about the structure of power and authority in the Church that have exhausted the inner creativity of many Western churches.

The 50th anniversary celebration of the publication of this book and the emergence of Catholic theology in Africa was held at the Catholic University of West Africa (French Abidjan) in 2007. It was the consensus of the African theological community at that gathering that the task of African theologians now is how to use the vibrant Christian imagination of African Christian consciousness to create a new African ecclesiology that will bring abundant life to our suffering people. What are the new paths that are opened to African churches today for helping to realize the design of God's kingdom for the people of Africa? How does the mission of the Church in Africa reflect God's dream for Africa? How can the Church be an oasis of hope in a continent long adrift from the global radar of development but remembered more for her persistent crises than for her inner riches and strength?

The search for abundant life, for peaceful and prosperous societies, has been at the center of African life and religious and social organizations as well as political and communal networks. Prior to the advent of Christianity and Western intervention in Africa, various African peoples have ordered their societies through a catena of religious frameworks. This was because a religious imagination was the *norma normata* of a truly African worldview. What today is called African Traditional religions permeated the life and meaning-making structure of African peoples. African Tradition as such had a common similarity with the Christian faith in terms of the goal of religion (abundant life) despite many differences in creed, legal code, ritual processes, and cultic norms and practices. If Christianity positively impacted European civilization, it makes sense to ask how it is impacting African civilization in our challenging times.

Aware of the pluralistic nature both of Christianity and of African societies and the place of the Church as the center for the articulation, celebration, and transmission of the Christian message, the contributors in the volume ask these fundamental questions: How is the Christian message to be communicated so as to enable African Christians to bear witness to the Good News in every aspect of their lives? What is the face of Jesus in African Christianity? Are there some influences on African christological symbols based on the Hellenistic construct upon which Western Christianity was spread in Africa? How can we evaluate the mission of the Church in Africa among African Christians who enthusiastically embrace and celebrate their Christian faith? In other words, what positive imprint does Christianity leave on the lives and societies of African Christians? Is their moral life any better or different from that of their non-Christian African brothers and sisters with whom they live and work in their societies? Are they the salt and light Jesus Christ envisions Christians to be? Does the Christian message have the potential of affecting African civilization positively, as it once did in Europe and other continents that have embraced Christianity?

The authors of this volume are driven by an evangelical passion and love for Africa, the Church, the gospel, and the Christian movement. We wish to follow in the glorious footsteps of our ancestors, the "*prêtres noirs*" in making some proposals on the path that is opened to the Church in Africa in the search for abundant life, love, peace, solidarity, communion, and a sense of shared destiny.

The contributors to this volume are all at the cutting edge of theological formulation in their diverse studies. Like the "*prêtres noirs*," most of them are studying or have studied in North America or Europe, and are working in or involved at different levels of church life and academic commitment in Africa, North America, and Europe. All the contributors to this volume were born after the decolonization of Africa and the beginning of the indigenization of African churches in the Roman Catholic tradition. Most of them were evangelized by local priests and religious, unlike the "*prêtres noirs*," who were all evangelized by Western missionaries. All the contributors to this volume share a common desire for a new kind of church in Africa, and a common hope that the resurgence of the Christian faith in Africa represents a third wave for global Christianity that carries immense hope for the achievement of abundant life for Africans.

This work is significant in many ways. In the first place, it is not only descriptive and explanatory; it is rooted on strong quantitative and qualitative approaches needed for a critical study of African history. The authors have direct access to the data of the Faith at the grassroots, reified in our own experience of the Faith in action (or inaction) and our studies of African history in general and African Christian history and doctrine in particular. In addition, the essays are grounded in biblical theology, admitting multiple frames of reference and integrating diverse hermeneutical keys in order to proceed systematically in engaging the data of the Faith both from the point of view of historical and dogmatic analyses, analysis of African Christian experience, and African condition in general, and the perspective of wider concerns of global Christianity.

The essays are designed to be prophetic and personal, concerned more with proposing concrete theological and realistic pastoral recommendations for the Church in Africa than in simply enunciating dogmatic and doctrinal truths or validating theological positions through

Introduction

proof-texting from magisterial or dogmatic documents. As young African clerics and religious, we are troubled about the state of the Church in Africa and the conditions of our African brothers and sisters. We are also concerned about the future of the Christian faith in Africa. We pray for and wish to work with our lay brothers and sisters, as equal partners and co-disciples of the Lord, in the search for how to improve the practice of the Christian faith through an assessment of its practice.

Theologically, we envision this work as a contribution to the long-standing debate on the meaning, content, and goal of African ecclesiology. It is also our own modest answer to the question raised by Pope Paul VI at the end of the Second Vatican Council: "Church, who do you say that you are?" This work is also inspired by the theme of the Second Synod on the Church in Africa, which defines the identity of the Church in Africa as salt and light. The Church can become an instrument for bringing about reconciliation, justice, and peace to the African continent by showing in her identity, ecclesial life and mission that she is the source, and agency for abundant life for God's people in this beautiful continent. Abundant life is understood here as the flourishing of the human and cultural life of Africans which leads to human fulfillment and the actualization of the gifts of God to the land and peoples of Africa. It is also conceived as the realization of the temporal and ultimate purpose of life for all people in this continent, and the promotion of sustainable life for nature and the environment as well. The transformative theological praxis for realizing this goal is presented in these essays using tools of critical history, biblical and theological analysis as well as socio-cultural engagement with African social context in its beauty and ambiguities. These essays are concerned with theologically articulating a better future for Africa through a critical engagement with the African social context, the life and witnessing of the Church in Africa, and through an appeal to the resurgent and buoyant spiritual momentum within African Christianity.

The Church in Africa faces serious challenges that reflect Africa's troubling social context. These challenges we project in these essays are unique to Africa and require a unique approach. The self-identity of the Church in Africa—our way of "being Church" in Africa—must give a Christian response to meeting these challenges and will have strong implications for theological, liturgical, canonical, and pastoral practices in African Christianity.

Introduction

In chapter 1, Stan Chu Ilo, develops an African theology of abundant life through a thoroughgoing exegetical and biblical Christology, using the Gospels of John and Mark. African theologies, he argues, should be based on a sound biblical theology, a critical understanding of Christian history and doctrines, a cultural hermeneutics of the christological symbols employed in the theologies of Christ in African Christianity, and a hermeneutical phenomenological immersion in African social and religious contexts. The credibility of the churches in Africa, he argues, depends on who the churches say, by their inner life and external acts, that Christ is.

In other words, how does the glory of Christ shine forth in the life of the Church? How does Christ illumine the structures and pastoral practices of the Church, and how have the gospel values become the concrete norm for the life of the churches and the lives of African Christians? In a concrete sense, how have the gospel values and the life of Christ shaped the lives of the Christians and the societies in which they inhabit, and how does this reality empower African Christians to work with other members of their communities in building a better society where the abundant life is available to everyone?

In chapter 2, Emeka Xris Obiezu attempts a response to the most frequent question the Church in Africa struggles with each time it is confronted with the reality of the enormous sufferings beleaguering the African continent: *What must we do?* This work takes for granted that the type of compassion that responds effectively to African situations must transcend the traditional understanding of mere individual instance and private charity to include socioeconomic and politico-moral concerns and actions. It thus seeks on one hand to explore the ways the Church can demonstrate its commitment to this new dimensions of compassion, an opportunity it finds in the ongoing discussion on African development. On the other hand, it seeks, within the context of *Ecclesia in Africa*, a hermeneutical tool for such participation. It identifies this tool in the metaphor of "family of God's people," used by the document to describe the Church in Africa.

Hence, the whole work is committed to demonstrating through critical analysis, how this metaphor, "Church as the family of God," can, instead of detracting, enrich, reconstruct, and contribute to a new way of relating that consciously and deliberately leads to a civilization that will be at the service of true community. One important question explored here is: How does the concept of "Church as the family of God's people" serve the liberative, ethical, and compassionate principles—solidarity, autonomy, relationality—in a non-exclusive manner?

Joseph Ogbonnaya examines how the Christian faith is lived out concretely, in the daily lives of the people, in chapter 3. The Church can only be the salt and light of African societies by how she shapes the minds and morals of African Christians, imbuing them with a sense of hope and transformative grace. This informs a people's understanding of the true and the false, their judgment of right and wrong, as well as their deliberations, decisions, and subsequent actions in accordance with the dictates of the gospel. As people of God baptized in Christ, African Christians as members of the Church, the clergy, and the laity, find meaning and purpose amidst the changes and chances of life because of the Christian faith which they have embraced. This chapter is an appraisal of what the Church is for Africans as they weave together the variables of their lives.

This chapter addresses two questions: (1) Do African Christians see the Church as relevant to them; that is, does the Church make any meaningful difference in improving their human condition? (2) What areas of her life should the Church in Africa improve to serve as salt and light for Africans? By making use of available statistics, this chapter assesses the African Church as salt and as light and makes recommendations on the way forward. Specific attention is paid to the African Church's response to the socioeconomic and cultural challenges facing Africa in a globalized world.

In chapter 4, Alex Ojacor analyzes the African situation, beginning with the threats that the continent is facing. In spite of all those threats, he argues, Africa is endowed with a wealth of cultural values and priceless human qualities. These are human values that can contribute to an effective reversal of the continent's dramatic situation and facilitate revival. This is what the second part of the chapter deals with. There are signs of revival, and there seems to be hope in the horizon. Africans, he emphasizes, are a people of hope. African cultures have an acute sense of solidarity and community life. Indeed, community life in African societies expresses the extended family. If Africa preserves this priceless cultural heritage and resists the temptation of individualism—which is alien to her best traditions—then, there is cause for hope for an African renaissance, with the Church in the forefront of both cultural and spiritual revival needed for a new Africa.

Introduction

In chapter 5, Ebere Amakwe takes up the challenges of the information age in Africa, especially its impacts on African women. As the wave of Information and Communication Technology (ICT) continues to blow stronger, women of all classes, ethnicities, and nationalities are encountering the monumental changes produced by its global impact. Studies on the societal effect of ICT have shown that the ICTs have winners and losers, beneficial consequences, and harmful applications: issues that have been raised are the digital divide, inequality in access, and sexual exploitation (fruits of the former). This article maintains that these problems need to be solved, especially as they affect African women. To do this, the following points are important:

(a) girls and women must be educated to cultivate interest in the study, use, and pursuit of careers in ICT

(b) the needs and dignity of African women must be globalized through ICT

(c) women need to become part of the ICT system

(d) regulation policy must be developed on the part of governments and states.

In chapter 6, Bekeh Ukelina Utietang takes up the question of the challenge of evangelization for the Church in Africa. While the Church in Africa is growing tremendously, it is his position in this essay that this growth is not sustainable unless the Church in Africa develops a solid ministry of evangelization that takes into account the cultural heritage of Africa and the culture of love taught by Jesus Christ. This essay looks at the weaknesses of the current work of evangelization in Africa and proposes four concrete ways in which the Church can become the salt and light in Africa.

The conclusion summarizes three fundamental challenges facing the African Churches today: accountability, identity/autonomy, and religious freedom/inter-religious dialogue; the ramifications of these challenges; and why and how the Churches in Africa should respond to these challenges.

These essays are intended to stimulate discussion on the state of the Church in Africa and the future of the Christian movement in Africa. Many other issues that could not be covered in this volume because of space limitations, we intend to take up in the future. Questions about formation of priests, religious, and lay pastoral agents; the specific nature and direction of Catholic charities and Catholic schools; the problem of lack of accountability in our churches; the relationship between the local churches in Africa and the universal Church; collegiality; the state of the religious communities in Africa, especially indigenous religious orders; polygamy; subordination of women; celibacy; widowhood practices; and childless marriages, among others.

This work is also limited by the fact that all the writers belong to the Roman Catholic Church and, naturally, draw from their experience from that tradition. However, most of the challenges facing the Catholic Church in Africa also face African Christians in other denominations. Indeed, ecumenical dialogue is urgently needed in African Christianity, in that African Christians realize that the historical and cultural issues that led to the doctrinal and denominational divides in the Western churches do not speak to the serious needs and pathos of contemporary African Christians.

So, clearly, in this book, we have not said the last word. This is only an invitation to African Christians to a deeper and far-reaching conversation on how the Church in Africa can better serve God's kingdom, as salt and light, and offer abundant life to our people.

—Stan Chu Ilo and Joseph O. Ogbonnaya

1

Beginning Afresh with Christ in the Search for Abundant Life in Africa

Stan Chu Ilo

> *As servant of the Word, the Church lends its voice so that the world may hear God. But in Scriptures, God does not only speak; God also listens. God listens especially to the just, the poor, the widow, orphans, the humble, and the persecuted. Mysteriously enough, God listens to those who have no voice. The Church must learn to listen the way God listens and must lend its voice to the voiceless.*
>
> —Bishop Louis Tagle of Imus, Philippines

Introduction

AT THE BEGINNING OF THE Third Millennium, Pope John Paul II (*Novo Millennio Ineunte*, 1–4) called on the Church to start afresh from Christ, to fix her gaze on the founder of the Church, whose word and deeds drew the early Church along the path of prophetic witnessing and authentic Christian living. During the Second Vatican Council, Pope Paul VI released his first encyclical, *Ecclesiam Suam* (August 10, 1964), which was less discussed but contains important inspirational teaching on the identity of the Church as rooted in Christ. The Second Vatican Council did not produce any specific christological document, but we could find some teachings on the person and works of Christ in *Dei Verbum*. However, one of the points raised by Paul VI, taken up at the extraordinary synod of 1985 dedicated to Christ, is that the Church can know herself better and carry out truly her prophetic ministry and the work of evangelization when she experiences Christ in herself in both her inner life and external works (*Ecclesial Suam*, 8). This is an important message which has constantly re-echoed in the teachings of successive popes, culminating in the recent work of Benedict XVI, *Jesus of Nazareth*. The call for the Church in Africa to become "salt and light" to the world and to help bring about the building of God's kingdom requires a foundational first step that demands a richer and more intimate contact with Christ. African peoples (Christians, Muslims, practitioners of African Traditional Religions, etc.) who wish to see Our Lord are looking up to African Christians and the Church in Africa

Ben Witherington III begins his impressive work *What Have They Done with Jesus?* by pointing out that Western society has been churning out strange theories about Jesus with increasing regularity.[1] These theories, according to him, are radically removed from the biblical evidence and the faith of the Christian community. His concern is shared by many Christians beyond the Western world, especially in Africa, where the name of Jesus has a reverential and spiritual hold on the life and destiny of most African Christians. However, Christianity, unlike Islam, is not a religion of the book. Christianity is a religion that grew out of personal relationships, personal love, and contacts between Christ and his small circle of friends. Christianity began as an oral proclamation validated by the transformative presence and power of the Lord and by the living faith and prophetic lives of the followers of Christ, who built new communities of love, faith, hope, and witnessing that were rooted in the words and deeds of Christ.

The truths of the faith that gave birth to the Church were not generated from texts, but rather by the oral proclamation and deeds of the Master and his subsequent followers. Christianity was born from the wounded side of the Lord, and through the miracle of Easter, which vindicated the message of the Messiah and determined for all eternity the

---

1. Witherington III, *What Have They Done*, 11.

futures of those who follow his path and that of entire creation as well. The unity of revelation is found in the mystery of salvation in Christ. This is our highest truth and in itself it is a totality that goes beyond what the texts of Scripture present.

In a sense, the timeworn theological debate over the Jesus of history and the Christ of faith becomes irrelevant when one underlies the inseparable link between faith and history for the Christian. The word proclaimed is not different from the personal encounter with the Word made flesh. Christ preached is not different from Jesus encountered historically, because the authority of the Word proclaimed draws from the authenticity of the witness or preacher, whose life flowing from a deep intimacy with the Lord proclaims the Word. Throughout all ages, the goal of all Christian spirituality and life has been to make Christ present in the lives of individuals and societies. This is why the best interpreters of the Scripture are the saints whose lives point to and reveal the person and works of Christ. The person that the early Christian communities proclaimed was a Christ whom they encountered, whose reign they had accepted, and whose mission, project, and destiny became also theirs as well. The scriptural evidence was a testimony of lived experiences, and not a mere invention. The faith of the early Church was intimately linked to the lives of the early Christians; it also shaped their personal and group history. The unfortunate separation of history and faith, especially within Western Christianity, presaged by the Enlightenment, led some historical-critical biblical scholars to wrongly extrapolate the same mentality in the faith of the early Christian community whose culture, life, and faith had Christ at the center.

The evidence of the Word made flesh is an ongoing testimony attested to in the Church in all that she has and all that she is, including the Word that is written in Scripture. Once the priority of this testimony as faith and life is given, with the concomitant flow of the grace and truth into the heart of the Church, the particular forms in which the Word is made manifest in Scripture—preaching, liturgy, the Church's undying tradition, and the prophetic witness of the people of God among others—assume an organic unity. This creates a compact of faith in the Christian which does not separate the Bible and the Church, or the Christ of faith and the Jesus of history, since the Church gave birth to the Scripture and is, at the same time, sustained by the Word. In addition, the early Christians were giving testimony to a living Person. Their faith, which was prior to and continuous with their witnessing, was not separate from the source of their witnessing: Christ the Lord. In the same vein, one could say that the Christian—who, as Jerome emphasizes, should give testimony to the faith of the Scripture (the revelation of the Son of God)—is the bulwark of the Church.

In the search for the foundations of the Christian faith in Africa, we need to begin with a deepening of the testimony from Scripture, tradition, and the living faith of the Church in the divine identity of Christ. The reign of God, which Christ brings, can only be built on the foundation of the word and deed of the Lord and his followers.

The oldest known definition of *theologian*, found in a third-century document, is one who shows the divinity of Christ. Most theologies of Christ in African Christian thinking have wrestled with the challenge of showing the true face of Christ, in order to help African Christians to see their own face and the face of the Church in Africa. Unfortunately, one can make the same remark like Witherington: "What have they done with Jesus in Africa?" The images of Christ in contemporary African Christianity have not shown clearly the transcendence of Christ and his immanence in history in the present painful and challenging African social context. These images in African theological writings are speculative creations, often not rooted in biblical evidence; nor do they reflect or respond to the liturgical practices and pastoral challenges facing African Christians.[2] As Alonso Schokel points out: "Christ did not only speak

---

2. There are many works on African Christology which one could consult for different symbols that African theologians are working with: Stinton, *Jesus of Africa*; Bediako, *Jesus and Gospel in Africa*; Mugambi and Magesa, *Jesus in African Christianity*; Shorter, *Jesus and Witchdoctor*; Nyamiti, *Jesus, Ancestor of Humankind*; Pobee, *Afro-Christology*; Schreiter, *Faces of Jesus*; Nyamiti, "African Christologies;" Bujo, *Christmas*; Ukachukwu, *African King*. See Goergen, "Quest." This article is a good summary of the various trends in African Christology today. It is important to note that his survey concludes with an ethnographic study of African experience with regard to the person of Christ. His survey results show that the Christ that his respondents verbalized is not what the theologians are thematizing in African Christology. His results are similar to my own findings in my ethnographic studies with the Maryknoll Insitute for African Studies, Nairobi, on the interaction of Gospel and culture in selected ethnic groups in East and West Africa. African theology is removed from the experience of the African people, and bridging this gap is what is needed for theology and faith to mutually enrich and correct each other in Africa. A more helpful christological study in recent scholarship is the work of Victor I. Ezigbo, *Re-Imaging African Christologies*. Ezigbo argues that the Christology that aims to engage concretely with both the Christ-event and the complex contexts of Africa should construe Jesus the Christ simultaneously as a question and an answer to the theological,

words; He is a Word, an expression, in His very being and in his acts and speech. Therefore, since Christ is the ultimate revelation of God, any new knowledge of God must consist in penetration ever deeper into the fullness which dwells in Him, all of the New Testament is one, since it derives from and speaks of this mystery."[3]

The images of Jesus presented in African theology have often been based on inadequate cultural hermeneutics and anecdotal and scattered references to biblical evidence, without any thoroughgoing exegetical commitment in the explication of the data of Scripture. Holding the two together is very important in recovering and redirecting African christological dialogue. More importantly, centering emerging christologies on the living faith of the Africans, such that they relate to, form, and transform the faith development and the social context of the Christian community, is very essential. We may not be able to fully undertake such a task in this chapter, but we wish to show that it is possible to develop an image of Christ that relates to the African socio-cultural context and is faithful both to Scripture and the Christian tradition.

I shall be using the christologies of John and Luke in showing how the vertical and horizontal dimensions of time and history meet in Christ. I will conclude each of the two sections of this essay by showing how the life of Christ should be placed at the center of the churches and societies in Africa for the transformation of the Black continent. It is not possible to span the entire gamut of Johannine or Lucan Christology in this short work, so I have chosen Herod's question in Luke 9:9 and the Good Shepherd analogy of John 10:10 as two texts that will help us to get a clear picture of the person and work of Christ.

Who Then is This about Whom I Hear Such Things?

The section of Luke 9 of interest in my analysis begins in verse 7. The account says that Herod the Tetrarch *heard about all that was happening* (verse 7). He was puzzled because there was a diverse opinion on the part of the populace about whom Jesus was; some thought he was John, or Elijah, or any of the old prophets. These puzzles led Herod to ask the question: "Who then is this about whom I hear such things?" Upon

---

cultural, religious, anthropological, spiritual, and socio-economic issues with confront, shape, and inform these contexts (xiii).

3. Schokel, *Inspired Word*, 104.

closer examination, one could easily discover that Herod's perplexity is a deliberate hermeneutical ploy by Luke to establish the divine identity and authority of Christ, as well as the authority of his witnesses, the early Church: Who is Jesus? Who are his witnesses in history? What was the content of "these things" that Herod heard about Jesus?

We will use both exegetical and theological approaches here, two distinctive frames of reference: history and faith. Before Herod's question, the divine identity of Jesus has been previously questioned four times in Luke's Gospel in the course of our Lord's Galilean ministry. In each case, the operative pronoun used is "who" Τίς, or the longer definitive question τις εστιν ουτος (Who is this?).

(1) The first place that the divine identity of Jesus is raised in Luke is in 5:21. In this episode, the scribes and the Pharisees are the ones asking the question in relation to Jesus' offer of forgiveness to the paralytic: "*Who is this man* talking blasphemy? *Who* can forgive sins but God alone?" The question here relates to the authority and claims of Jesus as God. In this encounter, Jesus doesn't claim to be God—but he doesn't have to. His action of forgiving sins is properly understood as identical to the divine activity of the God of Israel, as understood among the Second Temple religious elites (the Scribes and Pharisees), as well as the ordinary Jews who were his listeners. Only God can forgive sins; if Jesus is forgiving sin directly without any appeal to God, and without following the requirements of the law, his Jewish listeners then understand his action as a "claim" to divinity in continuity with their understanding of the God of Israel.

(2) In Luke 7:19, John's disciples come to Jesus with the question: "Are you the one *who is* to come or shall we wait for another?" Here again, Jesus' response is to point to his action: "Go and tell John what you have heard and what you have seen" (Luke 7:22).

(3) In the encounter with the woman who was a sinner, the people with Jesus at table raise the question: "*Who is this man*, that he even forgives sins?" (Luke 7:49).

(4) In the calming of the storm, we again hear the same christological question: "*Who* then is this, who commands even the winds and the sea and they obey him?" (Luke 8:25).

The question of Herod is, therefore, in continuity with the Lucan narrative motif of presenting the divine identity of Christ as a reality discoverable in his actions (which everyone and all nations could see and believe) and not in his words.[4] Here, it is important to note that the distinctive character of the claims of the Christian community in the past—and the claim of the Christian community today—is that Christ brought God to us.

No other religion makes such a claim. It is only Christianity that claims that God is so near to us, that he walks the path of life with us and makes his tent with us. Pope Benedict XVI reiterated this point when responding to the question: What did Jesus bring, if not world peace, universal prosperity, and a better world? "The answer is very simple: God. He has brought God. He has brought God who formerly unveiled his countenance gradually, first to Abraham, then to Moses and the prophets, and then in the Wisdom Literature—the God who revealed his face only in Israel, even though he was also honored among the pagans in various shadowy guises. It is this God, the God of Abraham, Isaac, and Jacob, the true God whom he has brought to the nations of the earth."[5]

How the Christian communities of today manifest the presence of God in their group and personal lives, and how they transmit the power and presence of God as salt and light to the wider communities in which they are located and beyond, determines the validity of their claim to the presence of Christ among them.

The Christian community is immersed in a world that is hearing so many words and seeing so many deeds, but the word or deed that stands out, like that of Christ, must relate to the deepest concerns of men and women about the meaning of their lives, and their ultimate destiny. The

---

4. That is not to say that Luke places less value to the words of Christ, but Luke was concentrating in his narrative on the efficacy of Christ's actions as witnessing to his words, showing his divine identity and the authority displayed which is also given to his followers. Analogically, one could state that the efficacy of a medication is determined not by what the label says, but what it does when it comes in contact with a sick person. The divine offer of salvation in Christ is for all peoples, and all could see this divine action in the action of the man Jesus. This question "Who is this?" is not repeated after chapter 9. Many exegetes, including Bock, Fitzmyer, Schurmann, Bobon, Schramm, and Talbert, agree that since this question ("Who is this . . .?") is not repeated in Luke after chapter 9, the most logical thing is to look at the inner logic of this ninth chapter in order to discover within this chapter, the answer to Herod's question. We shall, therefore, concentrate on how this question is significant in Luke and how it is answered in this chapter, with regard to the divine identity and mission of Jesus Christ. That question is a hermeneutical key to understanding the Christology of chapter 9 of Luke's Gospel and sheds great light on the Christology of Luke in general.

5. Benedict XVI, *Jesus of Nazareth*, 44.

account of the Christian community must be a light to the world in terms of deeds that translate into testimonies of love, grace, and truth. Herod's question is to be interpreted within the wider context of the preceding events that led to his question. It is also to be understood within the context of *what is going forward* in the chapter. The question is later answered in a definitive way in chapter 9 through a series of events in the life of Jesus culminating in Peter's confession in verse 20. Peter's response to the question of Jesus: "But who do you say that I am?" (vs. 20) is "The Messiah of God." Before Peter gave this answer, the other disciples had already told Jesus that some thought that he was Elijah (a thought which corresponded to the report that Herod received about the unique ministry of Jesus in vs. 8, which was that many people thought that, in Jesus, Elijah or John had come back to life).

A critical interpretation of chapter 9 of Luke's Gospel clearly shows the Christology of divine identity of Jesus in Luke. We shall concern ourselves with the essential elements of the chapter, which reveal the Christology of divine identity. In addition, I believe that there is so much in this chapter that we can grow into in our faith journey and encounter with Christ. The underlying concern here is that the divine identity of Christ is not a title which is conferred on him by the Christian community in an arbitrary manner, but one that draws directly from his Word and Deeds in the lives of Christians, the Church, and the world at large. In addition, what resonates in the Christian community, and the report that goes out beyond the community of faith about Christ, is pivotal to the fidelity, commitment, and success of the work of evangelizing the world.

In choosing this theological approach, I wish to emphasize the biblical truth that the self-evidence of God in creation and in a unique way in Christ, and in the Church is the most credible testimony of God's existence. Since this *self-presencing* has been committed to the Church as her mission and *raison d'être*, the authority and validity of the Church stands or falls to the extent that she presents the true face of the Trinity in the lives of Christians. Thus, the puzzle and even doubt of the divine identity of the Son of God that is still on the lips of many—like the Herods of today—cannot be answered simply through words, arguments, and claims, but through pointing to the action and presence of Christ, especially in the Christian community.

The Lucan community gave such an account in this passage under study. Particularly in Africa, the claims the Church and Christians make about Christ need evidential referents in both the kind of life that African Christians live and the kind of society they help to create in their respective communities. In the early Christian community, there were already rich signs and witnessing to the word and deeds of Christ, which was able to sustain the community in its difficult journey of implanting the faith in a complex and hard line religious and political orthodoxies around them. Such witnessing to the faith in the early Church was also able to topple the structures of sin and injustice, trouble the oppressive powers and authorities that exploited the people and held them in chains, and showed through the Christian community that a new and better way of living was possible.

The main outlines of the Christology of Luke (in terms of Jesus' divine identity and the nature of his Messianic ministry) are already clear at the conclusion of the Galilean ministry of Jesus and summarized in the episodes in chapter 9 of Luke's Gospel. The main outlines of this Christology are:

1) He is the Spirit-anointed Messiah, a prophetic Messiah—the Messiah of God, the Son of God.

2) His messianic ministry entails preaching the good news of the gospel to the poor, curing the sick, freeing those bound by Satan, restoring sight to the blind, forgiving sins, and calling sinners to repentance.[6]

Chapter 9 of Luke's Gospel is, therefore, a mini-summary of the content of the Gospel of Luke, because it sets out in an orderly fashion the mission and identity of Christ. It also adumbrates precisely the ways through which he will carry out this mission through his passion and death—an account around which the rest of the Gospel develops. This is why I pay close attention to the question of Herod and how it reveals the divine identity of Jesus and his mission. Joseph A. Fitzmyer argues along the same vein when he writes: "[In chapter 9] Luke has here woven into it a subsidiary treatment of Jesus of Nazareth to which one should perhaps more closely attend. It is an identification of him that gradually builds up, with titles and other elements, which makes it a crucial section in the Gospel as a whole, especially since this identification serves in its own

---

6. Matera, *Christology*, 58.

way as an important prelude to the Travel Account and to the function which this part of the Gospel has."[7]

David L. Balch[8] argues that Herod must have raised this question of the identity of Jesus for political reasons. Herod must have become afraid that a new kingdom was about to topple his political kingdom, because the chapter begins with the sending out of the disciples of Jesus to the ends of the world to establish Christ's kingdom. In addition, their mission was to be in continuity with the nature and mission of Christ, which he had already demonstrated in his powerful works and proclamation. It is no surprise that Herod was delighted toward the end of the life of Jesus to see him put to trial and eventually put to death (Luke 22:8). When Jesus sent the disciples out, he gave them "power and authority." In addition, "sending out" (as was done by Jesus in Luke 9:2) was a colonial-territorial political gesture; for example, the colonial occupiers of Africa until independence sent out colonial officials to Africa, as a way of claiming and maintaining authority over the land and people of Africa.

Herod the Tetrarch, therefore, raises questions about the identity of this man, who he thinks wishes to topple his political kingdom by establishing a new one.[9] We learn from the first part of Herod's compound sentence (9:9a) of the fate of John. The second half (9:9b), where Herod asks about the identity of Christ, already points to the fate of Jesus: the cross and resurrection. Already, within the question of Herod, lies the great truth that the fate of the prophet of God is death and rejection; however, there is the highly paradoxical narrative assumption that God's great power is not defeated by the killing of God's prophet. This is evident, for instance, in the case of John, whom Herod killed but could not prevent from fulfilling his mission of pointing to the Messiah. In the same way,

---

7. Fitzmyer, "Luke, Chapter 9," 138.

8. Balch, "Luke," 1121.

9. Since our main concern is not the identity of Herod, but rather how his question offers a hermeneutical key to understanding the Christology of chapter 9 of Luke's Gospel, we shall not concern ourselves in this brief study with the question of which Herod is being referred to here. There are many Herods found in the Synoptic Gospels, beginning with the Herod who ordered that all male new babies should be killed in Matthew 2:13–18—an account which we do not find in Luke. However, it is significant that while Mark uses "basileus" (king) to identify Herod in Mark 6:16, Mathew uses both βασιλευς and the Lucan τετρααρχηες (tetrarch) to identify this Herod, who was the political ruler of Galilee and Perea from 4 BC to AD 39.

even if Herod was to kill Christ,[10] he would not prevent the inevitability of the coming reign of God or the absolute newness that begins with Christ.[11]

Already here, we can make a connection with the suffering and pain that people encounter in Africa, and the failure of governments in some African countries that make life difficult for Africans. The prophetic ministry to which the Church and Christians are called to embrace will inevitably call for sacrifice and pain—and sometimes death—but the forces of evil cannot stop the reign of God from coming about in Africa, if the people hold onto Christ and follow his path as shown by the Church.

What is, however, interesting in Herod's question is that the deeds of Jesus did not go unnoticed by the highest political authority in the land. The presence of Christ always unsettles the structures of sin, undermines the foundations of anything evil, challenges the tepid, uproots the unjust, confirms the righteous, and comforts the weary. At all times and in all places and circumstances, the presence of Christ stimulates interest and uncertainty in those who see his deeds or "hear" about them.

Darrel L. Bock, however, notes that uncertainty about Jesus, as we see in Herod, comes only when one views Jesus as an outsider. When one encounters Jesus in an act of faith and self-surrender, the Lord brings heaven to the person's soul.

The challenge of our times is that of making Christ present in our societies so that he can change our lives and our cultures. The fact that there are many who do not know Christ in Africa, or many who cling to false images of Christ that leave them tottering constantly on the fringes of fear and self-deprecation, is a tragedy to be confronted. However, we see that even though Herod was an outsider, the deeds of the Lord were not unknown to him, though his interpretation of the Word and deeds of the Lord was negative.

---

10. Luke reports of two incidents of Herod's attempt to kill Jesus in Luke 13:31–33: "Just at this time some Pharisees came up. "Go away," they said. "Leave this place because Herod means to kill you." He replied, "You may go and give that fox this message: Learn that today and tomorrow I cast out devils and on the third day attain my end." And in Luke 23:8, during the trial of Jesus before Herod, we read, "Herod was delighted to see Jesus; he had heard about him; and had been wanting for a long time to set eyes on him; moreover, he was hoping to see some miracle worked by him."

11. On the absolute newness of Christ as revealed in the text and spirit of the Gospels, see Ignace De La Potterie, *The Hour of Jesus*, 188–90.

The Church as Salt and Light

Almost all regard Jesus as sent from God, but who exactly is he? The testimony that counts is from those who encountered him directly, testimony like that the disciples are about to give (9:20). But the issue of Jesus' identity needs to be considered by all. Even those in the highest places have to consider who he is. All must decide where they think Jesus fits.[12]

Fitzmyer and Talbert, based on extensive studies of this chapter of Luke's Gospel, believe that the motive of the question of Herod is irrelevant to the exegesis of the question. They hold that what *goes forward* after the question is what is significant for the Christology of Luke. The conclusion of the Galilean ministry of Jesus, as depicted in Luke 9—before the travel account depicted in the transitional statement "when the day for his being taken up were fulfilled, he resolutely determined to journey to Jerusalem" (v. 51)—raises a christological question: "Who is Jesus?" The materials we find in the chapter after Herod's question give the answer to the divine identity of Christ which was implied in Herod's perplexity. What follows will be a summary of the conclusions of some of the exegetical studies, that attempt to show that the Christology of this chapter is found not in Herod's question, but the answers presented in what *went forward* in the chapter after the question.[13]

There are six Lucan modifications of Mark in chapter 9.[14] These modifications are significant for the plot and development of the christological

---

12. Bock, *Luke*, 824.

13. For this section of our study, we have used the following exegetical sources: Talbert, *Luke-Acts*; Talbert, *Reading Luke*; Malherbe and Meeks, *Future of Christology*; Bock, *Luke*.

14. These six modifications are: (1) the use of the title Tetrarch for Herod in Luke instead of βασιλευς in Mark. (2) The reference to what Herod has heard is rendered in Luke as Τα γινομεθα παντα (all that happened). It is thus more generically formulated to include everything that Jesus did, not specifically to the miracles which are presented in Mark or Matthew as the object of Herod's perplexity by the word εκουσεν (he heard this—an object-specific kind of hearing) in Mark 6:14. (3) Luke is the one who reports that Herod was perplexed by what he heard of Jesus; the other evangelists note that the report of what Jesus was doing came to Herod. (4) Luke is the only one to use the threefold τίς (who?) which appears in this pericope, for the popular speculation about Jesus pointing to his concern with the divine identity of Jesus in this chapter. (5) The "Who is this about whom I hear such things?"—τίς δέ ἐστιν οὗτος περὶ οὗ ἐγὼ ἀκούω τοιαῦτα Καὶ ἐζήτει ἰδεῖν αὐτόν (Luke 9:9)—is distinctively Lucan. This, according to Fitzmyer, is a narrative device to pinpoint the function of the following episodes in chapter 9. "Herod is made to ask the crucial question, and the answer to it is provided in many ways in the episodes that follow; the question and the answer function as a prelude to the Travel Account itself and to its function in the Lucan Gospel" (Fitzmyer, "Luke, Chapter

theme of this chapter. In addition, this section also contains what NT studies call the "Great Omission." Luke omits the materials from Mark 6:45—8:26. Whether this was a deliberate omission because Luke had made references to those materials in some sections of his narrative, the Marcan priority has been toppled by this omission, or Luke's materials were supplemented by the so-called "Ur-Markus" or "Q," has not been conclusively resolved in NT studies.

The Divinity of Christ is Evident in His Person and Works

When we look at the nine subsequent episodes in the chapter, we can see that the whole narrative of the chapter is consistent with the "ordered account" that Luke set out to give in his Gospel. The gaps and omissions in the light of the dense and compact form of the narrative should be seen as one single movement. Thus, we have to read the whole chapter as one single pericope, even though there are discernable diversities in the materials, but all of them reveal the divine identity of Jesus and the witness of his disciples to the world around them. As Meier Sternberg argues, biblical narratives, as the words of omniscient narrators, are intelligible to, and authoritative for, readers—not because they are omnicommunicative, but because of the various layers of meaning that unfold at different levels of reading. The narrator may play games with the plot, but the truth value is open to all and can be discovered through the *regula fidei*. There is in biblical narratives a movement from truth to the whole truth, when the reader correlates the distance between minimal reading and rounded reading. The reader is led in faith to discover a truth in the disparate materials, which leads him or her in spite of temporal narrative displacement to the whole truth as an organic data of faith.[15] Matera agrees with this position when he writes: "The very concept of revelation presupposes unity, unless the God who discloses himself purposely seeks to conceal himself—in which case it would be better to speak of concealment than of revelation. Put another way, it would be strange for a believing community to affirm on the one hand that its Scripture witness to

---

9," 142). (6) The note about Herod's desire to see Jesus is also not found in Mark or Matthew, but only in Luke.

15. Sternberg, *Poetics*, 235.

God's revelation but on the other hand to be unconcerned about the inner unity of that revelation."[16]

I think this is what one achieves in giving a synchronic christological account of this chapter, like all NT christologies, they offer data for faith and theology; a conclusion that makes meaningless the divide between the Jesus of history and the Christ of faith.

We shall look briefly at five of the nine scenes that answer the question of Herod in this chapter and how they apply to the Church in Africa:

(i) The Feeding of the Five Thousand (vs. 10–17), manifesting Jesus' power to which Luke referred elsewhere as "a man commended to you by God with mighty deeds, wonders, and signs, which God worked through him in your midst, as you yourselves know" (Acts 2:22). Applying this, we can say that the Church in Africa cannot be credible unless it shows how the presence of Christ in the Church can help to respond to the hunger and starvation that insult the humanity of many Africans. We have to bring to our people the bread of justice, the bread of the Word of God, the bread of true freedom, the bread of fraternity, and the bread of unity. More than ever, our divided and traumatized continent needs to see in Christ that bread and fountain of life that unites all God's people in the garment of love and friendship. More than ever, the hungry, vulnerable, and defenseless children and women of Africa need to find in Christ through the Church the bread that can satisfy both spiritual and material hunger. More than ever, our confused world needs to listen again to Christ to find the road to the future and the truth about morality and faith.

(ii) Peter's Confession (vv. 18–21) that Jesus is God's Messiah (or the Anointed One of God) is a direct response to Herod's question "Who is this?" It does not contain the additional materials in Mark on the rebuke of Peter by Christ (Mark 8:32–33), or Matthew's presentation of the instruction and the affirmation that Jesus gave to Peter and the other apostles after the confession (Matt 16:16b–19).

The foregoing analysis shows that this chapter of Luke is not about Peter's leadership, as is appropriate in Mark and Matthew, but rather is an answer to Herod. The Church in Africa is challenged constantly to give an answer to the authorities of the day about the identity of Christ, through prophetic witnessing to Christ. More importantly, the text shows that

---

16. Matera, "Balance and Proportion," 126.

there are often points of diversity between what the political leaders think of the role of religion and the place of the Church and the Christians in society. At any of these points, the Church leadership is called to show the true face of Christ, the authentic message of love, truth, righteousness and justice. They should never compromise the truth or sacrifice the right answers required for a better Africa out of fear, deference, complacency, or an all- too-often marriage of convenience with the political and economic Herods of the day.

(iii) The first announcement of the Passion (v. 22), explaining that the Son of Man must suffer many things. This pre-Lucan element is retained in a modified form from Mark,[17] but Luke introduces the idea of those who shall make the Son of Man suffer many things (chief priests, scribes and the elders).

Talbert notes that this passage is significant in understanding the Christology of Luke in this chapter. This Christology, he argues, is similar to the great christological hymn of Philippians 2:8. It reveals that Jesus is the culmination of all that God has been doing in the history of Israel as Second Adam. His submission to God becomes anti-typical of the disobedience of Adam and Israel in the old dispensation. Jesus was true to the culmination of Israel's heritage. His passion is to be read as the newness in the understanding of the God of Israel, for it is only in understanding the new way of God's existence within history, can we appreciate the radical nature of the passion as offering the potential for suffering to be experienced as purification. The way of Jesus, then was from empowering through suffering to glory. Talbert further writes in this regard: "This concentrates all the attention on Jesus' prediction of the passion (9:22), the fate of Jesus. Implicit within 9:18–22 is that Jesus, while at prayer, came to the realization that he must suffer, die, and rise . . . The anointed one, endowed with the power of the Holy Spirit, will enter into his final glory only after rejection, suffering, and death. Furthermore, by putting the passion predication (9:22) in direct discourse . . . Luke makes it a part of the preceding dialogue. It becomes Jesus' prayerful response to Peter's confession."[18]

---

17. Mark in 8:31 writes Καὶ ἤρξατο διδάσκειν αὐτοὺς ὅτι δεῖ τὸν υἱὸν τοῦ ἀνθρώπου πολλὰ παθεῖν καὶ ἀποδοκιμασθῆναι ὑπὸ τῶν πρεσβυτέρων καὶ τῶν ἀρχιερέων καὶ τῶν γραμμαέων καὶ ἀποκτανθῆναι καὶ μετὰ τρεῖς ἡμέρας ἀναστῆναι (He began to teach them that it is necessary for the Son of Man to suffer.).

18. Talbert, *Reading Luke*, 103.

(vi) The Fourth Episode is the Transfiguration, giving the answer to Herod's question both explicitly and implicitly. The explicit answer is given by the heavenly voice that came down saying, "This is my Son, my Chosen One" (v. 35). Jesus may be God's Messiah and suffering Son, but he is "Son" and "Chosen One," underlying his divine identity. The appearance of Moses and Elijah, in glory with him, is significant. They discuss with Jesus his coming Passion and return in glory to the One who calls him "Son." These divine visitors depart, leaving Jesus alone. The divine charge 'listen to him' given in the presence of these ancient figures, point to the prophecy in Deuteronomy 18:15, where Moses foretells the coming of a prophet like himself whom Israel will listen to. The former prophets spoke of God; Jesus manifested God in himself as his Son. In him was the correspondence between message and messenger, such that the work and the person could not be separated, as was the case with the ancient prophets. Jesus is clearly identified as being in continuity with the prophetic tradition; but he is new in the sense that he is the One who is to be heard and followed in place of Elijah and Moses. According to Fitzmyer: "The christological affirmation here is that all that Moses and Elijah meant for Israel of old is now summed up in Jesus and that he is now the one—as Messiah and suffering Son of Man to whom all must now listen. The Transfiguration scene reveals Jesus for what he is; heaven identifies him."[19]

(v) The fifth episode is the miracle story of the cure of the possessed boy (vv. 37–43a). What is important in this Lucan use of Mark is not the depiction of Jesus as a great healer coping with demon-sickness, but the essentials of the story, which again supply an implicit answer to Herod's question: Jesus is one in whom God's salvific power is manifest; or, to put it more closely in the words of the episode itself, Jesus is the one in whom the majesty of God is made manifest. "And they were all astonished at the majesty of God" (43a), ἐξεπλήσσοντο δὲ πάντες ἐπὶ τῇ μεγαλειότητι τοῦ θεοῦ.

The other four episodes (the second announcement of the Passion, the strife of the disciples over who is the greatest, the sayings of the strange exorcist) all point to these five aspects of the divine identity of Christ or elaborate more on the elements of the Christology of divine identity in Luke. What is significant, especially with the question of who is the greatest among the disciples, is that the kingdom to which the disciples of

---

19. Fitzmyer, "Luke, Chapter 9," 147.

Christ are invited is not defined by a hierarchy of power and privilege, but rather by a circle of love and service. All are called to the table at which everyone is a firstborn son or daughter.

The first part of this chapter argues that Herod's perplexity in Luke 9 is christologically significant because of *what goes forward* in the same chapter. We agreed with the exegetical position that concentrates on the episodes after the question by Herod, rather than the position that concentrates on why Herod asked the question. Luke's answer—which he achieved through the modification of various sources from Mark and additions of some distinctive Lucan elements—is relevant for understanding both the Christology of the Galilean ministry and the subsequent Christology of the travel account in Luke and the whole Gospel. We discover—through christological statements made about Jesus or through his deeds in this chapter—his identity and the horizontal connection he has with all humanity, in time and history. Jesus is presented in Luke as related to John the Baptist (v. 19), to Elijah or the New Elijah (vv. 30, 36), and to the prophets of old (v. 19). He is God's chosen Messiah for the salvation of the world (v. 20), the Suffering Son of Man (vv. 22, 44), and the great healer who identifies with those who suffer and are held in chains by evil and sin (vv. 37–42). He is the New Moses (vv. 30, 36), a teacher (v. 38), a Master (v. 49), and one in whom the majesty of God is fully manifest in concrete action (v. 43a).

According to Fitzmyer, the Galilean ministry serves as a way of training witnesses (reference is made here to the quotation in Acts 13:31, "those who came up from Galilee to Jerusalem, who are now his witnesses to the people") for Jesus. This answers the question we raised at the beginning: Who are the witnesses of Christ on earth? Luke presents here an account that underlies the early Church's understanding: the One in whom she put her trust is One who has authority and is unambiguously included within the unique identity of the God of Israel.[20] Their lives and their faith pointed to Christ; their testimony was born in their personal encounter with Christ. We, therefore, note that the stated purpose of Luke of providing readers with an assured faith in Christ through an ordered account of the words and deeds of the Lord and his followers is achieved ἔδοξεν

---

20. Bauckham, *God Crucified*, vii.

κἀμοί παρηκολουθηκότι ἄνωθεν πᾶσιν ἀκριβῶς καθεξῆς σοι γράψαι κράτιστε Θεόφιλε (Luke 1:3).[21]

Luke tries to show that what the Church of his time was teaching about Christ is rooted in the words and deeds of the earthly Jesus. The gaps in the narrative are deliberate literary device to tell the whole truth. The main link in the narrative is both Jesus and God, and these episodes took place on his way to Jerusalem to meet his fate: death. Suffering, vulnerability, and even death are shown to be transformative and salvific.

The Lord's identification with those who suffer and the marginalized, especially evident in the Gospel of Luke, is a hopeful sign that evil and pain will not have the last say. The link between life and faith, between the words and deeds of Christ and the identity and testimony of the early Church, is the link that chapter 9 provides. In addition, the way the question "Who is Christ?" is answered here, in terms of mighty deeds, is also significant as a good foundational model in formulating christological symbols for African Christians.

To make sure that the authority behind this link and the Christology therein is not missed, Luke has Herod—a man of authority—pose the crucial question, "Who is this about whom I hear such things?" If the questioner has authority, the response given in the episodes in the chapter has greater authority, because it is from God and not from man. The guarantee of the mission and authority of the disciples, then, is the authority of Jesus himself—credible because it is from God, and of God, as manifested in the words and deeds of the person of the man Jesus. This divine guarantee given in Luke is shown in concrete sense in the Johannine text that we have chosen (John 10:10), for if Jesus brought God to us, it raises questions for many Africans:

- What does this God do for us?
- How can this God that Jesus brought to us grant us abundant life?
- How is this Jesus different from our ancestors for instance who brought blessing to their descendants?

---

21. "It seemed fitting for me as well, having investigated everything carefully from the beginning, to write *it* out for you in consecutive order, most excellent Theophilus" (Luke 1:3). See also Matera, "Balance and Proportion," 51.

Jesus, the Ultimate Source of Abundant Life for Africa and the World

Chapters 2–12 of the Gospel of John are generally regarded as the book of signs, because in it, John sets forth the meaning of Jesus in terms of his acts. This immediately shows a theological link between this periscope and that of Luke 9, that is, the works of Christ give evidence to his life and identity; in the same vein the works of Christians and the Church should give evidence of an identity that arises from, and points to Christ. John expounds the meaning of Jesus through seven signs—the miracle of Cana 2:1–12, the healing of the noble man's son (4:47–54), the healing of the sick man at the pool of Bethsaida (5:1–16), the feeding of the five thousand (6:1–14), the walking on the water (6:1–14), the healing of the man born blind from birth at Siloam (9:1–17) and the raising of Lazarus (11:1–14).[22]

Chapter 10 of the Gospel of John stands alone, but Raymond Brown suggests that it points the Gospel forward and serves as a transition between the words and acts of Jesus at the Feast of Tabernacles (John 7) and those of the Feast of Dedication (John 10:22). Our concern here is to understand verse 10 of this chapter within the wider development of its central theme—that Jesus is the Good Shepherd.

This verse is widely quoted in Africa; it has a rich christological significance for ordinary African Christians, hence the need to explore its rich biblical and theological significance. Because it has a hermeneutical key for understanding the meaning of life in Christ—because it speaks of good and bad shepherds—we see in this passage an essential biblical motif for understanding the meaning of ancestorship in Africa.

My reference to ancestral Christology here is to show the challenges African christological symbols face today. It is not enough to present christological titles borrowed from African cultural word, it is most important to show the continuity of the symbols with biblical faith, the living faith of the Church community, and the cultural world of Africans. But the question that needs to be answered is whether the biblical titles of Christ are unintelligible to African Christians—whether new titles have to be taken from the African cultural world to make Christ intelligible to Africans.

---

22. Davies, "Johannine 'Signs,'" 94.

My ethnographic studies in Kenya and Nigeria proved to me that despite the numerous christological titles being articulated in Africa, based on African cultural categories, most African Christians constantly referred to the biblical titles in their daily prayers. My proposal is that it will be helpful to show how the person of Christ revealed in Scripture and the Church's tradition can take flesh in the African world and lead Africans to a new reign of God, where justice and peace roll down from the heavens. Indeed, no cultural category is able to fully capture the fullness of Christ, but the reality of his reign can penetrate all cultures and be enriched by various cultures. Cultural analogies are rich but approximate appropriations of the biblical images of Christ.

In chapter 10 of John's Gospel, we can discover some theological and biblical hinge points around which we can insert the christological and ecclesiological status of ancestral veneration in Africa. Our survey will only be brief, given the limitation of time and space. In addition, because chapter 10 unpacks important aspects of Johannine Christology of life in Christ, one is challenged to seek a meeting point between this passage and the African understanding of life as lived fully by the ancestors and appropriated fully by the living through ancestral communion.

The presentation of Jesus as the Good Shepherd in this chapter has been interpreted by Raymond Brown, using A. Jülicher's division as having parabolic and allegoric components.[23] Some other Johannine scholars like Beasley-Murray and Barrett observe that this chapter is neither a parable nor an allegory, though it is related to both forms of utterance. The chapter, they argue, is a symbolic discourse in which symbolism and straightforward statement alternate and stand side by side.[24] We shall however, use Brown's classification, as it offers us significant insights for deeper understanding.

According to Brown, a parable is a simple illustration or illustrative story conveying a particular message or point about God as revealed in Christ, the human condition, creation, and history. An allegory, on the other hand, is an expanded series of metaphors wherein the various details and persons involved all have a figurative meaning. Chapter 10, from verses 1–5, presents various senses in which Jesus is the Good Shepherd; there are words about the gate, the sheepfold, the gatekeeper, the voice of

---

23. See Brown, *Anchor Bible: John I–XII*, 388–89.

24. See J. A. Du Rand, "A Syntactical and Narratological Reading of John 10 in Coherence with Chapter 9," in Beutler and Fortna, *John 10*, 94–95. See also Ball, *I Am*, 93–94.

the gatekeeper, etc. Verses 7–18 consist of allegorical explanations. These explanations bear important christological themes, essential in understanding the meaning of life in Christ. I will concentrate on two of the themes: *Jesus as the Messianic Shepherd of God* and *Jesus as the one who gives fullness of (abundant) Life*.

The fullness of life, or ultimate life, that Jesus gives is shown in this chapter to be essentially linked to the knowledge of God, or the revelation of God in Christ. Two ancient Christian documents among many show that the term "Good Shepherd," as a christological title, has always been identified in this chapter of John. St Ignatius writes: "He is the gate of the Father through which entered Abraham and Isaac and Jacob and the prophets and the apostles and the Church."[25]

Ignatius is applying the effects of the salvation of Christ to the Jewish patriarchs. The Shepherd of Hermes writes, "The door to the kingdom is the Son of God."[26] St Augustine was the one who clearly brought out the two dimensions of the Christology of this chapter on the Good Shepherd in his commentary on John's Gospel, *Tractatus in Evangelium Ioannis* (especially chapters 45–48).[27]

Augustine writes in a sermon that the Good Shepherd image applies to Christ in two ways, as both the door to the Church, through which one gains access to the Father and eternal life; and as the lamb who lays down his life so that the door of life will be opened for the flock. He writes also of the voice of the shepherd, speaking for all eternity, before the coming of Christ in flesh: "Before the advent of Our Lord Jesus Christ, when He came in humility in the flesh, righteous men preceded, believing in the same way in Him who is to come, as we believe in Him who has come."[28]

Augustine teaches that there is a change in the sound of the voice of the one who has come, but that the same faith unites the righteous men and women of the past who believed that Christ will come and those who believe that he has come. The footprints of God in the past showed the Patriarchs of Israel the way of God, while prefiguring the coming of Christ—who will not be spoken of but rather will speak of himself, to make God fully and truly present. The signs of this coming are found in

---

25. Brown, *Anchor Bible: John I–XII*, 394.
26. Ibid.
27. Augustine, *Homilies*, xlvi–xlviii.
28. *Tractatus*, XLIV, 9.1.

the course of history among men and women at all times who long for the fullness of life. They longed for the promises of the Good Shepherd who was to come, and therefore, share in some measure in his promises by keeping the precepts of love.

If we apply this Augustinian insight to the African ancestors, one can adapt the words of Hebrews 1:1:

> In the past God spoke to Africans through many African ancestors who lived good lives, who like the Good Shepherd lived life to the fullest by obeying their conscience and represented for the Africans the highest ideals of the African religious and cultural values. In our times, he speaks to us through Christ who has an ancestral kinship with us as the origin and archetype of all ancestors, who because of his intimate union with the Father and the Holy Spirit has brought to us the life of the Triune God. In Christ, the fullness of God is manifested and in his light we see the salvific significance of the lives of our good African ancestors who shared in the life of Christ through an identification in their own lives to the words and deeds of Christ.

Here, we find an interesting point for biblical and theological understanding that can help an African christological formulation.

In the chapter under consideration, Jesus condemns the false shepherds who are descriptively presented in Ezekiel 34:1–3: "Trouble for the shepherd of Israel who feed themselves . . . you have failed to make the weak sheep strong, or to care for the sick ones, or bandage the wounded ones."

The point here is that whoever sets up a selfish ideal, and falls short of the completeness of self-sacrifice, abridges the resources of life. He or she not only steals to satisfy his or her end, but he or she necessarily diminishes and destroys his or her own life. In the pursuit of a selfish end, the shepherds being condemned by Jesus waste life and the sustenance of life, even though they may not propose that destruction as the end of their action. This is the single truth which applies not only to the shepherds of Israel but to any guardian of the futures of life, whether at the micro or macro levels.[29]

Particularly within the Church, the "Good Shepherd" Christology is both a model and a challenge. If Church leaders cared more for the good

---

29. For a fuller understanding of the spiritual and universal implications of the Good Shepherd discourse, see Brooke Foss Westcott, *The Gospel according to St John*, vol. 2, 55.

of the Christians than protecting their privileges and power, the Church in Africa would clearly show the true face of Christ.

However, the chapter shows that Jesus did not mean this parable specifically to his immediate listeners—identified as the Pharisees and the Jews, who were already shown to be blind (John 9:39–41) and who were even thrown into greater blindness at the end of the allegory in chapter 10:19–21, when they began to dispute among themselves not so much the meaning of the allegories as the mental state of Jesus. Deeper studies done by Schnackenburg, Barrett, and Beasly-Murray show that Jesus' discourse should be taken not to refer to the specific narrative audience, but to embrace false messiahs within Judaism and redeemer gods of the pagan world as well as "Pharisees" who claim to hold the keys to the kingdom (Matt 21:13; Luke 11:52).[30]

The Life of Christ

Francis J. Moloney, in line with many other scholars like Rand and Fortna, proposes that chapter 10 should be read together with the healing of the blind man in chapter 9:39–40 if one wishes to understand the false "shepherds" to whom Jesus refers here, blind to the fullness of divine glory standing before them.[31] The Jews who came before Jesus rejected him and all who moved toward his revelation. This has been dramatically portrayed in 9:1–34. The claims of the "the Jews" to be the leaders of God's people are false. They are thieves and robbers, purveyors of a messianic hope of their own making. As the response of the man born blind to their interpretation of the Mosaic tradition has shown (9:24–33), the sheep have not listened to them.[32] Jesus is presented then as: "[the] Mediator who will provide what the sheep need for life . . . Jesus is the door through which access to good pasture is made available and by means of which a sheepfold is protected. Those who enter are saved (v. 9 εισελθε); those who go out (v. 9 εξελευσεται) find pasture. Jesus, the door (v. 7), offers both salvation and pasture and provides the sheep with abundant life (v. 10)."[33]

30. Ball, *I Am*, 96.
31. Moloney, *Sacra Pagina*, 300–312.
32. Ibid., 303.
33. Ibid.

It is through him that life came into the world (John 1:3–4, 17). In this sense, passing through the door has an christological meaning; to pass through that door (Christ) is to have the fullness of life. Life in Christ cannot be surpassed by any other life. The "door" words and the "Good Shepherd" word have an identical structure and are used together twice in this chapter, showing their intimate connection.

J. Martin C. Scott[34] argues that the Christology of the Good Shepherd is intimately connected with the "door" through which the sheep enter. They are complementary, not contradictory images. The whole section is about the relationship between Jesus, the Good Shepherd, and his flock. What Jesus offers, the source and origin of that which Jesus offers (the Father), and the nature of the relationship between the Good Shepherd and the Father, is the basis and model of the relationship between Jesus and his flock.

Jesus is the Good Shepherd who knows his sheep, and his sheep know him (9:14), but behind the mutuality of the Good Shepherd and his sheep lies the fundamental mutuality between the Father and Jesus; as the Father knows Jesus, so also does Jesus know the Father (v. 15a). The use of the conjunctive (*kalov* . . . "as") makes the Good Shepherd's role specific by showing that his role flows from the intimacy between the mutual knowledge of Jesus and the Father, which leads logically to the Good Shepherd laying down his life. "The thief takes the life of the sheep; the good shepherd gives his own life for the sheep."

In this image, John shows that Jesus offers something fundamentally and distinctively new from what has gone before him; his life is decisive for the future destiny of humanity. This is because even though the Davidic shepherd-messianic image is present in Jewish history, Jesus eclipses this because he lays down his life. In addition, the life he offers flows from his oneness with God and the Holy Spirit. Thus, in his sacrifice and his care for the flock, the love of the Father is fully and truly present as gift. Jesus, therefore, reveals the Father's love in its fullness and perfection.

Here, we might remember the magnificent saying of Irenaeus: *Dominus totam novitatem attulit semetipsum afferens*—in presenting himself, the Savior brought a total newness. It is no wonder Romano Guardini writes that Jesus is the absolute beginning: "If we accept the Incarnation, we admit that a vertical intervention has taken place in history, something

---

34. J. Martin C. Scott, "John," in Dunn and Rogerson, *Eerdmans Bible*, 1186–87.

which cannot be illumined by the past precisely because it was an invasion of the transcendent into history."[35]

In John's Gospel, we see a theological articulation of the intersection between vertical line of the Incarnation and the horizontal line of salvation history. At the vertical line, we see the coming of the Son of God as both a radical newness and an eschatological accomplishment. The hour of Jesus becomes the beginnings of when the shepherd who leads his sheep to green pastures bestows upon them the life of God's kingdom of salvation.[36] The self-gift of the shepherd unto death has no parallel in the Jewish texts that speak of the Messianic shepherd. The historical fulfillment of Israel expressed by the prophets (esp. Ezek 34) in which the people shall know God from the least to the greatest, and in which they shall find fullness of life and safety, is now realized in Jesus, especially in his laying down his life. The horizontal line also extends to all of humanity and creation in the longing for fullness of life. The newness that Jesus brings, which surpasses all our human imagination and expectation, was the desire of the African ancestors who, without knowing Jesus, belong to the horizontal line in salvation history.

The fullness of life is achieved for his flock by Jesus because he lays down his life so that his flock will have this same life that has been given, described in John 15:15–17 as all he has received from the Father. The verb used here of Jesus' knowledge of God (v. 15) is same as the one used in John 17:4 about eternal life which means "to know you the one true God and Jesus Christ whom you sent."[37] Knowledge *of* God is not knowledge *about* God in terms of propositions. It is to embrace personally, existentially, and communally (as a member of a flock), in faith, the revelation of the love and truth of God in Christ. To enter into the life of Christ means to enter into the superabundance of the life of the Trinity. Knowing Jesus means entering into this superabundant life in such a way that one's cup overflows with blessing (Cf. Ps 23). This is the abundant life that Africans are looking for in the churches.

The saving revelation of the fullness of God's love and life is found on the cross, on which the Good Shepherd lays down his life for the salvation of all. The cross stands at the center of history as the form of the

35. De la Potterie, *Hour of Jesus*, 189.

36. Beasley-Murray, *Gospel of Life*, 106.

37. On the textual and grammatical analysis of the verb γινοσκω, see Zerwick and Grosvenor, *Grammatical Analysis*, 317, 336.

revelation of the final Word of love to humanity and all creation. In this singular saving act, we see the shattering of national boundaries, the gathering of the scattered sheep of God, and the determination of the future destiny of humanity and creation. The ultimate life that Jesus offers is built on the simple truth of faith that the life of grace in Christ cannot be surpassed. Indeed, one can truly say that Jesus Christ is our home. In him is our heart at rest; in him are we truly at home. Christ is the answer to the homelessness of humanity. Christ is that true home that Africans seek, night and day, as an answer to the deepest needs of their souls and the strongest concerns of their temporal reality.

Africans are included in this fullness of life that Jesus brings. The gospel of Christ has been one of the greatest instruments in the ongoing transformation of Africa; the joyful tidings of the Lord have become a source of inspiration and consolation in its changing face. Africans are also entering in great numbers through the door of life as equal members with the rest of the Christian world in the sheepfold of Christ. Like the rest of their brothers and sisters in the Christian world, African Christians wish to have green pastures and find their true home in Christ.

Unfortunately, the story of Africa within the last four decades has been a story of death and decay, of devastation by leaders at all levels. It has been a story of fractured history and broken lives and societies; thus, the prophecy of Ezekiel in chapter 34 is far from being realized in Africa. Instead of rain being sent as the prophet promised, there are droughts and environmental degradation in many parts of Africa, especially in the African Sahel and in parts of the Horn of Africa. The prophet spoke of the devastation brought upon the land as they fall prey to foreigners; Africa has fallen prey to many Western powers, to the forces of globalization, to ecological and natural disasters. Fear and anxiety fill the land as diseases, hunger, starvation, and wars hunt the people by day and numb them by night. In the midst of all this, however, Africans troop to churches in large numbers as they search for the ultimate source of abundant life in Christ, who alone can guarantee them a future on earth.

Concluding Theological Reflection

In the articulation of appropriate Christologies in Africa lies a challenge of using traditional symbols and categories as interpretive keys to understand the revelation of God in Christ. However, this demands a deeper study of both the biblical evidence and a thoroughgoing cultural hermeneutics. While biblical and historical traditions are being studied deeply in African seminaries and theological schools, as well as by African theologians; African cultural hermeneutics—especially with regard to African Traditional Religions and worldviews—are only marginally present in theological imagination and consciousness in Africa. Our theologies of inculturation in Africa have been more a recycling of the same ideas because of the failure to profoundly engage African religions through social anthropology and cultural hermeneutics.

Jacob Olupona shows how socio-cultural studies could help African theologies so that African Christians can see themselves and their lives in the theological (christological) formulations coming up today in African Christianity, some of which evidently are as foreign to the African Christians as the theologies they tend to replace.[38] He argues that the basic question with which one should begin in any meaningful study of African religion for the sake of doing theology is the following: How did the Africans themselves experience their world in a fashion that we can still call religious?

This question is similar, he argues, to the one raised by the anthropologist Benjamin Ray, who proposed: "The debate about African 'monotheism' might have ended long ago if both sides had recognized that African Supreme Beings are like but unlike Western concepts of God."

The African experience of God is one in which the sacred and the profane tend to be symmetrical, and ordinary human experience is mimetic of the transcendence of the sacred.

Olupona calls for a phenomenological-hermeneutical investigation and interpretation of the mythological thoughts of African ethnic groups and culture zones. This could reveal the essence of Africa's religious worldview, allowing the materials to speak for themselves instead of having scholars impose onto the African cultural world a preconceived theistic formula borrowed from narrow Western theologies. Rosalind Shaw's magisterial essay which argues that African Traditional Religions are products of the paradigmatic status accorded to the Judeo-Christian tradition and of the associated view of religion as a text is significant here. This is because it calls attention once more to the need to avoid establishing homological linkages between categories of African religio-cultural

---

38. Olupona, "Major Issues," 28–29.

world and their Western cognates without a historical and hermeneutical phenomenological understanding of specific items within African religions and cultures.[39]

I will add that taking Western theologies as canons for doing theology in Africa is the greatest challenge facing African theologies. A horizon of totality fueled by the illusion of an integrated normative Christian culture—introduced in Western Christian theology through Aristotelianism, Neo-Platonism, and Thomism—has been the model for theology in Africa, especially in the Roman Catholic tradition. This approach, however, does not furnish African theologians the theoretical framework that should guide a socio-cultural and poly-methodical contextual theology in Africa today.[40]

Olupona further argues that a historical and scientific study of African Traditional Religions is an exercise in worldview analysis. Religious beliefs and practices in Africa are like nodes to understanding the intricate network of African cultural life. This will proceed at two levels: morphological phenomenology and hermeneutical phenomenology.

The first proceeds from field study or cultural immersion that puts the theologian directly with the religious elements in their concrete manifestations. One can then begin to clarify and classify the realms of meaning and essences tacitly residing in religious phenomena. This is necessary because most contemporary theologians (like all the contributors to this volume) were born and raised in the Christian tradition, without any direct contact with the data of African Traditional Religions.

Understanding African Traditional Religions and their influence on contemporary African Christian functional Christologies, rituals, religious gestures, symbols, and consciousness is more important than the

---

39. See Rosalind Shaw, "The Invention of 'African Traditional Religion.'"

40. Louis Dupre's 1994 Aquinas Lecture gives a very helpful insight on how theologies should reflect historical changes without losing their necessary character and being reduced to a mere chapter in the history of ideas. He argues that a horizon of totality, the condition for possibility of a metaphysical synthesis, is not in principle incompatible with the temporal emergence of ontological novelty. See *Metaphysics and Culture*, 35–41; see also Mark D. Jordan's essay "The Summa's Reform of Moral Teaching—and Its Failure" on the need to read Aquinas and some of the classical Western theologians in context because there are no unified totalities, even within Catholicism. As a result, attempts to use theologies like Thomas as canons to be followed slavishly through the years, without a sense of history, does injury to the cultural hermeneutics of which these masters were precursors. See *Contemplating Aquinas*, edited by Fergus Kerr, 41–54.

often extraneously-induced judgments theologians bring in evaluating them.

At the second level, the theologian proceeding from the essences and meaning discovered seeks to describe how they are expressed in cultural life. Here, one is concerned with naming the functional and symbolic nature of the religious beliefs or practices studied as they manifest in African Christian experience and worldview. In a real sense, such an exercise in cultural analysis and hermeneutics through the study of African Traditional Religions can give one a clear picture of the African society—seeing the people as they see themselves—so that one can understand the inner layer that shapes contemporary religious practices and tendencies in African Christianity not adequately addressed through Western theological systems.

Using one's findings to talk about the Christian faith, or using the meanings discovered to reinterpret the Christian message, will not alienate the people but will make them feel at home because the category is not a morphological identification randomly created or chosen by the theologian's apodictic dogmatic assimilation.

This task is particularly urgent in Africa because a hermeneutical privilege has been given to Eurocentered theological systems and christological symbols. The result of this is that the new voices and manifestations of post-Western Christian beliefs and practices from the other side of history are often seen as strange and even heretical. For instance, African theologies of inculturation have often proceeded with setting boundaries and rules for inculturation and dialogue with African Traditional religious beliefs, practices, and worldviews which many practitioners do not adequately understand. African culture and religions have to be understood on their own terms through a hermeneutical phenomenological immersion. The inner coherence of African culture or the lack of it has not been fully reflected in African theologies, nor have African theologians critically understood, appreciated, and named the patterns of continuity and discontinuity in African Traditional Religions found in African Christianity.

I argue that we need to demythologize a tendency in traditional Christianity to place Western theology as the epistemic model and pattern of divine revelation. If this is not done in African theological enterprise, it will be very difficult to show the face of Christ as he shapes a new Christian identity and Christian imagination in Africa through the cultural experiences of the African Christians and their very challenging social context. According to the African theologian Benezet Bujo:

> The Black African must rediscover his roots so that the ancestral tradition may enrich post-colonial people and make them adopt a critical attitude toward modern society. Then Africa will be able to breathe with a new life which neither idealizes the past, simply because one is black, nor treats the past as an idol. What is needed is a new synthesis. It is not a question of replacing the God of the Africans but rather of enthroning the God of Jesus Christ, not as the rival of the God of the ancestors, but as identical with God.[41]

My proposal is that the best place to begin is appropriate Christology. Happily, there are many African Christological formulations which have some promise. They can be refined with more biblical, cultural, historical and liturgical frameworks to meet the exigencies of a transformational theological praxis required for the troubling African social context. I am convinced that if the Church speaks more of Christ and not of herself, and that if the Church speaks convincingly of Christ as he is and presents him as he is through the life of the Church and that of Christians, she will have more appeal not only to Africans but to the whole world. Speaking about Christ in Africa will transcend mere proclamation, or appeal to authority, or mystifying ordinary Christians with strange and esoteric liturgies or "reverent" Latinized Masses. It will demand that the way of being Church in Africa should be the way that shows the face of Christ and leads to Christ. This path will seek to understand what African culture is about (through cultural hermeneutics), and what the inner core of Christianity is about (through Christology), as starting points for laying a foundation for deep faith that relates to the social context of African Christians and the biblical and historical context of the Christian message. These two dynamics must be held together, read, and interpreted through attention to their inner enrichment, in formulating the Christology that will not alienate the African Christian from his or her cultural world nor isolate him or her from the long stream of the Christian message with its many tributaries and multiple pasts.

Starting afresh from Christ means that the Church in Africa must show, through her life and witnessing, that Christ offers abundant life in every sense of the word in both its material and spiritual components,

---

41. Bujo, *African Theology*, 15–16.

an irreducible offer available to all who enter the Church. This means that the Church in Africa must speak the words of love and healing that Christ spoke, listen to the signs of the times and the cries of millions of Africans, and be the voice of those who have been condemned to die in a continent rich with human, material, and cultural resources, yet abounding with so much pain and suffering. The Church and Christians must offer an answer to the multiple challenges facing many ordinary African Christians and the constant uncertainty and tension that have been the lot of African societies.

The goal of all theological enterprise, especially in Africa, should be to present an image of Christ whom Africans can easily recognize as one with them; whom they can touch, hear, and follow, in order to transform the continent and transcend any negative cultural practices that make the abundant life in Christ less available to all. This will help to shape the liturgy, spirituality, ecclesiology, moral demands, and prophetic witnessing of Africans, all of which are in their formative and trial stages. I believe that this is where the Holy Spirit is leading African Christians today.

Africa is, in my opinion, the new center where the future of the Christian faith and the Catholic Church is being presently defined. The emerging polycentric map of Christianity means that we can no longer read the Christian past as a single history, nor perceive present challenges facing the universal Church, as demanding a univocal response, or one rule that fits all.[42] This polycentricism is not yet evident in terms of the marginal influence that African Christians have in the formation and development of Christian doctrines in world Christianity. This is because the churches of Africa have not attained financial autonomy and sustainability.

In the Anglican Communion, the churches in Africa have shown that commitment to the fundamental beliefs and practices of the Christian faith can no longer be sacrificed in the face of all kinds of social experiments that come from the West. In the Catholic Church, however, African Christians have not contributed much in shaping the policy of the Church of Rome. However, the demographics of Church growth and population, and the increase in vocations and African professional theologians, promises to "force" such a shift in the years to come.

In addition, a synchronizing tendency by the institutional Church will also not sustain any serious and deep Church life responsive to the

---

42. Gonzalez, *Changing Shape*, 16–17; see also Vanhoozer, "One Rule to Rule Them All?"

needs of the African society or accountable to the Lord for the "talents" that he has given to the churches in Africa. African bishops should consider the faith development and social context of their flock as their first loyalty. But it is left to African theologians to articulate a theology that is able to capture the imagination of the ordinary African Christians. Such a theology will inspire them to respond to Christ as their brother and Lord, to see him for who he is, and to work and walk with him in finding meaning in life and the strength to address the needs of the times.

Fortunately, Africans are beginning to define who they are both as Africans and Christians. They are beginning to realize that there are specific challenges that face them, and that they need to feel the presence of Christ in these areas. This begins with a redefinition of what it means to be a Christian and who Christ is to Africans. As Andrew Walls has pointed out, the new religious systems of Africa are distinctively Christian in that they not only magnify the God component that has always been present in African religion, but also identify that component with the God of Israel and of the Scriptures, and with the God and Father of the Lord Jesus Christ. That is to say, they bring the elements of African religious consciousness into connection with Christ.[43] How this definition helps them to answer the question that modern Herods raise to them about the identity of Christ—and what Christ does offer to those who follow him—depend on the identity of the churches that are emerging in Africa in their inner life and external relations, witnessing, mission, and outreach.

Some Recommendations and Questions

Particular or local churches in Africa should live in such a way that their lives become a witness to the presence of Christ. The priority of mission demands attention to the logic of the Incarnation: that we should suffer with those who suffer, be poor with the poor, and take a tent in the concrete life of our faith communities in Africa so as to be one with them in working out the ways and means of moving forward in the light of Christ. The questions any diocese or parish should constantly answer are (among others):

---

43. Walls, *Cross-Cultural Process*, 129.

Beginning Afresh with Christ in the Search for Abundant Life in Africa

- Who do we say that Jesus Christ is through our way of life?
- What stories are going out from the heart of our parishes, churches, and dioceses that people outside will hear and wish to join our Christian community?

The community of St. Luke told its own story—such an attractive story of love, courage, and solidarity that many people were drawn to them. How many people have joined our parishes and dioceses because of the love, respect, and service we render to one another?

The person of Jesus is not an invention of the early Church. The person they encountered and proclaimed was someone they knew personally. Our churches must seek a deepening of faith in Christ rooted not on some vague imagination, or even spiritual platitudes or mantras found randomly in religious worship.

How prophetic is our Church in the face of modern Herods in Africa who do not listen to the voice of conscience, nor respond to the pains of the weak? How do our churches defend the innocents who are defenseless in the face of modern Herods in Africa whose dictatorial tendencies have made the lives of their citizens unbearable? Are Church leaders part of the problem facing Africa, because some of them parallel the leadership failure of the wider societies, live above the Christians, and sometimes exploit them like the politicians?

How can the Good Shepherd analogy of John's Gospel become a reality in our churches? How can Church leaders become servants of the people, caring for the weak and the poor, reaching out to all beyond the borders of the Church, in order to help build a new society in African communities?

The Church in Africa must begin afresh by showing the true face of Christ. This should also be a concern to African theologians: Christ is neither our invention nor merely the symbol of our cultural imagination. Contextual theology has to be faithful to the terms and relations of its systematization and be attuned to the historicity of the data of faith available to it in its engagement with the data of history generated from the liturgical, cultural, socio-economic, and moral universe of African Christians. A critical hermeneutics of skepticism should be applied to cultural categories before using them as christological symbols.

2

The Church in Africa and the Search for Integral and Sustainable Development of Africa: Toward a Socio-Economic and Politically Responsive Church

Emeka Xris Obiezu, OSA

Introduction

THIS CHAPTER ADDRESSES THE CONCERNS raised by the working committee on the Second Synod on Africa in chapter 4 of the *Lineamenta*. In the light of the enormous suffering endured today by the African people and nations, what must we do, as "brothers and sisters"? Obviously, our Christian faith tells us that—by the way he went about all the cities and villages curing disease and every sickness, healing victims of suffering, and confronting structures of injustices—Jesus leaves us an example. Thus, in the African circumstances, he calls us to show compassion to those who suffer. Compassion is not just an important theme, or something for which only a few saintly people have a capacity. It is a fundamental imperative and basic to the Christian tradition. Compassion, as generally defined, is an effective way of responding to others' suffering through empathetic identification with their pain.

However, the complexity of suffering as experienced in Africa challenges our understanding and practice of compassion. It demands that we expand the horizon of Christian compassion beyond traditional understanding of individual instances and private charity that responds to the immediate needs of the sufferer, but does nothing more. As St. Augustine, an illustrious son of Africa, says in his commentary on the first letter of John: "You give bread to a hungry person; but it would be better were no one hungry, and you could give it to no one. You clothe a naked person. Would that all were clothed and this necessity did not exist!"[1]

Compassion, by the implication of Augustine's statement, means that we not only respond to the effects of suffering but also deal with its root causes. If we agree that suffering, as experienced in most African states, is manmade and often linked with structural sin or evil, then compassion should lead us to undertake some socio-economic and politico-moral concerns and actions, in compassionate solidarity with those who suffer. Most importantly, we should become more involved in the formulation of those social policies, so that they foster structural change—a matter of justice—and thereby substantially reduce the need for exercising charity.

The ongoing discussion on African development presents ample opportunity for the Church in Africa to demonstrate its commitment to the socio-political dimensions of compassion in solidarity with those who suffer. This is why I have titled this essay *African Church and Sustainable Development of Africa: Towards a Socio-economic and Political Responsive Church*. Following the directives of the *Lineamenta*, this project seeks, within the context of the First Synod, to develop a Christian hermeneutical principle that will enable the Church to participate in the ongoing discourse of African development.

Sustainable development has assumed center stage as people try to respond to the many problems that plague the African continent. One after the other, African scholars are discovering the inefficiency and inappropriateness of some of the already tested attempts at reconstructing Africa—badly battered by cases of incessant conflicts and economic, cultural, and socio-political malaise.

Unlike neo-classical economists, who identify economic issues as the sole cause of Africa's predicament, traditional Africans look beyond economics. They consider issues of division—ethnic and religious—as worse factors militating against sustainable development of the African people. These factors endanger if not peace, at least the pursuit of common good of the society.[2] While Africans do not denigrate economics-based

1. See Augustine's commentary on 1 John 8:8.
2. See John Paul II, "Post-Synodal Apostolic Exhortation, Ecclesia in Africa," in Browne et al., *African Synod*, 247.

solutions to African specific cases, they insist that any attempt toward a true development of Africa must include the issues of division. In view of this, the demand for a paradigm shift has become more urgent in the African discourse.

Some African Christian theologians agree with the need for a paradigm shift. They maintain that theology addressing the peculiar African situation must be distinct—African friendly, and contextual in issues, language, and method. Thus, in order to respond to different facets of sufferings endured by Africans, these theologians claim that a true African development must be not only sustainable but integral. Focusing on the African concept of life and humanity itself as ontologically "relational" and "bound together" in a fundamentally communal perspective,[3] African theologians agree that issues of division are truly indispensable in the agenda for development in Africa. Hence, it has become the challenge in Africa to provide theologically descriptive and normative basis for social inquiry aimed at decreasing domination and increasing freedom in all their forms, especially of the most disadvantaged people in the community.

The metaphor of "family," used by the Post-Synodal Apostolic Exhortation *Ecclesia in Africa* to describe the Church in Africa, provides a critical hermeneutic for a fruitful and effective Christian witness of compassion in the world of politics and economy in Africa. This essay will demonstrate how the metaphor of "Church as the family of God" could, instead of detracting, enrich, reconstruct, and contribute to a new way of relating that consciously and deliberately leads to a civilization at the service of true community. One of the questions I shall explore here is how this metaphor, "Church as the family of God's people" serves liberative, ethical, and compassionate principles—solidarity, autonomy, relationality—in a non-exclusive manner.

I will begin with a short presentation of suffering in Africa, a short phenomenological description of the socio-economic and political situation of Africa—with an awareness of the risk of oversimplification and of the need for modifications in specific areas. This presentation will explore the meaning of integral and sustainable development, especially as it applies to Africa, identifying the historical and politico-economic barriers to true development. It shall present one interpretation of what *Ecclesia*

---

3. John Paul II, *Ecclesia in Africa*, 45.

in Africa means by *Church as family of God*. Lastly, the metaphor shall be evaluated within the context of critical self-reflexive engagement with the aim of identifying its challenges and prospects as a critical hermeneutical liberative concept that responds more directly to the issues of division.

Background: Sufferings in Africa

Socio-political and Economic Condition of Africa

The situation in Africa cannot fail to touch consciences. Africa has largely become a continent of economic decline, political instability, human insecurity, and environmental devastation. Take West Africa as an example. According to the Economic Commission for Africa in its workshop in preparation for the Fourth African Development Forum (ADF IV) on Governance for a Progressing Africa, in December, 2003, four of the five countries listed on the bottom of the UNDP Human Development Index (2003) were located in West Africa. All the countries of the subregion were located in the bottom 25 percent of the Human Development Index.[4] Typical of this region—and indeed, of all African regions—are the lack of basic needs, education, and health facilities and services. The situation is made worse by the growing HIV/AIDS pandemics that ravage the entire continent, gravely reduce its workforce to less than half the population, and alarmingly increase the death toll of young parents, leaving a teeming population of orphans with a high mortality rate.

Another striking feature of African suffering has been the unprecedented scale and scope of internal crisis. In the African western subregion alone, more than two million people are believed to have died in violent armed conflict. The story is worse in the Horn of Africa, where people have experienced and continue to experience one of the horrifying genocides and carnage in human history. Beginning with Rwanda and then Somalia and Darfur, Sudan, and the Congo, the world has experienced terrible tragedies of killing, raping, destruction of property, and forced displacement.[5] Lastly, the African environment bears testimony to reckless destruction and inordinate use of creation that reveals a sense of disconnectedness between humanity and nature.

---

4. UNDP, "Report (2003)," 1.
5. Mohamed, "Darfur Crisis," 4.

The story of suffering in Africa, especially from poverty, is entrenched in heartbreaking contradiction. Considering Africa, a continent of such enormous landmass, who can comprehend that its citizens are fighting for land? How can a continent of such incredible wealth—human and natural—wear poverty like a breastplate? Africa is seemingly steeped in religion, yet also steeped in much sin. It boasts many politicians, but no political class. Africa struggles to develop, but is not growing[6] in socio-economic, environmental, or human dignity terms required for sustainable and integral development.

The origins of these phenomena are often multifaceted, ranging from economic inequalities and social injustice to competition for scarce resources, lack of democracy, ideological issues, and political tensions.[7] Apart from all this, historical disparities between ethnic, tribal, and religious groups and social exclusion of segments of the population appear to be the most significant. This is so because these disparities have given rise to discord and antagonism that bear heavily on the very core of existence in Africa, which we recognized earlier in the introduction as ontologically "relational" and communal. Indeed, Africa—as described by Musa Dube, one of the African leading contemporary Christian theologians—is a "bleeding continent." If something is not done, and done quickly, she will bleed to death.[8]

In response to this plea, various attempts have been made to salvage the continent from this fate. Above all, it goes without saying that Africa is also deeply beautiful, strong, and spiritual. Sources of African strength must not be glossed over by any response to the African predicament. The "family" metaphor, once again, is chosen above others in this work because it enables us to contribute to empowerment models as well as deal with victims and victimizations.

---

6. Matthew H. Kuka, Rev. Fr., cited in Ojakaminor, *Happenings*, 11. Africa is the "second largest of the earth's seven continents, covering, with adjacent islands, about 30,300,000 sq km (about 11,699,000 sq mi), or about 20 percent of the world's total land area. In the late 1990s some 760 million people, or about 13 percent of the world's population, inhabited Africa." See *Funk & Wagnalls New Encyclopedia*.

7. Second Committee on Human Development and Civil Society, *Countries Emerging*, 2.

8. See Musa Dube, in Getui, "Role of Women," 19.

Responding to Africa: Toward a Sustainable and Integral Development

Popular Approaches—"Economic Growth and Sustainable Development"

Until recently, African problems have always been perceived as economic; hence sustainable development has been basically pursued via economic strategies.[9] In order to improve the lot of their people, many African nations have (consciously or not) experimented with several economic and development models. According to the authors of *An Alternative Strategy for Africa's Sustainable Economic Development: The Case for a Non-NEPAD Approach*, within the last five decades, there are five dominant paradigm in Africa's development strategies, *viz.*

(1) Arthur Lewis' two-sector growth model of 1950s

(2) the inward-looking industrialization (Import Substitution) model of the 1960s

(3) the growth-with-equality paradigm of the 1970s

(4) the neo-classical paradigm of the 1980s

(5) the sustainable economic development model (macro-economy) of the 1990s, and also the New Partnership for Africa development (NEPAD) of the first decade of this century.

Arthur Lewis' model was originally developed to deal with the unemployment condition created in the Caribbean countries and other Third World Countries by the effects of World War II. The model proposes that these countries should provide tax holidays in order to attract firms from the mainland of the United States to make use of the surplus

---

9. Sustainable development finds its more articulated economic nuance in the work of the "World Commission on Environment and Development," otherwise known as "Brundtland Commission." The commission was set up by United Nations General Assembly in 1987 to address the economic related crisis to environment. The commission assuring that world economic development can comfortably coexist alongside sound environmental policies identifies this coexistence as "sustainable development." Thus, it defines sustainable development as "development that meets the need of the present without compromising the ability of the future." However, this concept has obviously been applied to the African situation as attempts to resolve its numerous crises assume prominent position in the discourse. See "Alternative Strategy: Case for a Non-NEPAD Approach," 4.

labor in these countries. His model celebrated as "Economic Development with Unlimited Supplies of Labor," was adopted by the United Nations especially its agency, the Food Agricultural Organization (FAO), and other funding agencies. By 1963, this paradigm was in practice in Ghana under President Kwame Nkrumah. Prebisch and Singer developed the Import Substitution Industrialization (ISI). The idea is to substitute domestic production of previously imported simple consumer goods and then substitute through domestic production for a wider range of more sophisticated manufactured items. Growth-equity paradigm came as a result of the disenchantment with the trickle-down theory associated with the two previous economic development models. This paradigm promotes development by empowerment and grass-roots approaches. The neo-classical paradigm of 1980s originates from the Bretton Wood institutions (The World Bank, and International Monetary Fund, IMF). The paradigm insists that African nations seeking economic assistance, reconstruction, and admittance into the world trade and economic community, undertake Structural Adjustment Programs (SAPs). Among other things, under the SAPs, the development polices in Africa had to focus on market-oriented reforms, export-promotion and the laissez-faire system. New Partnership for Africa's Development (NEPAD) was introduced on October 23, 2001, by African heads of states as an "African solution to African problems' or Africa's answer to globalization and/or alternative paradigm for Africa in the twenty-first century—with emphasis on partnership."[10]

Unfortunately, most of these reconstruction models failed to sustain growth and reduce poverty in Africa. The majority of Africans continue to lack access to potable water, health care, and education, and easily preventable communicable diseases ravage societies. Some of the economic development models—for instance, Lewis' model of development—were criticized because they mainly concentrated on output and failed to take into account income distribution, welfare, and human satisfaction.[11] Hence, some of their economic policies, such as SAPs, were rightly described as "cures that are worse than the disease."[12]

10. See Lewis, *Economic Growth*; see also works by Michael P. Todaro, Raul Prebisch, Hans W. Singer, and William F. Steel and Jonathan W. Evans, referenced in "Alternative Strategy: Case for a Non-NEPAD Approach," 1–10.

11. "Alternative Strategy," 4.

12. Elliot, "Cure," 14.

The Church in Africa and the Search for Development of Africa

This is because these neo-classical development paradigms are based on a philosophical principle alien to the African people. Such a principle promotes a non-relational, or impersonal, type of condition that undermines the ontological principle of relationality and "bound-togetherness" that defines the African people—who exist because they are related. It encourages individualism and maintains the imperialism and hegemony of the capitalist West, which welcomes and integrates the African local hegemonic elites into the global circuits of accumulation through a variety of mechanisms.

On the other hand, while the governments were directly concerned with these economic developmental experiments, the NGOs and other stakeholders—local and international—were primarily concerned with the immediate relief of the suffering of the African people and provided material aids and other logistics to meet the here-and-now needs of the suffering poor. Consequently, the structured injustices remain in place.

The Catholic Church in Africa remains one of the major players in this campaign—"operation-salvage the bleeding Africa." Time and again, the Church vocally affirms that commitment to a better Africa is a constitutive part of its mission and evangelization in Africa. In *Ecclesia in Africa*, Pope John Paul II cast a compassionate look at the dark moments of slavery and colonization, along with political, economic, and social realities that reveal an alarming yet hopeful situation of Africa. He not only indicates how these came about but also outlines how they can be remedied in the spirit of the gospel.[13]

From its earliest missionary activities to this day, the Catholic Church in Africa has been committed to providing educational institutions, hospitals, food banks, clean water programs, homes for destitute, and such. Most recently, through its department for justice, peace, and development—Justice, Development, and Peace Commission (JDPC), present in most local parishes and dioceses—the Church has included a socio-moral and political dimension in its compassionate response to the African situation.[14]

But, like the economic-based approach, these attempts by the Church and other NGOs fall short of meeting the envisioned true development of

---

13. John Paul II, *Ecclesia in Africa*, 6.

14. The full job description of this commission is yet to be appreciated, since they often end up doing the work not much different from that of St. Vincent De Paul—collection and distribution of money and material relief to the poor.

the African people. They fail mostly because they do not address the fundamental issues of divisions that have always been at the base of so many African problems. In some cases, agencies such as the Church were even indicted as fueling or widening the gulf of division in many African communities, and accused of maintaining the status quo that created these divisions. The colonial era comes to mind here immediately. As Musa D. Dube writes: "The success of the 19th century colonial imperialism in Africa depended on three agents—God, gold, and glory—and the most veritable of them was God."[15]

Through its dualistic spirituality, the missionary Church dichotomized between "articulated Christianity and lived Christianity"—a belief of discontinuity between this life and the life after,[16] and thus kept the people out of the political and economic administration of the African states. It was this same spirituality that divided the African communities, as it set the boundary between the saved and the damned, between baptized Christians and African traditional religious worshipers; in some cases, baptism was a necessary prerequisite to receiving Church-given charity. This is one of the challenges presented to the metaphor of "Church as family of God."

Toward a Paradigm Shift—"Integral and Sustainable Development"

With all this, it became obvious both to African developers, within and without Africa (including the Church), that the prevalent narrow economic definition of sustainable development by neo-classical economists is deficient and does not effectively respond holistically to the African needs. Sustainable development, African economists and social scientists argue:

(1) should expand to include not only economic growth but also improvement in socio-cultural and political dimensions

(2) needs should include fair redistribution of resources among the various groups in the society.[17]

---

15. Dube, *Postcolonial Feminist*, 6–9.
16. McCormick, "Social Responsibility," 1–3.
17. "Alternative Strategy," 9.

To the list as well can be added a concern of the religious—an inclusion of "spiritual and ethical imperatives in overcoming selfish attitudes and lifestyles which led to unsustainable development."[18]

An overarching theme underlying the above challenges is a focus on the special needs of women, children, the elderly, and, most recently, those living with HIV/AIDS, as these vulnerable groups invariably comprise a majority of the affected population. "The challenge here is on how to integrate the needs of these groups in the entire reconstruction process."[19] Recognizing this, *Ecclesia in Africa* introduces the concept of integral developments into the discourse. It defines integral development as "implying respect for human dignity, and this can be achieved in justice and peace."[20] It sees the security of the individual and respect for basic human rights as the cornerstones of political and economic stabilization. With this new understanding, more African scholars looked beyond economics as they search for possible causes of lack of development in their continent.

Ethno-religious Division and the Problems Militating Against Sustainable and Integral Development in Africa: A Search for Alternatives

Sustainable and integral development has not succeeded in Africa for many reasons: human insecurity, lack of accountability and transparency, popular participation, adherence to the rule of law, electoral credibility, economic mismanagement and entrenched culture of public corruption, and the adverse effect of the present global political economy. Over and above all this, the issue of ethnic and religious division appears paramount. Many of these others can be linked to this one issue.

We Africans know how so much we are tied to our religions,[21] ethnicity, culture, and traditions. As is noted by Stan Chu Ilo: "In Nigeria,

---

18. African Regional Advocacy Workshop on Human Rights and Sustainable Development, 2 (Nairobi: 11 May 2002).

19. Second Committee on Human Development and Civil Society, 4–5.

20. See John Paul II, *Ecclesia in Africa*, 69; cf., Browne et al., *African Synod*, 254.

21. According to John S. Mbiti, "It is religion, more than anything else, which colors their understanding of the universe and their empirical participation in the universe, making life a profoundly religious phenomenon. To be is to be religious in a religious universe" (*African Religion and Philosophy*, 262). Also, Geoffery Parrinder argues that

people identify themselves more by their ethnic origin than by their national identity. One is first a Yoruba, Ogoni, Hausa-Fulani, Igbo, etc., then a Nigerian. The priority of the ethnic identity in Africa over the national identity is ontological as well as historical. People can connect with their ethnic identity in terms of their personal history, their cultural traditions, their language, way of dressing, customs, etc. What is referred to, for instance, as a Nigerian culture is a nebulous concept. It is true of other African countries."[22]

According to Naomi Chazan et al., ethnicity—or a sense of "peoplehood"—has its foundations in combined remembrances of past experience and in common inspirations, values, norms, and expectations.[23] It is defined here in line with Fredrick Barth's idea as "a distinct group in society self-consciously united around shared histories, traditions, beliefs, cultures, and values, which mobilizes its membership for common political, economic, and social purposes."[24] In Africa, it is said that "the blood of tribe is thicker than the water of baptism."[25] This idea thus makes the politics of indigene and non-indigene a very serious issue in Africa.

Ethnicity and religion in Africa often lead to bad administration of economy and politics that have left African grappling with the vicious circles of poverty, socio-political conflict, and underdevelopment. This bad administration is often characterized by unequal distribution of power and resources between groups that are so divided by ethnicity, religion, or language. For instance, according to the April 2004 report of *Human Rights Watch* on Nigeria, throughout Nigeria, non-indigenes are forced to cope with state and local government policies and practices that exclude them from many of the material benefits of Nigerian citizenship.[26] The situation is in most cases created by politicians, who then use these

---

"the African people are deeply religious, so much so that material and the spiritual are intertwined, the former serving as the vehicle for the later. This life and the next are scarcely divided by a narrow stream of death" (*African Traditional Religion*, 27–28).

22. Ilo, *Faces of Africa*, 104.

23. Chazan et al., *Contemporary Africa*, 106.

24. Barth, *Groups and Boundaries*, in Chazan et al., *Contemporary Africa*, 13–14.

25. Shorter, "Curse of Ethnocentricism," 27–32, cited in Ogbonnaya, "Contemporary Nigerian Church," 79.

26. See "They Don't Belong Here: Government Discrimination Against Non-Indigenes," *Human Rights Watch* (April 2006) 7–15.

polarizations to score political "points" by pitting one religion or one ethnic group against another.

This is one of the causes of insecurity in Africa, often associated with armed rebellion, destabilization of national economies, and untold hardship on the citizenry. On one hand, it breeds dissatisfaction on the part of the excluded; on the other hand, it increases the incentive of the beneficiaries to hold to political power indefinitely. Additionally, such polarization is often sustained by the proliferation of small arms and light weapons. The horrendous carnage in Rwanda was ethnocentric—between the Hutus and Tutsis. The September 7, 2001, Jos bloodbath in Nigeria was between the Hausa-Fulani and the indigenes of Plateau state. The ongoing Darfur, and renewed Somalia-Mogadishu, conflicts are both ethnically and religiously motivated.

This is why it has become urgent, as African scholars maintain that any true sustainable and integral development must first attend to the concerns of these divisions. Theology that is true to people's struggles for a full life cannot overlook this concern. Therefore, as we turn to the next section of this work, we shall be considering some of the following questions:

- What do Christian ethics and compassion have to say in the wider public debate of sustainable and integral development in Africa, especially in attending to the divisions of ethnicity and religion?
- Should theologically informed perspectives be involved in a discussion like this that is clearly political, social and economic?
- Is there anything distinct that Christian ethics can offer? [27]

I have identified the metaphor "Church as family of God" as one hermeneutical tool for engaging these questions aimed at providing spiritual, compassionate, and ethical imperatives in overcoming selfish attitudes and lifestyles which led to unsustainable development.

---

27. This set of questions is adapted from Douglas Hick's method, "Christian Ethics and Theology in a Pluralistc Society," in his *Inequality and Christian Ethics*, 85.

"Church as Family of God" at the Service of Integral and Sustainable Development in Africa

Family of God: The Synodal Definition

The concept of family was used by the African Catholic bishops in their first synod in Rome to define their Church in a way distinctively African, yet scriptural and faithful to the traditions of the Church. The model employs the language of community to define the Church as viewed by the Second Vatican Council: "people of God, mystical body of Christ, flock and sheepfold."[28] In a special way, the synod fathers recognized that "the future of the world and of the Church passes through the family," especially in Africa where family is "the foundation on which the social edifice is built." The use of this concept stresses the anthropological significance of the reality of the family for the African continent. "For this image emphasizes care for others, solidarity, warmth in human relationships, acceptance, dialogue and trust."[29] To these should be added participation, autonomy, accountability, and the like.

Thus, the synod most eloquently indicates that "religious language of faith becomes empty and meaningless unless it contains a recognizable reference to real human experiences and the autonomous structures implied in them."[30] In a very remarkable way, it sets a new tone of evangelization in Africa, one that will aim at: "building up the Church as Family, avoiding all ethnocentrism and excessive particularism, trying instead to encourage reconciliation and true communion between different ethnic groups, favoring solidarity and the sharing of personnel and resources among the particular Churches, without undue ethnic considerations."[31]

The synod also understood the overpowering threat present-day civilization presents to the African family. Therefore, the assembly devoted a deal of time and energy to the topic of the family. Above all, the synod concludes that for the metaphor to retain its active role, both as an evangelical model and ethical imperative, it must be remodeled—first, by resisting all the negative influences from outside the borders of Africa;

---

28. See F. Kabasele Lumbala, "The Church as Family in Africa," translated by John Bowden, in Cahill, *Family*, 93.

29. John Paul II, *Ecclesia in Africa*, 63.

30. See Schillebeeckx, *Church*, 210–13.

31. Ibid.

second, by dealing with some possibilities of negative proclivities inherent in the concept by focusing on the Holy Family of Jesus, Mary, and Joseph—"prototype and example for all Christian families."[32]

The Metaphor of "Church as family of God" as a Hermeneutical Liberative Principle

Critical Self-reflexive Engagement

The authenticity of any theology today is, according to Mary Jo Leddy, dependent on its capacity to intersect with other perspectives and realities.[33] This implies that theology possesses the ability to sustain a self-reflection and criticism. By this fact, the discourse has to be "questioned by and questions other discourse, is protected from nothing, is forbidden no intellectual space, is permitted to press its own critical demands anywhere." The underlining goal of self-critique involves "calling into question the assumptions underlying our customary, habitual patterns of acting, feeling, and thinking, and being prepared to act differently on the basis of this critical exposure."[34]

Assuming without qualification that the family metaphor aptly provides Christian ethicists with an ethical and compassionate tool to deal with cases of division in Africa, however, is an oversimplification. As we shall soon discover, the concept of family, and the special qualification "family of God," have some inherent proclivity to support, rather than overcome, divisions. Therefore, as a liberative Christian ethical and theological tool that offers descriptions, guides for action, and ways to assess the signs of our time, this concept of "Church as family of God" cannot escape self-critical evaluation to which every theological model ought to be subjected.

We must be able to ask the following questions about the concept of *family* in general and *Church as family of God* in particular:

---

32. Sanks, *Salt*, 80–85.

33. See Mary Jo Leddy's foreword to Schweitzer and Simon, eds., *Intersecting Voices*, 7; and Jobling, "The Bible and Critical Theology: Best Friends or Unstable Ally?" in ibid., 156.

34. Legge, "Inclusive Communities," 290–91.

- What is and what is not *family*, and what is or is not *family of God*?
- Who belongs; who is welcomed, or excluded, and why?
- Does this *family of God*, specifically, Church communities, provide alternative community spaces with room to learn about different needs and abilities to meet them and to participate in the conflict and negotiations required to meet different groups and needs?[35]

Understanding the Internal Dynamics of "Family"

Answering the question of what is and what is not a family of God, we first acknowledge that the concept *family* is an ambiguous one, commonly used today with many variations. Scholars such as Lisa Sowle Cahill, Brian W. Grant, Carolyn Osiek, and Charles J. Reid, Jr., unanimously agree that family, as we have it today in modern industrial societies—often narrowed to the "nuclear" family, a married couple with children—has come through a wild set of passages warranting changes in shapes, sometimes fundamentally.[36] As they put it: "In most of the world's cultures, 'the family' institutionalizes intergenerational biological relationships, expanded and perpetuated by means of marriage between kinship groups."[37]

The family is the basic unit of social structure of African society. Of the three basic levels of a typical African society—namely, tribe, clan, and family—family is the strongest source of identity and inclusion. These civilizations see the family and lineage as the foundation and conduit through which God's blessings and traditions are passed from one generation to the next. Family "extends both vertically to the ancestors and descendants and horizontally to relatives, as well as, to such unrelated persons as slaves, freepersons with legal bonds to the family, and servants."[38]

The traditional African family shares common similarities with the family structure of ancient Israel and other civilizations in the Ancient Near East.

---

35. Ibid.

36. Cahill, *Family*, 93; also, Grant, *Christian Families*, 1; Carolyn Osiek, "The New Testament and the Family," in Cahill, *Family*, 1–9; and Charles J. Reid Jr., "The History of the Family," also in Cahill, *Family*, 10–17.

37. Cahill, *Family*, 93.

38. Ibid., 19–23.

In its earliest use in the Jewish and Christian Scriptures, family is translated by two correlated Hebrew words—*mishpaha* and *bayith*.[39] *Mishpaha* is a broader concept, translated as "family" and designating those who are of the same kind, have the same essential features; it is the essential factor of the community, all forms of a whole, a homogenous community with its own characteristics. *Bayith*, on the other hand, designates a more intimate grouping; a household—all who live within or around the dwelling—and "represents kinship in its most intimate sense."[40]

Brian W. Grant suggests that, irrespective of any differences in the use of *mishpaha* and *bayith*, neither represents anything as limited or exclusive as the contemporary nuclear family.[41] Families in African and related cultures do not function as social units in isolation; they are open to other persons not directly related by blood to the particular families. Family structure is also a means of contact with the wider societies. Tribes are units of social and territorial organization of units of clans; clans are made up of numbers of related families.[42] In the same vein, it is important to note that, irrespective of the "otherness" of the outsiders, respect and hospitality to the "other" are primary virtues in African culture. In essence, family relationships portray both some exclusive and inclusive traits.

Land and biosphere also play an important role in understanding family structure in Africa. It is vital that those who work for the integral and sustainability of Africa keep this in mind and not exclude environmental concerns as they seek reconciliation, peace, and justice for a divided Africa.

In most African cultures, lands are owned by families. They are sacred because they are source of link between present generations and their ancestors and gods. Equally, it is by the land and other creations that a god nourishes, sustains, and protects his people. Before the advent of

---

39. Grant, *Christian Families*, 11–12.

40. *Bayith* is from the Hebrew root, *beth abh*, "father's house." There is no clear distinction biblically in the use of *mishpaha* and *bayith*, as family and household are often interchangeably used by the Scripture, both the Old and New Testaments. See Grant, *Christian Families*, 48–51, quoting Johannes Pedersen, *Israel: Its Life and Culture*, vol. 1 (London: Oxford University Press, 1973).

41. Grant, *Christian Families*, 12.

42. Cahill, *Family*, 23.

Christianity, many African tribes preserved some forests, lands, and species by dedicating them to gods—family gods. In the Igboland of Nigeria, the family god is personified as land, *ala*. Therefore, in a traditional African setting, land is not easily transferable to non-members of the family—not even to governments. At the same time, inordinate use of nature is highly abhorred and often classified as taboo, considered as one of the serious offenses. Such offenses are punishable by banishment into exile until the land is purified.

From our understanding of a traditional family, some basic characteristics that define this relationship are important to us as we consider the family metaphor's liberative potential. Traditional African families provide opportunities for productive and economic units. For instance, all the early African agrarian family contributed to the household and local community's economy, leading to a high level of interdependence between the sexes and among generations and groups. The families are equally a "matrix of ethical life."[43] One basic African family value is the emphasis placed on solidarity as a paradigm of compassion, grounded in the interdependence of members that is necessary for survival and continuity. Unity is very important to an African.

In Africa, individual identity is defined primarily in relation to the family: duties, responsibilities, and prerogatives one holds within one's family and by virtue of one's family role in the social network. Thus, against the egocentric definition of the self-based on the philosophy of Descartes—*ego cognito, ego sum*—"I think, therefore I exist," an African says *ego pertineo, ego sum*—"I belong, therefore I exist." This African philosophy provides an ethical and compassionate framework that ensures autonomy and relationality with relative amount of mutuality, freedom, and equality that justifies our very existence as "being for relationship."

This relationship, as we have seen, is not anthropocentric only. It provides for an all inclusive relationship that sees humanity as ontologically related to creation. As Prof. Ikenga Metuh states: "For the African, man is a force in the midst of and in union with other forces in the universe actively interacting with them."[44]

On the other hand, the family in the traditional Africa can be a nexus of social inequalities maintained, as Lisa S. Cahill observes, by

---

43. Legge, "Inclusive Communities," 288.
44. Ikenga-Metuh, *African Traditional Religions*, 181.

"structures of precedence and subjugation" because of the patriarchal and hierarchical nature of the structure.[45] Even though one can notice some improvement on this level today, women are always and easily relegated to the background, as family roles and social functions reflect a *public-private* split. While men belong to the public spheres of politics and employment, women are confined to the domestic, backbreaking private life of childrearing, caring for the elderly, hauling water, farming and gathering firewood, going to market, preparing family meals, etc. This whole attitude reflects on child preference, education, and empowerment of different children based on sex.

Stories of African women, most times, are stories of exploitation and discrimination—politically, economically, culturally, and religiously, rooted in the family structure. The male child is educated and trained for professional jobs at the expense of the female child.

As an example: in the Northern part of Nigeria, school enrolment of girls lags significantly behind that of boys—the ratio is approximately eight boys to one girl.[46] Again, of the over 67 million Nigerian women out of the total national population of 130 million, there are only three women out of the 109 elected senators in the National Assembly. In marriage, women are still considered the men's bought property, and can be disposed of at any time he deems fit. So, while it is easy for the man to divorce his wife at the flimsiest excuse—e.g., not being pleased with the taste of her cooking—it is difficult and almost impossible for the woman even with the most cogent reasons, even a threat to life. One result is that African women are the worst victims of HIV/AIDS pandemic.

Nevertheless, women have also enjoyed some privileges in the traditional African family structure and had access to sources of economic, cultural, and political power. In a pre-colonial and pre-Christian Nigerian Igbo society, women had right to a personal farm, harvest, and business, to which their husbands have no express right except with their wives' permission. Also, women participated actively in the governance of the traditional society through the various women's associations, such as *Umuada*—"the daughters of the clan." Their male counterpart,

---

45. *Ba'al*, one of the Hebrew roots for the word family is translated, according to Johannes Pedersen, with the connotation of man—as the possessor or master of the house and its occupants, and also designating his sovereignty within this household. See Johannes Pedersen, quoted in Grant, *Christian Families*, 13. See also Lisa Cahill, *Family*, 27.

46. Adebowale, "Nigeria Latest," 6.

Umunna—"the sons of the clan"—never made decisions without consulting the women's group. It was the solidarity and autonomy that came from these associations that empowered the Igbo women to rise up against the British government in Nigeria in 1929 when the government imposed taxes on them.[47]

Various family values such as self-identification with one's family, loyalty to family above all else, collective identity, pride, and devotion to the mutual well-being—primarily of family members and others in one's own clan—can develop strong traits of ethnocentrism: antagonism, competition, or reciprocal favoritism among families, clans, and tribes. These also provide for a solidarity that services a kind of "politics of cronies, and patron-client relation"[48] typical of many African nations today.

For instance, administration of economy and politics are corruptly bent to serve the needs of the family or ethnic group of the one in charge—assuring the good of some and denying that of others. Thus, as the leaders put the needs of their relatives first in their administration, their relatives do everything to defend them (their family members in power), even in the worst cases of corruption—looting of national treasuries. This type of understanding of solidarity is evident in the blood conflicts that support despotic and tyrannical leaders like, Charles Taylor of Liberia, Mobutu Seseko of Zaire republic, Robert Mugabe of Zimbabwe. Recently, there was a case in Nigeria where community members took to the street to protest the arrest and detention of a state governor who was incarcerated in London for money laundering. The most heartbreaking thing about the story is that the governor did not in any way improve the life of this community. But simply because he is one of their own, they would rather do anything to save him than to see him face public disgrace, tantamount to their community's disgrace. In the olden days, the reverse was the case. Such an offense was considered a disgrace to the family and community. One who commits that was never welcomed home. The fear of banishment helped curb such acts in those days.

At the same time, because an African believes that a child will always remain a "child" to its parents, parent-child relationships can be manipulated or abused to inhibit the full development of young people, who will always be seen as children, too immature to make decision or to take

---

47. See Uchem, *Women's Subordination*, 37–38.
48. Ilo, *Face of Africa*, 290.

responsibility. This is why gerontocracy has survived in many African nations—making no room for innovations or fresh ideas in public administration. This is also a reason why unemployment of youth is on the increase in many African nations. Employers will always insist on years of experience as a major criterion for employment—thus perpetuating the recycling of the "old brigades," as they are called, in offices, without any limit or strict orders to when they must retire. What we have seen here is a clear illustration of structural sin: "A particular system, (a historical system of relations between people) easily creating a series of situations which make necessary—and thus apparently reasonable—that conduct which favors one's own greed or that of one's family at the expense of the life and dignity of many others."[49]

These exclusivist structures are what Christ anticipated when he insisted in the Gospels that those who would prefer mother, father, or siblings to him are not worthy to be his disciple. And again by calling those who were not biologically related to him his folks, in place of his blood relations (Matt 10:27–28; Luke 8:21), he challenges Christian families to break the yokes of exclusivity; he thus intends his Church to be an archetypal of a liberative family.

The Church as Family of God

According to the Acts of the Apostles, as a result of the Apostles' preaching, many came to believe in Christ. They formed a community of believers, united in heart and mind. They held everything in common; no one called anything their own, and no one lacked anything s/he needed (Acts 4:44–45). This became the prototype of what today is known as the Church, the *family of God*. Though the early Christians were somewhat removed from family identity, they structured their community in a pattern that is similar to, yet distinct from, the traditional family system.

By identifying God as Father, the Church as *family of God* follows the structure of African and Ancient Near East families, structured around

---

49. Fitzgerald, "Economics," 224. The nuance Fitzgerald brings to the understanding of structural sin in relation to our topic—family in particular, and sustainable and integral development of African people in a broader sense, is that, "as a personal sinner, an individual is seen as both responsible for and as a victim of these oppressive social structures." Often, the sinners do not come to know immediately the consequences of these actions to the poor because the effect is felt in the remote and rural areas.

the father as the head of the household. However, as Lisa Cahill submits, "the metaphor shifts loyalty from the *paterfamilias* to God alone." She maintains that this metaphor does not necessarily have to be understood in "patriarchal" terms: "Indeed, it can challenge human fathers to forego prerogatives that derive from their power over their dependents, if God's fatherhood is imbued with divine qualities of mercy, forgiveness, and perfection that Jesus urges the disciples to imitate."[50]

Again although the early Church considered loyalty to the community very important, it was not in the manner of the traditional family that commands intense loyalty and grants security in the society for those of its members first. The Christian family advocates a new form of community in which loyalty to family hierarchy is superseded by solidarity with other believers in a mix of family and class standings. So, in contrast with association by biological kinship, the Christian form of family provides for a more inclusive association. It collapses the wall of distinction between race, tribe, clan, and families, and adopts a classless community approach, where "there is no longer Jews or Greeks, there is no longer slave or free, there is no male or female" (cf. Gal 3:28). The New Testament perspective on the family, therefore, provides us with a prime example of a socially transformative family, engaged with cultural realities and committed to a positive and constructive renegotiation of natural human relations and bonds.[51]

However, it's not unlikely that, sometimes, this type of community becomes as exclusive and discriminating as the structures it tries to reconstruct. This happens each time ethical values are couched in a privatized language intended for those who believe and act as "we" do. In that case, Christian community, just like traditional family, "declines into a parasitic enclave of comfort and security for a few amid growing disorder and imbalance."[52]

---

50. Cahill, *Family*, 31. On the basis of the divine qualities that Christ intends his disciples to imitate, one may agree with Cahill, especially as she makes the assumption of the non-patriarchal undertone of the fatherhood of God. But looking at how culturally nuanced this concept is and the role it plays in the administration of the Church—past and present, one may not totally subscribe to the non-patriarchal epistemological tendencies of this fatherhood. I am coming from the theological inclusive and communitarian background such that will position the Church comfortably as a sacrament of true community in the African gender-laden societies.

51. Ibid., 19.

52. Legge, "Inclusive Communities," 290.

This is apparent in the history of Christianity in Africa. At one time, the Christian community—instead of providing for an inclusive and borderless community—created division in communities, as well as between humanity and nature. Sometimes, as it is in the family system, affiliation with the Church determined who received help from the Church and who did not. In some instances, education and other social services administered by the Church, in those early missionary days (which still persist in some forms and places today), were refused to children of unbaptized parents. In other cases, as in our earlier example from the colonial period, the Church has been accused of loyalty to the status quo that creates and maintains these divisions in the socio-economic and political arena. As Kwok Pui-lan, a Chinese Christian feminist, maintains: "Many missionaries, both male and female, accused indigenous traditions of being oppressive to women without the slightest recognition of the sexist ideology of Christianity."[53]

Appropriating this observation within the African context, Rose Uchem points out that in Africa, some Christian pastors make use of biblical passages and writing of some Church fathers that are highly misogynist to support the subordination and marginalization of women.[54] These scholars expose us to the dialectical approach required as we reinterpret and adopt the metaphor of *Church as family*; Christian critical

---

53. Kwok Pui-lan, as cited in Dube, *Postcolonial Feminist*, 32.

54. Such Biblical passages that Uchem refers to include Eph 5:22; and 1 Cor 11:3, where Paul demands that women render an unqualified submission to husbands who represent Christ the head of the family. In 1 Tim 2:11–12, Paul commands that the woman should not be allowed to teach or to have authority over men. He advised that women should be quiet. In 1 Cor 14:34–35, Paul maintains that "it is shameful for a woman to speak in the Church" and thus suggests that if she wants to know something she should consult with and know it from her husband. Among the Church fathers, John Damascene calls women "sick-ass . . . A hideous tapeworm . . . the advance post of hell." John Chrysostom says of women, "among all savage beasts none is found to be so harmful as woman." Of course, Augustine and Aquinas debated as to whether or not a woman has a soul and is capable of being save on her own. Their conclusion was that she might be saved only through her attachment to a man in marriage. This is from Pauline teaching in 1 Tim 2:15, where Paul holds that a woman can only be saved through maternity. See Uchem, *Women's Subordination*. Now the interpretation of the New Testament texts cited above is much debated by scholars. Whether, when interpreted against their original contexts, they really support the subordination of women is not agreed. Perhaps they do not. But what is clear is that in the history of Christianity they have certainly been *used* in that way.

hermeneutics need to address the selfishness and divisions militating against sustainable and integral development of the African continent.

In summary, just as the *Church as family of God* is obviously a human reality, so is it also a product of human activity. The Church is socially constructed; therefore, it is possible that, based on its rich resources and inspiration from the Gospels, the metaphor can provide a theological rhetoric to support advocacy for human dignity, of rights of the disadvantaged, and, hence, the sustainable and integral development of the African people in general. On the other hand, it could also serve to increase and maintain the suffering of the marginalized and, indeed, the unsustainable development of the entire continent.

Therefore, as a hermeneutical principle that provides theologically descriptive and normative bases for the struggle to refashion an integral African continent that "enables the kind of sharing that can ensure, against great odds, that none among us are oppressed, marginalized, homeless, hungry, lonely, or alienated," this metaphor places on the Church some inescapable responsibilities.

Challenges of "Church as family of God" at the Service of Sustainable and Integral Development

With the "family" metaphor, we understand better the operations of structures of our society. In that society, the Church as Christ's witness is called to a mission of ensuring an inclusive, universal love and peace, structured around compassion, that seeks to remove every barrier that excludes people.[55]

The paradigm asks a set of questions which the Church in Africa and individual Christians must struggle with at all times, as they attempt to respond to the sufferings of their people in this new dispensation of sustainable development of Africa. It wants to know how the Church understands its social and political role:

- How is the Church related to society?
- What internal dynamics are operative in the Church and how do these affect the Church's public role?

---

55. Hay, "Bible and Outsider." See also kairoscanada.or/e/refugees/reflection/bible/outsider.

These questions could be grouped into two subdivisions—responsibility *extra ecclesiam* and responsibility *intra ecclesiam*.

First, the Church in Africa has to embrace responsibility toward reconstructing Africa as a necessary component of its mission in Africa. The Church in Africa, understood as family of God, should include the whole African continent in its scope. With the hermeneutical guide provided by this metaphor, the Church addresses various family-oriented types of division that bring about bad administration of the politics and economy of the nations and increase sufferings endured by the poor of the society. The Church must identify with projects aimed that enabling Africans to transcend our individual communities to a more inclusive community that will, in solidarity, see to the human flourishing of all.

What I propose here, in accord with the thoughts of John Macmurray, is that our search for sustainable and integral development in Africa would already be half-realized if everyone was recognized and related to as a *person*,[56] without distinguishing whether he or she is rich or poor, literate or illiterate, man or woman, from whatever region, tribe, or religion. In other words, while I, like Macmurray, admit that it is difficult to maintain friendship with everyone, I believe that we can advance a collective sense of mission, partnership, and commitment growing out of friendship[57] associated with the family character where we are first related—either as parents, or brothers and sisters. This is one of those areas where this metaphor is at the service of the ethical principles of solidarity, autonomy, participation, and human dignity.

In a nutshell, in today's Africa, this metaphor challenges the Church to a threefold compassionate responsibility—to recognize, to reflect, and to respond. The Church should be alert and sensitive to recognize the ills of our society, critically reflect on them in the light of the Church's role as salt to the earth and light of the world, and committed to actions that effectively respond to these ills in a manner that ensures the development of the African people and continent.

---

56. See Macmurray, *Persons in Relation*, 118.

57. Friendship for John Macmurray is the "normative form of personal life—a community unity-pattern." According to John Costello he was aware that "'friendship' could easily be seen as a soft and woolly category, one that modern canons of objectivity, so distant from Aristotle's, would not even allow into philosophical discourse." See Costello, *John Macmurray*, 160–61.

In Africa, the moral credibility to effect change in the public sphere depends a lot on the moral background of the individual's family. In the parlance of the metaphor of the family, the critical role of the Church as the artisan of a new humanity in the African world means that the Church must rise above the wholesome values of the society. Barnabas Okolo writes: "The Church should never be so affected by these values that its power and freedom to act are neutralized and rendered ineffective. If this happens it gradually becomes the slave of the system rather than its transformer. For it cannot whole-heartedly nor effectively oppose the society if it shares exactly the same mentality and values as the society."[58] In other words, the Church in Africa must first look inward itself and embark on radical conversion that will liberate it from the inherent internal contradictions that negate a true community of inclusive solidarity, mutuality, equality, and freedom.

The appropriation of this metaphor enables the Church to see itself as in a mirror and acknowledge as never before the areas where it resembles the state in the use of family's oppressive tendencies; that it can—and has, in some instances—been enslaving, just like the state. Then, Christians will begin to realize with Augustine that the Church can be both "city of God and city of man [sic] at the same time." As Gregory Baum, observes in interpreting Augustine: "The City of God becomes present wherever people love and serve one another, but it gives way to the city of man, the proud city, when people become self-centered, pursue their own advantage, betray their friends and abandon social solidarity."[59] In this mirror, the Church sees how it has been marred by the symptoms and traits of clericalism—dominance, intolerance of pluralism, conformism, fear of risk, secretive use of power, anxiety, joyless security, rejection of oppositions, and ultimate apathy.

The grace to carry out the conversion comes from the gospel as the normative basis of ethical formation of the Church. First, in the way and manner that Christ critiqued the purity system and temple practices that oppressed and marginalized many people, the Church is called to challenge and reevaluate its focus—questioning what comes first in the mind and agenda of the Church. In its order of cult, the worship of God, and administration, a true human love and concern should be at the heart and

---

58. Chukwudum Okolo, "Liberation Theology: The Nigerian Connections," in Uzukwu, *Religion and African Culture*, 183.

59. Baum, "Meaning of Hope," 79–83.

The Church in Africa and the Search for Development of Africa

center of the Church's mission. Such consideration should probe which values the Church is more interested in and would want to be identified with: human fulfillment or gigantic edifices. Sometimes, the erection and maintenance of these structures make the Church susceptible to the baits of some oppressive, corrupt benefactors and benefactresses.

So, for the Church in Africa to be a "microcosm which can serve as the concrete model of what a fully inclusive community might look like and as catalyst, within the conditions of current political and economic realities, for actions intended to bring that community into existence,"[60] it must be accountable and transparent in all it does. For example, the Church cannot promote good working conditions, just wages, and regular payment of workers' salaries, without first treating its own employees with this love and justice. It cannot insist on a government policy that makes adequate provision for the poor without the poor and their concerns occupying a prominent place in the programs of the Church.

Likewise, the Church cannot fight the subordination and subjugation of women in the African socio-political economy without first recognizing and granting women equal opportunities, according to their potential, to creatively and freely participate in the life and administration of the Church. This will involve creating equal training and opportunity in Church administration for men and women, priests, religious, and laity alike, indigenes as well as non-indigenes.[61] In another dimension, if the Church—the sacrament of community which it is called to be—attempts to overcome denominational differences and cozy separateness it presently maintains in relation to other Christian Churches, it then can model the possibility of inclusiveness to divided African societies. The Church

---

60. Kirkpatrick, *Community*, 230.

61. As it is the case, theology is still regarded today as a special and sacred discipline meant for candidates for the priesthood alone. On rare occasions do we see religious women and laity encouraged to study theology and admitted into theological schools. Often it has become a tool of intimidating the religious women and laity in particular by the clergy who by their exclusive knowledge of theology parade themselves as demigods and the only true interpreters of the mind and will of God for the laity. In my own opinion this attitude equals that of the elites in society who make qualitative education and special knowledge a prerogative of the rich that subdues and keeps the poor perpetually on the margin of history emanating from the traditional family practice that discriminates against the girl-child in education and privileging of some children at the expense of others.

has to make concrete moves toward becoming genuinely ecumenical, and encourage a healthy and mutual interfaith relationship.

As concerns the place of the environment in the pursuit for sustainable and integral development in Africa, this metaphor challenges the Church to learn from the compassionate way African families deal with their environment, based on their idea of interconnectedness between families and nature, to develop a new way of dealing with our environment. This new way should reverse the prevalent arrogant superiority and callousness that follow from a single interpretation of the creation story of Genesis and other biblical texts[62]—an attitude that gave birth to the *theology of dominion*—that the earth exists just for us.[63] We replace this with a new theology that sees the whole earth as the *creation of God* and therefore sacred,[64] recognizing that the world is not only God's handiwork but was declared good by him (cf. Gen 1).

Also, when God sent his only begotten Son into the world, he did not send him to condemn or judge the world but rather to save it (John 3:16–17). In view of this, efforts should be made by all African Church leaders and theologians to integrate this appreciation of the earth into their liturgies. One such attempt would be for Catholic preachers to see that concerns for the earth are heard often in Churches through their sermons and homilies, as well as in catechesis. Church authorities should, on a regular basis, have their eyes on the activities of those involved in various forms of healing ministry in order to guard against wanton destruction of forests and artifacts considered as evil.

Lastly, this new Christian critical hermeneutics does not, as Gregory Baum notes in the case of critical theology, create the impression that "all we need is the transformation of institutions, forgetting that we also need the conversion of heart."[65] "More than we need to convert bad systems," Ronald Rolheiser says, "we need to convert ourselves."[66] Thus, African Christians must confront those vices that have held us captive—greed, jealousy, and the lack of forgiveness, ability to compromise, or respect for

---

62. Stoeber, *Reclaiming Theodicy*, 42.

63. Larry Rasmussen, "Earth Community," quoted in Gnanadason, "Yes, Creator," 166.

64. This concerns the way we see humanity, other creatures, and God. Attitudes related to compassion enable us see the whole creation as a community. Ibid., 168.

65. See Baum, "Solidarity," 56.

66. Rolheiser, *Infinite Horizon*, 128.

others. We should eschew selfish "solidarity" that seeks to protect ourselves at all cost by covering up the wrongs of people related to us, while we see only the sins of others.

In places where injustice, oppression, and the like have created a gulf between peoples and classes, the Church can point to those elements in the African family structure that respond to the needs of reconciliation, peace, and justice. Two of such dynamics identified in this work are community prayer and forgiveness.

Prayer, from an African perspective, has a very strong community character—a sense of social responsibility and solidarity. It brings together families, relatives, friends, and neighbors in a way that dissolves any class distinction, thus providing a social forum for support. When we identify with the sufferers in prayer, we draw them close to our hearts and they feel the touch and support of our presence. Many a time, it is within prayer that the poor are blessed and reconciled with their oppressors. In this prayerful environment, the poor and the marginalized feel a sense of belonging and protection. Prayer is one of the means a suffering community lets God know what they want him to know and do about their lives, and also make a personal and communal commitment to work for the transformation of their community.[67]

Anger and hatred do not bring peace in relationships, even in the family circle; they prevent even dedicated people from forming cohesive movements for social change.[68] Without forgiveness, the oppressed easily turn into the oppressors. Forgiveness is simply understood here as the process that involves a change in emotion and attitude regarding an offender that results in decreased motivation to retaliate or maintain estrangement from an offender despite their actions, and requires letting go of negative emotions toward the offender.[69] For forgiveness to achieve its dynamic aim of compassion and integral, sustainable development, the victims must recognize that it is a very transformative power they possess and have the freedom to offer. On the part of the oppressors, it calls for acknowledgment and remorse for the violence done, a change of life orientation and direction, and restitution as a concrete, practical component to the process of forgiveness.

---

67. Okumu, "Christo-Pastoral Response," 5–47.
68. Cromwell, Review of *Compassionate Revolution*.
69. Philpot, "Apologies and Forgiveness," 6.

The Church in Africa should discover the power and grace in this spirituality of forgiveness. As its contribution to the rebuilding of the continent, the Church should encourage and create an environment where both oppressed and oppressors can mutually seek healing from evils committed against the poor, inside or outside the Church in Africa.

Conclusion

Clearly, African problems are far more than solely economic in nature. The role of issues of divisions, undoubtedly, cannot be overlooked nor overemphasized. Economy-based solutions alone cannot sufficiently ensure the sustainable and integral development of the African people. Hence, the demand for a shift in paradigm, one that will reflect on the division-related issues, is inevitable. A critical appropriation of the metaphor of "family" can provide one means of participating in this public discourse.

In some senses the Christian family, *Church as the family of God*, bears a remarkable resemblance to the traditional African family. But far beyond that, *Church as the family of God* teaches that family fidelity and responsibility need to be combined with altruistic social action that makes it possible for families and the Church to participate in the common good of the society, in its full ramifications: justice, peace, human dignity, and the integrity of creation. In other words, the Church is a socially transformative family that seeks to make the Christian moral ideal love of neighbor part of the common good.

Unfortunately, just like in the African system, there are some elements of this family-Church that can sanctify injustices, reinforce social inequalities, and polarize communities. However, if the socially transformative responsibility of the Church is taken seriously, "family values" can be modeled on the bonds and affection faithful to kinship and assist social inquiry toward beneficial development. This will be possible if the Church models its family principles on the responsive love exemplified in the New Testament by Christ and the early Christian community.

I believe that, drawing on the New Testament model, the Church has the potential to empower all to be human-centered, self-respecting, other-regarding persons in relation to one another. It can provide means of reconciling the estranged, eliminating divisions, and healing wounds of apartheid and oppression by furthering harmony and mutual forgiveness.

The Church in Africa and the Search for Development of Africa

It can help advance human solidarity, redress injustice, and rehabilitate and reintegrate those separated from the communities by addiction, HIV/AIDS, and marginalization.

In union with the stance of the New Partnership for Development of Africa, I close with an ancient African proverb: "When spider webs unite, they can tie up a lion." I believe that, apart from becoming more involved in policymaking, collaborating with other stakeholders in justice-making will immensely enhance the Church's effort and commitment to integral and sustainable development of the African people. According to Dean Brackley: "Self-sufficiency sabotages social agendas, abandons society to its own inertia, in practice, its most powerful and least scrupulous members."[70]

In our compassionate woork for justice, we search with others. We don't start from scratch but rather draw from the wealth of wisdom creatively and critically. We reach out to others for advice and experience. As we have seen, solidarity is one of the values of the Church. And, as *Ecclesia in Africa* puts it, the image of Church as family of God favors solidarity and the sharing of personnel and resources among particular churches, without ethnic considerations.[71]

However, I expand the scope of this solidarity to include sharing and learning from the experience of churches in other continents, such as Latin America; the emerging critical Christian communities in North America—Canada, for one; and other civil stakeholders and various Non-Governmental Organizations committed to justice-making. It necessarily has to include engaging in creative dialogue and collaboration across various cultural and religious divides.

Pastoral Recommendations

For the African Church to successfully implement the proposals set out in this essay, the following pastoral recommendations have been suggested.

Since a JDPC (Justice, Development, and Peace Commission) exists in many parishes, dioceses, and countries of Africa, the activities of this commission should be expanded beyond its present sole concern with material relief and sourcing for grants to include more advocacy

---

70. Brackley, *Call for Discernment*, 164.
71. John Paul II, *Ecclesia in Africa*, 63.

initiatives. This will require those who work in this commission to be ready to take an active part in the activities of their particular local or national governments, as well as those of other stakeholders in development programs. It also demands adequate training of JDPC staff in the areas of socio-political and economic analysis and other relevant disciplines dealing with integral, sustainable development. Where such a commission has not been established, initiatives should be taken to create one.

Mahatma Gandhi reputedly said, "Be the change you expect to see." In its activities, beginning with the pastoral lifestyle in parishes, the African Church must ensure justice, transparency, and equity. This includes providing significant equal opportunities for the integration of all the various sectors into the life of the Church, according to each person's or group's abilities.

For instance, a pastor dealing with a particular issue of concern to the whole community should adopt a decision-making process that would involve the entire community in the resolution of the problem. This enhances the importance of shared life and mission and promotes a sense of belonging, an important aspect of integral, sustainable development.

In responding to the reality of internal divisions, parish communities with a diverse or multi-ethnic demography must first appreciate this diversity and then positively harness its energies, all the while treading lightly to avoid any manipulative or oppressive action.

These recommendations are made with full awareness of the undesirable tendency to generalize issues and to presume a concept or practice from one culture or region inevitably applies to the whole of Africa. These are not hard and fast rules that must apply in every instance. It is for each parish and diocese to discern what is feasible in the unique circumstances of their particular church and milieu.

3

The Church in Africa: Salt of the Earth?

Joseph Ogbonnaya

Introduction

OUR SUBJECT MATTER IS A question aimed at assessing the performance of the Church in Africa.[1] Are the churches in Africa seen as salt and light? That is, do they give taste to the food of life? Do they give flavor/meaning to the lives of African Christians?

How do they impact the life of African peoples? As salt, do they preserve life, enriching the culture and tradition of the people, or have they become tasteless? If so, are the people aware? What do the people do about it? Hang onto their Church, abandon it, seek to inform it? If so, for how long will they remain as Christians within the Church?

Are the churches in Africa the light by which people see; the guide to their lives? Are they able to dispel the darkness of people's lives? Do they have light themselves, or are they blind guides leading the blind? Are they sacraments of salvation for the teeming population of Africa, converting in the millions to faith in Jesus Christ?

1. By "the Church" here, we refer to the Catholic Church. So when we say churches in Africa we shall be referring to the various Catholic churches in Africa. This in no way implies that the other Christian churches are not seen as salt of the earth for Africa. We acknowledge that they, in many and in various ways, are involved in the life of Africa and are contributing to the socio-economic and political as well as the religious life of the people of Africa. It is just that our subject matter is limited to the African Catholic Church.

The Church as Salt and Light

Do the African peoples find solace in the Church in their plight—in their sufferings, anxieties, sorrows, frustrations, joys, and hopes? With a people reputed to be deeply religious, does the Church satisfy the deep yearnings of African spirituality—or are African Christians forced to seek solace and satisfaction elsewhere, while remaining nominal members of the Church? In effect, what type of light does the Church in Africa radiate: weak, bright, little glow, or full light?

The Church as the Salt of the Earth

Of course, the backdrop of our assessment will be the Gospel understanding of salt and light as defining characteristics of the People of God and Christian faith:

> "You are the salt of the earth. But if salt loses its taste, with what can it be seasoned? It is no longer good for anything but to be thrown out and trampled underfoot. You are the light of the world. A city set on a mountain cannot be hidden. Nor do they light a lamp and then put it under a bushel basket; it is set on a lampstand, where it gives light to all in the house. Just so, your light must shine before others, that they may see your good deeds and glorify your heavenly Father."[2]

By describing the individual Christian—and, by extension, the entire People of God—as the salt of the earth, Jesus meant that Christians and the Church must be examples of purity: holding high the standards of life, such as honesty, conscientiousness, morality, diligence in work, etc. S/he must be conscientious in speech, in conduct, and even in thought. In the ancient world, salt was the commonest of all preservatives, used to keep things from going bad and rotten; in the world today, the Christian, as the salt of the earth, must keep the earth from corruption. As the biblical scholar William Barclay explains: "The Christian must be the cleansing antiseptic in any society in which he happens to be; he must be the person who by his presence defeats corruption and makes it easier for others to be good."[3]

The Church as the salt of the earth must promote good over evil; she must not only preach justice but see that it is done. She must, by the

---

2. Matt 5:13–16.
3. Barclay, *Matthew*, 116.

example of her life and ministry, keep corruption at bay in all facets of human life. By recognizing impurities in people's attitudes and values and purifying them, the Church will rightly be the salt of the earth. She does this well in her ministry of reconciliation, whereby peace is made not only between God and humanity but within humanity itself.

Last, but not in any sense the least, another quality of salt is that it adds flavor to things. The Church as the salt of the earth lends flavor to life. She gives meaning and zest to life. Food without salt will be insipid; similarly, a Church that is not the salt of the earth will be colorless and uninteresting, dull, lifeless, and useless.

As the sacrament of salvation (*Lumen Gentium* Arts.1, 9, and 48), the world's sole sanctifier, in line with the mission of its founder and head—Christ, the absolute action of God, and the universal sacrament of encounter with God—the Church must be the salt of the earth, upholding values and standards in life. As the *sacramentum* of the world's salvation, the Church appears as the communion of faith, hope, and love (Arts. 8, 64, 65), as well as the Church of the Trinity. Moreover, she is not just the Church of hierarchical power and sacraments, but also the Church of the charismatics (Art. 12) and the Church of martyrs (Art. 42). Finally, the Church sees herself as the Church of the poor and the oppressed (Art. 8, 41).[4]

It is only by rising to the challenge of this image of herself as working for the integral salvation of humankind that the Church can truly be seen as the salt of the earth. This implies mediating in the socio-political, socio-economic, and socio-cultural life of the people, and remedying wrongs through reconciliation, justice, and peace. This is the barometer of our assessment of the Church as the salt of the earth in Africa.

Let us begin by painting a picture of the situation as things stand in Africa today.

The Contemporary African Scene

The contemporary picture of Africa is one of "failed" states, marred by chaos and anarchy, corruption and greed, hyper-inflationary trends, poverty and disease, ethnic rivalries, and religious conflicts.[5]

4. Rahner, *Church After Council*, 72.

5. The Synodal Assembly for Africa sadly had this to say about the continent: "One common situation, without doubt, is that Africa is full of problems. In almost all our

The *Lineamenta* for the Second Synod for Africa decried some of these worrisome situations in Africa including the widespread deterioration in the standard of living, insufficient means of educating the young, the lack of elementary health and social services with the resulting persistence of endemic diseases, the spread of the terrible scourge of AIDS, the heavy and often unbearable burden of the international debt, the horror of fratricidal wars fomented by unscrupulous arms trafficking, and the shameful, pitiable spectacle of refugees and displaced persons.[6]

But, paradoxically, all this bad news is accompanied by a significant increase in the number of conversions to Christianity. According to the *Statistical Yearbook of the Church 2003*, in 1978, Catholics numbered about 55 million (12.4 percent of the African population); in 2003, they numbered almost 144 million (17 percent, 25 years later). According to 2004 statistics, the faithful now total 148,817,000, with 630 bishops and 31,259 priests, of whom 20,358 are diocesan and 10,901 religious. Moreover, there are 7,791 lay brothers, 57,475 consecrated women, and 375, 656 catechists. Membership in the African Catholic Church keeps on growing. The *Pontifical Yearbook 2007* indicates that of 1.115 billion Catholics worldwide—an increase of 1.5 percent of Catholics compared with the 1.098 billion the previous year—there was a 3.1 percent increase of Catholics in Africa, while the population has grown by slightly less than 2.5 percent. The increase in the number of priests and religious is put at 3.55 percent. As the Vatican statement noted: "Asia and Africa proportionately had more priests; [they] together provided 19.58% of the world's overall number in 2004; in 2005 their contribution had risen to 20.28%. In 2005, of every 100 candidates to the priesthood in the whole world, 32 were American, 26 Asian, 21 African, 20 European and one from Oceania."[7]

Going by the above statistics, the Church in Africa numerically is surely a vibrant Church, with great prospects—a citadel of hope for the future of Christianity as a religion, with great potential for evangelizing

---

nations, there is abject poverty, tragic mismanagement of available resources, political instability and social disorientation. The results stare us in the face: misery, wars, despair. In a world controlled by rich and powerful nations, Africa has practically become an irrelevant appendix, often forgotten and neglected" (John Paul II, *Ecclesia in Africa*, 40).

6. Lineamenta #8.

7. "Number of Catholics and Priests Rises, Pontifical Yearbook of 2007 Releases Data." Online: http://www.jknirp.com/numcat.htm.

the universal Church. As Pope Benedict XVI acknowledged, Africa "is the great hope of the Church."[8] Likewise, as the salt of the earth and the light of the world, the Church is expected to have made and to be making significant improvements in the life of Africans. Evidence of this abounds in such areas as health care, education, provision of social amenities like pipe-borne water, and the presence of community banks that provide loans to individuals and cooperative societies for small-scale businesses. In fact, in many African countries, the Church is the only viably functioning institution enabling people to continue to live and hope in a better future.[9]

However, the sad reality in the growth of Christianity in Africa includes the continuing African condition of poverty, penury, and want. In the words of a Kenyan author, George Kinoti:

> Experts tell us that Christianity is growing faster in Africa than on any other continent, at the same time the people are rapidly becoming poor and the moral and the social fabrics of society are disintegrating. Christianity is not making a significant difference to African nations. Why should this be so? The main reason is that we . . . failed to apply the gospel to the whole life and limited it to spiritual life only. We read the Scriptures selectively, placing emphasis on those (verses) that talked about salvation and neglecting those that talked about justice and material well being.[10]

Kinoti's statement lends credence to the situation of endemic poverty and disease under which African peoples live today. And, as deeply religious people, African Christians run to God through the Church as the sacrament of salvation for relief. The Church will surely be seen as irrelevant if, through its ministry, it is unable to lift African peoples up in many visible ways. As Julius Nyerere, the former President of Tanzania, said:

> Unless we participate actively in the rebellion against those social structures and economic organizations which condemn men to poverty, humiliation and degradation, then the Church will become irrelevant to man and the Christian religion will degenerate into a set of superstitions accepted by the fearful. Unless the Church, its members and its organizations, express God's love for man by involvement in the present conditions of man, then it will

---

8. Benedict XVI, "Discourse," 7.
9. Lineamenta #6.
10. "The Shifting Contexts of Sin," in Ryan, *Structures, Seeds*, 15.

become identified with injustice and persecution. If this happens, it will die—and, humanly speaking, deserve to die—because it will then serve no purpose comprehensible to modern man.[11]

Although the Church exists as a sacrament to proclaim the good news of the kingdom of God and to accomplish the salvation of humankind, she cannot do this without paying attention to the well-being of human beings in the world. As the document for the engagement of the Church in the modern world (*Gaudium et Spes*) clarifies, the Church fulfills its mission notably "in the way it heals and elevates the dignity of the human person, in the way it consolidates society, and endows the daily activities of men [and women] with a deeper sense of meaning."[12]

Therefore, the Church in Africa must face more seriously both the vertical and the horizontal dimensions of her apostolate, intrinsic in her nature as a Church. One is reminded here of the beautiful and much-quoted words of the bishops of the world in the Synodal document *Justice in the World (JW)*: "Action on behalf of justice and participation in the transformation of the world fully appears to us as a constitutive dimension of the preaching of the gospel, or, in other words, of the Church's mission for the redemption of the human race and its liberation from every oppressive situation."[13]

Evangelization cannot go on without paying attention to the human condition of the people evangelized.[14] The Fathers of the Special Assembly for Africa noted this challenge: "In Africa, the need to apply the gospel to concrete life is felt strongly. How could one proclaim Christ on that immense continent while forgetting that it is one of the world's poorest regions? How could one fail to take into account the anguished history of a land where many nations are still in the grip of famine, war, racial and tribal tensions, political instability and the violation of human rights? This is a challenge to evangelization."[15]

---

11. Nyerere, "Church's Role," 119.
12. "Gaudium et Spes #40," in Flannery, *Vatican Council II*, 826.
13. Gremillion, *Gospel*, 514.
14. Pope Paul VI's *Evangelii Nuntiandi* emphasized this connection of the relationship between the gospel message and the concrete situations of human life. And Pope John Paul II restated this in his address at the Puebla Conference in Mexico January 1979: "The Church has learned that an indispensable part of its evangelizing mission is made up of works on behalf of justice and human promotion."
15. John Paul II, *Ecclesia in Africa*, 51.

And the human condition today, including that of Africa, cannot be divorced from the world of today. Therefore, we must pay attention to the prevailing condition of the world within which the Faith is proclaimed in Africa.

The Challenge of Globalization

The socio-economic, political, and cultural situation under which the Church in Africa exists and evangelizes today is marked by consumption and competition, capital and profit, subjugation and terrorism. Coupled with this are philosophical presuppositions of mechanistic and materialistic perception of human beings not as persons, but in terms of what they produce or consume. In common parlance, the Church today exists in an age of globalization, with all its attendant benefits and defects.

Globalization is built on self-interest and capital, as well as maximization of profits. It is founded on a mechanistic, organistic understanding of human beings as means to an end—as labor for production and consumer of goods and services—and as such, as expendable and subordinate to corporate organizations. Little wonder such international financial organizations as the World Trade Organization (WTO), International Monetary Fund (IMF), and World Bank insist on capital accumulation. Development is seen in terms of economic growth, without due consideration of the general well being or condition of the human person. Thus, while globalization has contributed greatly to economic integration of a world market and to information technology, it has had an adverse effect: accentuating the rich/poor divide in the world, and with it, insensitivity to human suffering. The major consequences of globalization include unregulated free-market imbalances in trade, accumulation of capital by the rich, and marginalization of the poor.

Africa and other Third World countries feel the impact of such socio-economic conditions and policies adversely. In Africa, globalization undermines the role of the state, cedes its powers to transnational corporations. This makes the state impotent in the face of the plight of its people and even compels it to withdraw welfare schemes that would cushion the effects of stringent economic measures.

Since the introduction of the Structural Adjustment Programs, which provided the launching pad for globalization in Africa, foreign economic policies have been introduced into Africa under the guise of domestic policy. These policies are drawn by the international financial institutions—the IMF and the World Bank—mainly to protect their own interests. For instance, the oil multinational corporations including Shell, Mobil, Exxon, AGIP, Chevron, Texaco, etc., in Nigeria fashioned a vision called Vision 2010 and sold it to the late dictator General Sanni Abacha who, in his bid for legitimacy, bought the policy aimed at subjugating the indigenes of the oil producing states whose farms and means of livelihood, waters etc., are destroyed by oil spillage. This General eventually executed the environmental activist from Ogoni, Ken Saro Wiwa, for speaking out against the environmental degradation his people were going through because of the oil spillage.

On account of globalization, more and more African countries have been plunged into debt; African life expectancy rates have plummeted; many people have been laid off their jobs; crime has increased; and violence has become the order of the day. All the promises of globalization[16]—combating poverty through growth in the private sector; creating avenues for employment, better standards of living and such—are reversed in Africa. Kwame Boafo-Arthur aptly summed up the impact of globalization on Africa thus: "Although one cannot deny the relevance of other compelling explanatory variables for Africa's classic underdevelopment such as civil strife, corruption in high places, high birth rates and, therefore, high population growth, etc., the fact still remains that the problems have been aggravated by globalization."[17]

Arguing against the backdrop of liberalization of trade and protectionism by the West—through which they flood their goods to developing countries, and yet subsidize their farmers, making it impossible for developing countries to compete in the unfair trade—Carol Goar specifies the effects of globalization arising from imbalances in trade on the developing countries of the South:

> Meanwhile, in Africa, local markets are being flooded with mass-produced Western exports. Domestic farmers can't compete, let

---

16. Pro-globalization theorists see globalization as the one and only system out there to lift humanity from poverty and poised to increase human wellbeing. According to them globalization is both economically and socially benign, increasing overall wealth and positively impacting poverty, literacy, gender equality, cultural autonomy, and diversity; cf. K. Ohmae, *The End of the Nation-State: The Rise of Regional Economies* (London: Harper Ellis, 1995), cited in Ilesanmi, "Leave No Poor Behind," 76.

17. Boafo-Arthur, "Dilemmas," 39.

alone export their meager produce. The continent's fledging textile industry is reeling from a WTO decision to throw open Western markets to products from China and India. Factories are closing, incomes are falling and jobs are disappearing... What experience has taught Africans and their impoverished Asian neighbors is that life was better before globalization; trade deals do more harm than good; and Western governments can't be trusted.[18]

Globalization is neither a linear, uniform, nor homogenizing process. Nor does it address inequalities in the international political economy. While pro-globalists might extol its successes, the fact that globalization creates inequalities is beyond doubt, at least in those parts of the world where people are left behind in the economic system and where policies aimed at advancing capital marginalize and increase the suffering of the poor, weak, and less privileged. And so our assessment of the Church in Africa as the "salt of the earth," for both Africans and the world, must show how she has contributed to human promotion of the African peoples and how she is responding to globalization.

One is led into posing various questions:

- In what ways has the Church in Africa lifted the African peoples from poverty, penury, and want?
- Has she been involved in development efforts in Africa? How does the Church in Africa respond to globalization?
- What is the Church doing to be relevant and to counter the persistent degradation of the human person arising from globalization?
- Should the Church do anything, or is it outside the tangent of her vocation to meddle in globalization?
- What type of spirituality should drive the evangelizing mission of the Church in Africa?

Since we have passed the age-old dichotomy of the Church and the world, the spirituality of the Church in the contemporary age must be different. The Church has redefined itself in the Second Vatican Council as the People of God, affected by the condition of her peoples and ready to ameliorate her conditions with determination to stand for justice and

---

18. Goar, "Protectionism's Fresh Appeal."

peace. How this is carried out will surely determine the Church in Africa as the salt of the earth.

First, let's examine the Church in Africa's involvement in human promotion.

The Church in Africa and Human Development

From the days of the missionaries to the present, the Church in Africa has focused its development strategy in Africa in two areas: education and health care. As of December 1998, the Catholic Church maintained 29,824 primary or secondary schools serving 9.6 million children, 6,754 secondary schools serving 1.9 million high school-aged students, and its universities and institutes of higher education had over 62,000 students enrolled.[19] The latest statistics shows a significant increase in the number of educational institutions in Africa. According to the *Statistical Yearbook of the Church 2001*, as of the end of 2001, there were 10,738 Kindergarten schools, 30,009 primary schools, and 7,488 secondary schools. Students in Catholic higher institutions numbered 37,750; community welfare institutions numbered 14,144.

In the area of health care, the Catholic Church is visibly present by the number of hospitals, clinics, dispensaries, and other welfare institutions it runs. The 1994 African Synod records that although Catholics constitute only 14 percent of the population of Africa, Catholic health facilities make up 17 percent of the health-care institutions of the entire continent.[20] In 1998, there were 817 Catholic hospitals on the continent, 705 orphanages, and 504 homes for the elderly, chronically ill, invalids, and handicapped.[21]

Through the dual emphases on education and health care, the Church in Africa has helped tremendously in fostering development of the continent. The products of its schools and higher institutions teamed

---

19. Cited in Zalot, *Sub-Saharan Africa*, 54.

20. John Paul II, *Ecclesia in Africa*, 38.

21. Cited in Zalot, *Sub-Saharan Africa*, 54. The number of hospitals run by the Catholic Church in Africa is of course more in number than the figure we have here. But this is the statistics within reach as at the moment of writing. For instance in Uganda alone, there are twenty-seven hospitals, over twenty-three health care centers and over 6,000 health care workers and is second to the government as the largest healthcare provider in the country. The same is true of many African countries at least countries in the sub-Saharan Africa; cf. http://www.ucmb.co.ug/data.

up, and fought for, political independence from their various colonial governments. Education has offered employment opportunities to significant numbers of Africans. Many more are involved in private businesses and are contributing to African socio-economic development.

And through health care, the Church in Africa boosts the lifespan of Africans. In many African countries, Church-owned hospitals end up being the most reliable health care system in place for the people. With the outbreak of HIV/AIDS, the Church in Africa pioneered efforts to diagnose and control the spread of the disease. For instance, records show that the first serological test for the diagnosis of HIV/AIDS was carried out in St Francis Hospital, Nsambya, in Uganda on May 23, 1986.[22] In Tanzania, Bugando Medical School, operated by the Catholic Church, trains thirty doctors a year—*half* of the newly qualified doctors in Tanzania.[23]

The Church in Africa and the Search for Social Justice

A story is told of a certain village by the bank of a river, known for its generosity and hospitality. One day, a group of villagers saw dead bodies floating by the river. They raked up the bodies and buried them. As the phenomenon continued, the villagers selected some people for the purpose of burying dead bodies from their river. While they did what was commendable for burying the dead, they failed to find out the source of the evil omen; they did not think that what was killing their neighbor at the other end could eventually get to them. And so after a while, the enemy crossed over to the generous villagers and slaughtered them all.

If Africa is impoverished, it behooves the Church in Africa, like any other institution in Africa, to find out why—and to be ready to do what it takes to better the lives of her flock. Thus, we come to our second question: Does the Church in Africa do anything toward finding out why its people are poor? What does it do to liberate Africa from poverty?

First, individual bishops, dioceses, national, and regional conferences of bishops, as well as theologians and lay people, perceive their being

---

22. See Daniel Guisti, "Faithfulness to the Mission of the Church in Healthcare: Points of Method Emerging from Reflection over an Experience" (January 2005); cf. http://www.ucmb.co.ug/data. The Church in Africa still needs to do more in creating awareness of the HIV/AIDS pandemic. We shall say more on this as part of our recommendations on the way forward for the Church in Africa.

23. International Finance Corporation, *Health in Africa*.

leaders and members of the Church as implying their being salt of the earth—that is, those who by their witness ought to purify and perfect the society. As individuals, however, they diagnose the cause of African malaise differently.

- In his intervention at the 1994 Special Assembly for Africa, (the African Synod), bishop Joseph Ajomo of Nigeria observed that "as leaders of the Church in Africa, we must distance ourselves from unjust rulers, dictators, the corrupt civil authorities, and assume our rightful place as "the salt of the earth and light of the world" (Matt 5:13–14).[24]

- For Archbishop Michael Kpakala Francis of Liberia, the problem with Africa is traceable to the tendency to the cult of personality worship and intolerance. Archbishop Albert Obiefuna of Nigeria agrees—and notes with regret that, indeed, the African Christian with his exaggerated ethnicism finds it difficult to accept the truth that the Christian man or woman in India is much more a brother or sister than the non-Christian brother or sister in the natural family (Gal 5:10).[25]

- Bishop Jean-Noel Diouf of Senegal sees inculturation and dialogue as the solution to the problem of Africa paralyzed by wars, famine, debt, unemployment, and poverty, decline of the educational system, AIDS and other endemic diseases, as well as the striking social crisis.

- For Bishop Zacchaeus Okoth, grassroot solutions should begin at the small Christian communities where inculturation, justice, peace, and communication through dialogue will receive greater attention.

Nevertheless, despite individual differences, various national and regional conferences of bishops of Africa[26] speak out as one through

24. Ajomo, "Interventions."

25. Archbishop Albert Obiefuna, cited in Ajomo, "Interventions."

26. There are nine regional conferences in Africa. These include: 1) Association of Member Episcopal Conferences in Eastern Africa (AMECEA), which includes Eritrea, Ethiopia, Kenya, Malawi, Sudan, Tanzania, and Zambia; 2) Association of Episcopal Conferences of Anglophone Africa (AECAWA), which includes Gambia, Ghana, Liberia, Nigeria, and Sierra Leone; 3) Inter Regional Meeting of Bishops of South Africa (IMBISA), includes Angola, Botswana, Lesotho, Mozambique, Namibia, South Africa, Swaziland, Zimbabwe, Sao Tome, and Principe; 4) Association of Episcopal Conferences of Central Africa (ACEAC), which includes Rwanda, Burundi, and the Democratic

The Church in Africa

communiqués against government policies that infringe on the human dignity of Africans. An example was the 1992 pastoral letter Living Our Faith, from the Catholic Bishops of Malawi. This pastoral letter helped in the democratic process of Malawi, although after its publication a number of the bishops were arrested, questioned, detained, and repeatedly accused of sedition by the Malawian police.

African bishops call their nations to prayer[27] and offer useful suggestions on prevailing socio-economic situations.[28] For instance, the Cameron Bishops Conference 1990 pastoral, *Les causes de la crise economique*, suggested an end to the Structural Adjustment Programme, cancellation of all foreign debts, and the creation of a new international marketplace based on solidarity and mutual interdependence.

The continent-wide body is the Symposium of Episcopal Conferences of Africa and Madagascar (SECAM), formed during the Second Vatican Council (1962–65) to enable the young African bishops speak with one voice on African issues and inaugurated as assembly of bishops on the occasion of Pope Paul VI's maiden visit to Africa in 1969.[29] It identified development and peace as the major areas Africa must tackle and achieve. Heavily influenced by the social teachings of the Church and the Synod of bishops' documents *Justice in the World* as well as *Evangelii Nuntiandi*, the bishops, faced with the problems of Africa, emphasized the

---

Republic of Congo; 5) Association des Conference Episcopale Regionale de l'Afrique Centrale (ACERAC), which includes Congo, the Central African Republic, Cameroon, Chad, Gabon, and Equatorial Guinea; 6) Conference Episcopale Regionale de l'Afrique de l'Ouest (CERAO), which includes Benin, Burkina Faso, Ivory Coast, Guinea, Mali, Mauritania, Niger, Senegal, Togo, Cape Verde, and Guinea Bissau; 7) Conference Episcopale de Madagascar (CEM), which includes Madagascar, Seychelles, Mauritius, Comores, and Reunion; 8) Conference Episcopale Regionale du Nord d'Afrique (CERNA), which includes Algeria, Libya, Morocco, and Tunisia; and 9) The Catholic Hierarchy of Egypt (AHCE), which includes Egypt and the Oriental Churches of North Africa; cf. Zalot, *Sub-Saharan Africa*, 186–87

27. Worthy of mention is the famous "Prayer for Nigeria in Distress," composed by the Catholic Bishops Conference of Nigeria in 1993, when the presidential elections were annulled, followed by political upheaval, and national crises threatened the existence of the Nigerian nation.

28. Cited in Zalot, ibid., 158.

29. Pope John Paul II traced the history of the formation of SECAM to the Second Vatican Council, where bishops sought to identify appropriate means of better sharing and making more effective their care for all the churches. Such moves gave rise to plans for suitable structures at the national, regional and continental levels. SECAM is an instance of such structures; cf. *Ecclesia in Africa*, 2–3.

connection between evangelization and human promotion. At the 1974 International Synod of Bishops in Rome, SECAM's report "Experiences of the Church in the Work of Evangelization" stresses integral salvation demanded by the Gospel. "Citing the fact that Christ himself is intimately concerned with the salvation of the entire person, the delegation holds that participating in development efforts and providing social services are not alien task[s] of the Church, but an integral element of the gospel message it is called to proclaim."[30] Thus their self-understanding, expressed in their mission statement, is:

> "To promote its role as a sign and instrument of salvation and to build the Church as a Family of God in Africa": to preserve and foster communion, collaboration, and joint action among all the Episcopal Conferences of Africa and the Islands. Accordingly, the Symposium, through the Episcopal Conferences promotes: (i) Propagation of Faith: stressing on primary evangelization of those who have not yet received the message of Christ, i.e., in-depth and on-going evangelization of the peoples of Africa and the Islands. (ii) Human Development: i.e., the integral liberation of the human person, Good Governance and Justice and Peace issues. (iii) Ecumenism: i.e., the pursuit of fraternal relations and interreligious dialogue with peoples of other faiths. (iv) Formation: i.e., the establishment of theological/pastoral institutions and research centers. (v) Consultation: i.e., on the major problems facing the Family of God in Africa and in the world as a whole.[31]

Through SECAM, the African bishops have spoken out with one voice against national and international injustices that keep Africa from attaining development. They have appealed to world leaders and international agencies for assistance to Africa's development efforts. They have also condemned the debt burden of Africa and the structural adjustment programs forced upon Africa by international financial institutions like IMF and the World Bank, which have robbed many African countries of welfare schemes and plunged them deeper into poverty that results

---

30. See Zalot, *Sub-Saharan Africa*, 147. Thus, as they did in the 1971 Synod of Bishops that produced *Justice in the World*, once more, in the 1974 Synod, they emphasized the importance of efforts to liberate people from oppression as the very demand of the prophetic function of the Church, and without which the Church will be rendered useless.

31. Cf. SECAM web site: http://www.sceam-secam.org/identity.html. Elochukwu Uzukwu acknowledged the role of SECAM in promoting evangelization as integral human promotion and its criticism of infringements of human rights; cf. Uzukwu, "Local Church," 6

in increased disease and illiteracy. As early as 1969, they emphasized the need for any assistance package to Africa to respect the dignity of the human person in Africa and not be attached to conditions that would negate African values. Applying the principle of subsidiarity, they insist on the right of African peoples to be involved in their own development.

SECAM does not just pass the buck of African underdevelopment on external factors. In its 1981 document *Justice and Evangelization in Africa*, the bishops identified corruption by Africans themselves as the major factor militating against economic development and called upon African Christians to realize that their faith calls them to authentic justice as part of the Christian ethic they profess. They are also aware of the place of authentic witness, starting with the Church itself. Thus, they state that in order to be truly a prophetic voice, the Church must be just within its own life. They urged the clergy to renounce flamboyant lifestyles that contradict the simplicity of the Gospel. The document also makes the following recommendations for justice in Africa:[32]

(i) education of the faithful in the social teachings of the Church;

(ii) proper relationship between justice and human development: SECAM appealed to all Africans in public office to "carry out their responsibilities with justice and impartiality; it asks that in public spending priority be given to meeting the basic needs of the people . . . and that public money never be employed for extravagant expenses."

(iii) on Politics: SECAM condemned "the rigging of elections, the suppression of freedom of speech, of free association, or of freedom of religion. It also condemns . . . the persecution, banning, or arbitrary imprisonment of those who profess political opinions that differ from the official position."

Globalization and the Church in Africa

No one doubts the benefits of globalization. Greater interconnectedness and interdependence, made possible by revolution in information

---

32. I am indebted to Josef D. Zalot's book *The Roman Catholic Church and Economic Development in Sub-Saharan Africa*, 150–54 (2002), for the citations from the SECAM document "Justice and Evangelization in Africa" under review.

technology; an improved standard of living, made possible by economic boom arising from free trade and the open market system; greater accountability and transparency, made possible by the demands and terms of trade; greater efficiency, made possible by competition bringing out the best in human creativity and ingenuity. The spread of democracy and more efforts at good governance, as well as respect for human rights, comes about at times from fear that maladministration affects trade and drives away investors wary of investment in unstable nations. This is because in globalization there is a connection between good governance, corruption-free regimes, provision of infrastructure, and economic advancement. The list can go on and on without end, depending on one's place in the global economy, good governance, and competitive spirit.[33] As Christopher Farrell notes: "A great transformation in world history is creating a new economic, social and political order: Communism's collapse and the embrace of freer markets by much of the developing world are driving huge increases in global commerce and international investment. The Information Revolution is forging strong links between nations, companies, and peoples. Improving education levels are creating a global middle class that shares 'similar concepts of citizenship, similar ideas about economic progress, and a similar picture of human rights.'"[34]

---

33. While appraising globalization positively, we must not forget to ask the question for whom and to what extent. The rich industrialized countries can appraise globalization and rate its success highly as Martin Ravallion of the World Bank Policy Research did; see Martin Ravallion, "The Debate on Globalization, Poverty and Inequality: Why Measurement Matters" (*World Bank Policy Research: Working Paper 3038*, 1–26). Because the benefits have accrued to them and are still accruing to them and may continue to accrue to them, going by the structure of economic globalization today that creates economic inequality. However, alongside this phenomenal affluence arising from globalization there is the increasing poverty of the world's poor, whose standard of living keeps on falling; who are exposed to violence, and who suffer dehumanizing indignities as a result of the affluence created by globalization to the few rich industrialized nations; cf. UNDP 1998 Report, 49. Simeon O. Ilesanmi's observation buttresses this fact: "Contrary to the jubilant declaration in certain international financial circles that the embrace of market-based development and great advances in the global circulation of goods, capital, and ideas are creating wealth and bringing new opportunities (World Bank 1995, 1), globalization has actually exposed billions of people to monumental risks. It has created an unjust condition of radical inequality and penury that is extreme, persistent, pervasive, and yet, avoidable. Africa is most overburdened by this condition because of the manner in which it is integrated into the global economy. By the terms of its integration, Africa is conditioned to never-ending impoverishment." Ilesanmi, "Leave No Poor Behind," 78.

34. Farrell, "Triple Revolution," 195.

However, as the system of globalization fosters homogeneity among people, there is the tendency for the dominant groups to swallow the minority; this inevitably brings about loss of cultural identity and, hence, loss of meaning and value, often resulting in chaos and confusion. And this is the major tension in globalization: the tension between culture (tradition) and development or civilization, between modern life and traditional values. The dichotomy between the two plays itself out in the open society in the tension between the individual ethics of life and communal norm; the secular and the religious, the sacred and the profane, religious extremism and tolerance. The result has at various times been either violence or reconciliation. Thus, the challenge of globalization remains keeping the two in a balance, as Thomas Friedman aptly observes:

> The challenge in this era of globalization—for countries and individuals—is to find a healthy balance between preserving a sense of identity, home and community and doing what it takes to survive within the globalization system. Any society that wants to thrive economically today must constantly be trying to build a better Lexus and driving it out into the world. But no one should have any illusions that merely participating in this global economy will make a society healthy. If that participation comes at the price of a country's identity, if individuals feel their olive tree roots crushed, or washed out, by this global system, those olive tree roots will rebel. They will rise up and strangle the process. Therefore, the survival of globalization as a system will depend, in part, on how well all of us strike this balance.[35]

I quote Thomas Friedman extensively, not because I adopt his market-oriented profit-making capitalistic brand of globalization that must don the "golden straitjacket," irrespective of its adverse effects on the poor, weak, and infirm. Nor do I support the reform measures of the international financial institutions that have taken over governance and dictate the economic policy in many developing countries including Africa; but, rather, to show the tension in the world today sharpened by the new system of globalization. As we noted earlier, African poverty and increasing incidence of disease, including HIV/AIDS, results partly from the withdrawal of social welfare packages by African governments adhering strictly to the "golden straitjacket" of economic globalization.

---

35. Friedman, *Lexus*, 42.

It is to this globalization—political-social-economic imperialism and tendencies to "universal" civilization, or monoculture—that the Church in Africa must respond. The Industrial Revolution left Africa behind because she was enslaved during the period; her labor provided the raw materials for the growth of the industries. Today, if care is not taken, the revolution in information technology might overtake Africa and again leave her behind, something that enduring poverty in Africa inadvertently facilitates (how many children in Africa today know how to use a computer?).

As a consequence, Africa in the future, just as now, may not be able to tell her own stories; she may not have control of mass media. She may well be relegated to merely an appendage in the global communications machine, resurfacing on the world stage only when tribal conflicts and wars are flashed on screen, therefore continuing to portray how savage she and her people are to a civilized world.

The unpredictable power supply in some African countries and its complete absence in others, as well as absence of and/or decaying social infrastructures, are also worrisome aspects of considering the future of Africa in the new era of globalization. The Fathers of the Special Assembly for Africa (1994) lamented:

> The developing nations, instead of becoming autonomous nations concerned with their own progress toward a just sharing in the goods and services meant for all, become parts of a machine, cogs on a gigantic wheel. This is often true also in the field of social communications which, being run by centers mostly in the northern hemisphere, do not always give due consideration to the priorities and problems of such countries or respect their cultural make-up. They frequently impose a distorted vision of life and of man, and thus fail to respond to the demands of true development.[36]

Furthermore, and perhaps most importantly, African cultural values appears to be most seriously hit in the system of globalization. Globalization has made migration easier; a quest for a better standard of living has made emigration almost a necessity for Africans. This has brought lots of strain on marriage, family, and Christian faith, with increasing rates of divorce, domestic violence, and abandonment of the Faith in the quest for basic survival in foreign lands.

---

36. John Paul II, *Ecclesia in Africa*, 52.

Furthermore, the present wave of secularization with its tendencies to materialism further distorts African cultural values, thereby weakening its ability to integrate the dialectics of African communities. If one may ask, where is our sense of fellowship when we are divided ethnically and tribally? Where is honesty and selflessness amidst so much lying, greed, and corruption? What have we done with transparency and accountability in the face of grandiose worship of money? What has happened to African sense of chastity as she hawks her daughters and children to prostitution overseas? The situation is precarious: Africa struggles with the problem of cultural identity arising from the various heritages she has inherited from her traditional culture, Christian life, and Islamic religion.

The Imperative of Culture

Globalization, therefore, makes attention to culture an imperative. And the Church in Africa cannot ignore this. Actually, the first African Synod (1994) made inculturation its central theme, in order to harmonize Christian faith and culture. An inculturated Christian faith becomes meaningful to the African and pays attention to the various conditions of the African peoples—no longer foreign, but native to the African life. Such Christianity allows Africans to be who they are and equips them to weave together the variables of the globalized world of today. Only an inculturated Christian faith will give the African the spirituality for liberation—for the reconciliation, justice, and peace much needed for development in Africa. Pope John Paul II, during his visit to Malawi, offered inculturation as a challenge to the Church in Africa: "I put before you today a challenge—a challenge to reject a way of living which does not correspond to the best of your traditions and your Christian faith. Many people in Africa look beyond Africa for the so-called 'freedom of the modern way of life.' Today, I urge you to look inside yourselves. Look to the riches of your own traditions, look to the Faith which we are celebrating in this assembly. Here, you will find genuine freedom—here, you will find Christ, who will lead you to the truth."[37]

But thus far, inculturation has been liturgical only, with the Eucharist celebrated in various native languages of Africa; in the use of local instruments used in sacred music; and in liturgical vestments sewn using

---

37. Ibid., 48.

African textile materials. In other areas of life, attempts at inculturation have been heavy on words and light on action. While attempts are being made to study the African traditional religion, the religion from which most conversions to Christianity are made and the custodian of African culture,[38] the process of inculturating the Christian faith has been rather too slow. Cultural problems are still handled as they were by the missionaries over a century ago. Some rich cultural values and practices are condemned outright, without proper investigation of them. Members of the clergy set up ad hoc committees to adjudicate cultural issues they do not understand. Peculiar African perspectives that deal with the spirit world—ancestral veneration, witchcraft, and water spirit cult phenomena—are either swept under carpet as if they do not exist or are treated as neurotic or schizophrenic, in a Eurocentric manner.

Cultural institutions like masquerading, marriage, and title taking are not treated any differently. Masquerading is banned as an evil cult; indigenous cultural titles are condemned as tainted with evil due to certain sacrifices associated with them; and some marriages, contracted validly in the customs and traditions of the people, are declared invalid. Little wonder that today many people, especially among the educated elites, discard Christianity, while a good number mix their faith with their traditional religious beliefs and practices. The gap between theory and practice of inculturation results from concentrating on theological principles, justifying inculturation that swallows up the practice itself. Augustine Onyeneke rightly notes: "Much work on inculturation, mainly by theologians concentrating on theological principles, showing how desirable and how feasible the movement ought to be, but hardly descending to practical ways and examples of inculturation in concrete life."[39]

---

38. In a letter of March 25, 1988, mandating the Episcopal Conferences in Africa and Madagascar to include the study of African traditional religion in the seminary curriculum, the then President of the Secretariat for Non-Christian Religions, Francis Cardinal Arinze, cited six of these cultural values to include: "sense of the sacred, respect for life, sense of community, family, spiritual vision of life, authority as sacred, and symbolism in religious worship."

39. Onyeneke, *African Traditional Institutions*, 18. Two other factors militating against inculturation of Christian faith in Africa are the theological divide between inculturation theology and liberation theology; and the financial dependence of the Church in Africa to the Western Church. On account of the former, there is mutual suspicion among theologians in the various camps in Africa. Since he who plays the piper as the saying goes, dictates the tune, the Church in Africa leaders are afraid of implementing

The anomalies in the life of African people thought to uphold rich cultural values is a clarion call on the Church in Africa to integrate African cultural and religious values—that in themselves are in consonance with the Gospel values of love, justice, and peace—into Christian faith. What this means in the search for social justice and in the life of the Church as the salt of the earth is that, as people begin to accept and reconcile their faith with their culture, Christian faith and love can take root in the whole life of the people.

Christian faith could thus become a transforming force through which people can overcome the otherworldly spirituality that prevents the people in large part from seeing social injustice as something they should fight to change. This could go a long way toward sensitizing people to the importance of overcoming poverty, fighting the culture of corruption, and holding their leaders accountable for use of the nation's resources. Thus, inculturation becomes a powerful factor in the struggle for justice. As Peter Schineller observed:

> Since inculturation is inevitably linked with the struggle for justice, it will at times be a challenge to the ruling powers. Inculturation grapples with the issue of the religious culture of people in the face of the Christian faith, as well as the major questions of poverty, injustice, marginalization in our world . . . Much resistance will come to a prophetic voice when it addresses these issues and tries to inculturate Christian faith in a sinful, often unjust world. Persecution and rejection are marks of the true Church, the Church that is trying to inculturate gospel values of justice and peace in a world that is often unjust and violent.[40]

It ought to be emphasized, then, that the issue of social justice is a great challenge confronting the Church in Africa. She can no longer tackle it merely by exhortatory words, addresses, and communiqués. The socio-economic, historical, and political landscape of Africa demands more prophetic roles in terms of open denunciation, education, and mobilization of the people to reject, to fight, and to uproot unjust structures that oppress, marginalize, impoverish, and dehumanize African peoples. There will be no African Church if there are no Africans.

---

inculturation to the full for fear of loosing the financial assistance from Rome and other sister Churches in the West.

40. Schineller, "Inculturation," 56.

The Church in Africa also cannot exist independent of the context and life situations of Africans. Therefore, improving the lot of Africans must be one of the constitutive dimensions of the ministry of the Church in Africa. So inculturation and liberation must go hand-in-hand if inculturation is to be put into practice. As Jean-Marc Ela aptly notes:

> A Church that seeks to say something to today's African cannot content itself with an authentically African liturgy, catechetics, and theology. The modes of expression of the Faith have sense and meaning only if the Church is deeply involved in the battles being waged by human beings against conditions that stifle their human liberty. The participation of the Church in these battles, then, becomes the necessary condition for any liturgy, any catechesis, any theology in Africa. It is in the vital experience of the communities and of their striving for life, liberty, and justice, that any reference to Jesus and his mission—a mission of the liberation of the oppressed—will find genuine sense and meaning.[41]

Recommendations

In the light of the foregoing discourse, we recommend the following toward the Roman Catholic Church being the salt of the earth.

1. The Church must give authentic witness aimed at living the gospel values, so as to satisfy the thirst for God by the people of God, its body of Christ. In this regard, the lifestyle of the clergy must reflect the condition of the people. Clergy need to be rigorous in self-examination to ensure that, while they are entitled to maintenance, their compensation should not be out of line with the conditions of the people to whom they minister.

2. Training the laity as the agents of evangelization is important. Through homilies, symposia, conferences, seminars, etc., the laity can learn how to step up to their civic responsibilities. Bible study and fellowship sodalities etc. should emphasize social analysis. In this way, faith and action is integrated.

3. HIV/AIDS is ravaging Africa and is the number-one weapon of mass destruction militating against any development effort, as it kills experts and skilled manpower and drains resources. The Church in Africa should do more than it does now to combat the disease. She should create

---

41. Ela, *African Cry*, 132.

awareness by talking about the disease publicly, discussing its causes in order to remove the stigma, and helping in the care of the afflicted.

4. As a religion, the Church in Africa must come to grips with the reality of globalization and be able to understand its internal dynamics, especially economic globalization. The socio-economic condition of African today was created as a consequence of (among other factors) the Breton Wood agreement. It should be able to speak out in clear condemnation of structural adjustment programs without a human face that keep many African peoples perpetually poor and malnourished. Christians and other religionists perpetuate capital outflow from the continent. She must not allow herself to be caught up in sharing in the booty of the few African technocrats who benefit from a system that holds other Africans down in poverty and want. If she does, she will be caged.

She has to understand the dynamics of market-oriented economy before involving herself in it. She must not become an agent that corrodes the cultural traditions of Africa in preference for Eurocentric culture masquerading as Christianity. Therefore, she must open her eyes to the effects of globalization and be ready, through Christian tradition, to preserve the cultural values of African peoples.

5. In a pluralistic society like many countries of Africa, with multiple heritages, the Church in Africa must pay close attention to dialogue and be able to unite with other religions to a common cause for the good of the continent. The divide-and-rule attitude that pits the Church in Africa against other religions does not help in bettering the socio-economic life of the people. It only gives the technocrats opportunity to distract the people by playing religious politics while looting the treasury and disregarding infrastructural development.

6. The African Church does not seem to have caught on to aspects of ecological devastation, in spite of erosion and other disasters like drought, famine arising from insufficient rain, etc. At times, she embarks on development projects without due regard to the environment. I have not come across any document from any of the regional bodies on ecology or on the need for an ecological spirituality.

4

The Church in Africa and the Search for Abundant Life: Signposts for Renewal and Transformation of God's People in Africa

Alex Ojacor

Africa: The Bad News

WHENEVER WE TALK OF AFRICA, what strikes immediately is the suffering continent. Africa is full of bad news. According to Thabo Mbeki, Africa is passing through a "dark night." It is a continent "consumed by death." So we begin with the bad news.

The continent of Africa is faced with multiple challenges. In spite of Africa's richness in human and material resources, in cultural traditions, and in our embracing of faith commitments, the general image that people have of our beloved continent is that of conflict, war, poverty, suffering, disease, violence, and injustice of every kind. We highlight a few of them below to show the gravity of the problem.

Diseases

Africa is a host of many diseases that have claimed millions of her people: malaria, Ebola, sleeping sickness, HIV/AIDS, *et al.* Up to 25 percent of the African population is infected with HIV/AIDS. Although our approximately 750 million people constitute only 12.5 percent of the world population, we contribute up to 75 percent of the world cases of HIV/AIDS.[1]

Political Instability

In the last four decades, thirty-five out of fifty-three states in Africa (about 66 percent) have been wracked by conflict, much of it internal. At least twenty-three African heads of state or government (which is nearly half of the heads of state) have military backgrounds, among them men who have led armed rebellions against the state. Africa has a shameful history of violence, exacerbated by slavery and colonialism, which continues to this day. Her children are at the mercy of destructive forces unleashed by criminals and gangsters, tyrants and dictators—violence, fraudulent elections, bribery, corruption, and above all, an obscene passion for wealth that is a cause of all these ills.

Poor Leadership

Africa has a chronic cancer of corruption, economic mismanagement, and bigotry. African leaders loot their countries' wealth with impunity, bleeding their own kin to death, impoverishing their countries and perpetuating corruption. Independent Africa has witnessed more incidence of human rights corruption, injustice, and oppression than it did in colonial times. Many political leaders own public lands and assets wrongly, or take social positions to enrich themselves.

Poverty

Africa has about 60 percent of the world's natural resources, while most of our people live on less than $1 a day! Forget about the rosy figures presented to us of so-called strong economic growth and macro-economic success; Africa remains the poorest continent in the world. The rosy figures represent only some areas. Distribution of welfare gains has varied across regions, sectors, and social/economic groups. The poverty gap and the depth of poverty have increased especially in rural areas. This poverty

---

1. See UNDP, Human Development Reports 1990–97.

is multi-faceted: low levels of income, physical insecurity, poor health, low education, and disempowerment.[2]

This state of affairs has led to a dependency syndrome that has eroded our self-confidence, initiative, and creativity. Some just flee for low-paying jobs or a life of dependency in the developed world, sometimes in very degrading circumstances.

Climate Change

Climate change may be the greatest challenge facing humanity in this century, a challenge in which the world's poorest countries and the world's poorest people—the bulk of which are in Africa—will bear the brunt.[3]

These and many other factors conjure up frightening images of savagery in contemporary Africa. Africa has to rebel against them, to banish the shame, and the only way out is to look back on Africa's past achievements and find hope for the future. There is no need to indulge in self-contempt. Admittedly, the picture may be bleak—but it is not the whole picture. This limited optimism is what is challenging African theologians, such as the writers of this book, to discern numerous signs of incipient African revival in the present situation. I for one am happy to be pointing to the signposts of hope and renewal.

Africa: the Good News

Not all is bad news in Africa. Archbishop Buti believes that Africa's internal criticism has been exaggerated by Western observers and their ardent followers, giving rise to pessimism that is unjustified.[4] This mind set has become known as "Afro-pessimism," a feeling of despair among foreigners and even among Africans themselves, but we refuse to label Africa as "the hopeless continent." There is an unarticulated part of Africa that is not cited: its glorious past. This includes the emergence of *homo sapiens*; the numerous cave paintings; the art and architecture of ancient Africa;

---

2. UNDP, Human Development Report 2000.

3. The Human Development Report 2007/2008 shows that climate change is not just a future scenario. Increased exposure to droughts, floods, and storms is already destroying opportunity and reinforcing inequality. Meanwhile, some believe that the world is moving toward the point at which irreversible ecological catastrophe becomes unavoidable.

4. Thlagale, "Religion and Renaissance," 16–22.

the centers of learning at Alexandria; Ethiopian Christianity, and more. Africa hosted Joseph and his brethren in time of famine and also gave refuge to the Holy Family. Africa was the seed ground of Christian saints and theologians like Augustine, Tertullian, Cyprian, and other Fathers. These must be recalled to give us hope.

More recently, several events have happened in Africa that bring hope to even the worst of pessimists: to name two, the acquisition of independence in all African countries and self-governance. These countries, despite what Mveng calls "structural poverty,"[5] have continued to persevere and exist until today. There are emerging social structures that are improving life for Africans, even if they do not match those of the developed world.

A 2006 World Bank report[6] states that 2005 may have been the year when Africa "turned the corner" from poverty and debt to prosperity and wealth. In a continent that was once dependent on foreign aid, there are now sixteen countries that have achieved annual growth rates in excess of 4.5 percent for more than a decade. Several African countries—Senegal, Mozambique, Burkina Faso, Cameroon, Uganda, and Ghana—are on course to cut the number of people living in poverty by 2010.

Enrolment in primary schools has increased continent-wide, from 72 percent in 1990 to 93 percent in 2004, and literacy rates have risen to 65 percent in 2002, from a previous rate 50 percent in 1997.

In the ecclesiastical arena are springs of hope as well. At a meeting with diocesan clergy of AOSTA on July 25, 2005,[7] Pope Benedict XVI noted that vocations are increasing in the Southern part of Africa; indeed they are so numerous that it is proving impossible to build enough seminaries to accommodate all the young men who want to be priests. He attributes to this *inter alia* a certain enthusiasm of faith because they are in a specific period of history. In a sense, it is springtime of faith in Africa.

The Church as Family of God in Africa

The theme of the Plenary assembly of the Symposium of Episcopal Conferences of Africa and Madagascar (SECAM), the special Assembly for

---

5. Mveng, "Impoverishment and Liberation," 157–58.
6. http://www.britainusa.com/.
7. Address of His Holiness Benedict XVI to the Diocesan Clergy of Aosta at Introd Parish Church, Aosta Valley, 25 July 2005.

Africa of the Synod of Bishops held in 1994, was *The Church as the Family of God*. This image emphasizes the special character of the Church as a communion, easily the most outstanding trait of life in Africa. It was the bishops' hope that an exploration of the African family as an image of the Church will contribute in no small measure to a better understanding of the nature, mission, and destiny of the Church in Africa.

There are still people in this twenty-first century, both non-Africans and, unfortunately, some alienated Africans themselves, who find it very hard to believe that African cultures can add to the understanding of Christianity and Church. Any African model is suspect, while Eurocentric theological, biblical, liturgical, moral, and ecclesiastical models are sacrosanct—in effect, making the European model synonymous with "Christianity." This needs to be seriously addressed in the wake of the Africa being the hope and beacon of the Church today. Now is the time for counter-evangelization. In this way, Africa can define itself and position itself in the life of the Church. It is therefore right and fitting that the rich model of African family was used in the Synod.

The African experience of family is much wider than the word suggests in Europe and America. This idea is supported by Mbiti, who says a family in Africa includes children, parents, grandparents, uncles, aunts, brothers, and sisters who may have their own children, and other immediate relatives.[8] He adds that the family also includes departed relatives and unborn members still in the loins of the living. As the bishops of South Africa expressed in their inter-regional meeting during the preparations for the Synod, African traditional culture is centered on family.[9] Speaking to the Catholic laity in Harare, Zimbabwe, Pope John Paul II rightly said, "African traditional culture is centered on the family. Africa cannot flourish unless its families survive present social upheavals. The African family must find new strength, reaffirm the positive values contained in tradition, and assimilate a more personal dimension of understanding, commitment and love."[10]

We certainly recognize that African cultures, like all cultures, are dynamic. Unfortunately, we cannot fail to note that the African family is in mortal danger. The migrant labor system, social and geographical

---

8. Mbiti, *African Religions and Philosophy*, 106.
9. Browne et al., *African Synod*, 45.
10. Pope John Paul II in his visit to Harare, Zimbabwe, 11 September 1998.

The Church in Africa and the Search for Abundant Life

mobility, unemployment, housing shortages, rural-urban migrations, internal displacement due to civil wars (placing people in squalid "displaced person" camps), refugees, the corrosive influence of the Western neo-pagan culture, and the many factors are destroying the traditional family and its many positive values. It is only, as the Pope said, by assimilating a more personal dimension of understanding, commitment, and love that African family culture can be saved.

This theme of the Church as family in Africa runs through the African Synod and is repeated several times to underscore its importance. The African family is a model of the living Church: it includes everyone. It is the basis of unity and solidarity because it means sharing roles and involving all. It emphasizes small communities, fitting the ecclesiologies developed by several African theologians based on the family, clan, and tribe. As the bishops pointed out, they owe much to African theological reflections on this point to bring new life into the Church; this will be one of the greatest contributions of African Church to the universal Church.

This sense of community is not only expressed in the family but permeates the whole of African society. The African is a citizen of the whole world, open to life and receptive to new ideas. African culture is not a discriminating culture. There is a sense of community and hospitality—a trait that any visitor will not fail to discover. In the words of Stan Ilo, they do not understand the language of exclusion or racial bar. Any animosity between tribes only occurs in the political and economic balancing game.[11] The African loves "newness" and very easily interacts with anyone of any culture or color. In Africa, people know each other and share their joys and sorrows with each other. The sense of community is alive and vibrant, even in the midst of urbanization and westernization.

The Hope of Africa: Signposts of Renewal and Transformation

In spite of Africa's present dire predicament, there are already signs of an incipient renaissance. As far back as April 1998, Thabo Mbeki (even before he succeeded Nelson Mandela as President of South Africa) used the phrase "African renaissance" in a lecture he delivered to the United Nations University in Tokyo.[12] In August the same year, he broadcast his

---

11. Ilo, *Face of Africa*, 296.
12. Mbeki, "Mbeki speaks."

"African Renaissance Statement." And, on the eve of the millennium, he made his "Our African Century" speech to the South African National Assembly.[13] In October 1998, an "African Renaissance" Conference was convened in Johannesburg, followed by the foundation of an "African Renaissance Institute" and the creation of a ministerial committee on African Renaissance in the South African Government.[14] In November 1999, another Conference on African Renaissance was convened at the Africa Centre in London.[15] Numerous writers of all shades and opinions since then have published reflections that provide a roadmap toward African renewal and transformation: we are people of hope.

This concept of African Renaissance used by Mbeki is not new in the history of cultures and religions, either. In 1864, St. Daniel Comboni had already talked of his "Plan for the Regeneration of Africa," with "regeneration" synonymous with "renaissance."[16] Rebirth implies a previous existence, but it also celebrates a new reality, a creative transformation of the old. We are talking here of a deeper and more vital concept than just "cultural revival" or "cultural retrieval," which merely suggests the identical recovery of a past experience, as some Africans would like to have.

Other heroes and heroines have also helped shape the new Africa making its appearance at this moment of history. We can look to both the past and the present for these signs of hope. Individuals like Leopold Senghor, Archbishop Kiwanuka Joseph (First African bishop south of the Sahara in modern times), Kwame Nkrumah, Julius Nyerere, Oliver Tambo, Nelson Mandela, and Desmond Tutu (African nationalists); John Mbiti, Sr. Theresa Okure, and John Mary Walligo (African theologians); Martha Karua (Nobel prize winner), Ellen Johnson Sirleaf (the first African woman president), and Justice Julia Ssebutinde (Presiding Judge in Special Court for Sierra Leone at the International Criminal Court) have greatly contributed to African renaissance. Artists like Lucky Dube, Miriam Makeba, and Chaka Chaka have brought new hope to the African continent. Prolific writers such as Wole Soyinka, Chinua Achebe, Okot p'Bitek, Ken Sarowiwa, and Ali Mazrui have set a precedent in African literature that is making Africa more aware of itself in the global context.

13. SABC, "African Renaissance Statement."
14. Haffajee, "Midwives."
15. Davies, "African Renaissance?" 18
16. Shorter, *African Imagination*, 40–42.

The Church in Africa and the Search for Abundant Life

If we take the example of South Africa, skeptics who have always presented Africans as brutal and murderous were brought to shame when apartheid ended. To their utter amazement, the oppressive, dehumanizing reign of apartheid was followed not by orgies of retribution and revenge by Africans on Whites but by the extraordinary Truth and Reconciliation commission, a process of forgiveness and reconciliation. Nelson Mandela is one of the world's most revered statesmen today because he demonstrated magnanimity and generosity of spirit in his willingness to forgive his tormentors and the oppressors of his people. He is today an icon, a saint of forgiveness and reconciliation, in a world that has become ruthless and belligerent—as demonstrated by terrorism throughout the world and the famous war on terror led by the mighty United States.

Other encouraging signs and movements across Africa have emerged within the last few years. There is a growing intolerance of dictators and human-rights abusers. Former leaders, even presidents, can face the wrath of the law for crimes against their people.[17] There are signs of emerging hope of democracies in many African countries. The winds of change are blowing in Africa, and people are demanding, ever more insistently, the recognition and promotion of human rights and freedoms. National oppressive leaders can no longer hide in the name of "non-interference in internal affairs of a country." Action against dictators and those usurping legitimate governments through undemocratic means can no longer do so without raising international eyebrows. Cases in point: Darfur, Somalia, Sierra Leone, Liberia, and most recently, Kenya—where warring parties were pressured to have a government of national unity. ECOWAS, ECOMOG, the African Union, etc., are all examples of a concern by Africans for Africans themselves. Gradually, we see the development of democratic institutions and structures in the African continent. Even if they're far from perfect, at least they're moving in the right direction. The right questions are being asked.

It is interesting, though not surprising, that such examples of humanity should be regarded as an inspiration for the moral renewal which underlies the concept of the African renaissance. Although sometimes presented as an agent of division and war in Africa, religion does occupy

---

17. The case in point is the trial of Charles Taylor, the former president of Sierra Leone, and many others who have been indicted by the International Criminal Court. Some warlords, like the Lord's Resistance Rebel leaders of Joseph Kony of Uganda and others in the DRC, are wanted to answer charges in the International Criminal Court.

a very central role in this African renaissance, and the abuse of religion does not invalidate its potentially positive contribution. According to Buti Tlhagale, African renaissance seeks to bring out what is noble in humanity. It is a new orientation—a radical shift in the scales of preference, this adoption of spiritual values that have been overlooked. To him it is, therefore, a form of religious development.[18]

Stan Ilo, in his book *The Face of Africa*, prefers to call this an Afro-Christian vision. I totally agree with him when he says that hope is a principle that sustains belief in the rich possibilities of the future for Africa. Ilo builds up an Afro-Christian vision of hope as a theological category; it is that there can be no transformation of any society, and no emergence of a culture of hope, without the integration of a religious component into the whole reality. When we look at the religious revival at work in Africa even within traditional, conservative, established churches, we are filled with more hope. For many established historical churches experiencing decline in the West, the hope for their continuity and revival is in Africa.

Recommendations

The African renewal and revival is, first of all, a discovery by Africans themselves—a confidence-building voyage of discovery into their past without remorse or shame. It is a rediscovery of Africa's soul and a restoration of her self-esteem. It is a mass crusade for Africa's renewal. It is a determination to learn and a desire for genuine liberation. In the words of Wangari Maathai, the Kenyan Nobel Peace Laureate, 2004, it is important that a critical mass of Africans do not accept the verdict that the world tries to push down their throat so as to give to and succumb. The struggle must continue to nurture new ideas and initiatives that can make a difference.

The political and economic objectives of the African renewal and revival include eradicating hunger and poverty, promoting economic growth and integration, developing infrastructures, eliminating HIV/AIDS, creating a non-racial and non-sexist society, and restoring human dignity. The social and moral objectives include the abolition of militarism in governance and one-party states, the democratic empowerment of the people, the elimination of corruption and the abuse of power, the

---

18. Tlhagale, "Religion and Renaissance," 16–22.

resort to peaceful means of conflict resolution, and solving the problem of brain-drain. The religious objective is to redefine and position Africa as a beacon of hope for Christianity.

In the words of Mbeki, such a program is a call to rebellion against tyrants and parasites, but a call as well to generate new knowledge and apply this knowledge for beneficial social change. For this to happen, Africa must become a learning society, with a friendly intellectual environment. Africa must be brave enough to gear its academic courses to suit our African experience and needs. Africa has a right to see the world from its own perspective and model—to not only integrate its own practical wisdom and skills within the new technology, but to resist intellectual and economic colonialism.

Religion in general, and Christianity in particular, can contribute to the regeneration of humanity through the discipline of sacrifice and self-denial. From a purely pragmatic point of view, religions cross the boundaries of African states and can help to provide the intercultural and inter-ethnic dimension of this new society of Africa. All communities of faith share in what Tlhagale calls a "mystery of fellowship," which they try to live. The Church is, in fact, a model—even a laboratory—of this new society proclaimed by the African renaissance.

The content of salvation positively entails the remission of sins, the removal of evil, freedom and new life for the children of God, and the hope for eternal life. That means that liberation from structures of sin and injustice is part and parcel of African renewal and salvation. Salvation also embraces the final redemption of our bodies (Phil 3:20). This is fully possible only through the transforming power and presence of Christ in African culture and life. This calls for us to be critical as well of any African cultures that may mitigate fullness and abundance of life.

Conclusion

It is true that Africa is challenged on many fronts: economically, politically, emotionally, socially, culturally, religiously, etc. This is cause for worry. Contemporary Africa can be compared to a man who went down from Jerusalem to Jericho; he fell among robbers who stripped him, beat him and departed leaving him for dead (Luke 10:30–36). Africa is a continent where countless human beings—men, women, children, and young people—are lying, as it were on the edge of the road, sick, injured, disabled, marginalized, and abandoned.

But it's not all bad news. Africa is endowed with a wealth of cultural values and priceless human qualities that it offers to the churches and to humanity as a whole. These human values can contribute to an effective reversal of the continent's dramatic situation and facilitate that worldwide revival on which the desired development of individual nations depends.

Africans have a profound religious sense—a sense of the sacred, of the existence of God the Creator and the spiritual world. The reality of sin in its individual and social forms is very much present in the consciousness of these peoples, as is also the need for rites of purification and expiation. These are ingredients and a recipe for reconciliation, forgiveness, and respect for human life that gives us much hope for the continent.

In African culture and tradition, the role of the family is fundamental. Open to this sense of family, of love and respect for life, the African loves children, who are joyfully welcomed as gifts of God. The Pope rightly said:

> The sons and daughters of Africa love life. It is precisely this love for life that leads them to give such great importance to the veneration of their ancestors. They believe intuitively that the dead will continue to live and remain in communion with them. Is this not in some way a preparation for the belief in the communion of saints? The peoples of Africa respect life which is conceived and born. They rejoice in this life. They reject the idea that it can be destroyed, even when the so-called "progressive civilizations" would like to lead them in this direction. And practices hostile to life are imposed upon them by means of economic systems which serve the selfish rich.[19]

Africans show their respect for human life until its natural end, and keep their elderly parents and relatives within the family.

African cultures have an acute sense of solidarity and community life. In Africa, it is unthinkable to celebrate a feast without the participation of the whole village. Indeed, community life in African societies expresses the extended family. If Africa preserves this priceless cultural heritage and never succumbs to the temptation of individualism, which is alien to its best traditions, then there is cause to rejoice: we are on the right track.

19. John Paul II, "Homily," 3.

5

Globalization and the African Woman: A Socio-Cultural Analysis of the Effect of Information and Communication Technology (ICT)[1] on Women

Bosco Ebere Amakwe, HFSN

Introduction

A GOOD SUMMARY OF THE social effect of digital and electronic technology is found in the words of "the patriarch of media criticism,"[2] Marshall McLuhan, who said: "The medium, or process, of our time—electric technology—is reshaping and restructuring patterns of social interdependence and every aspect of our personal life. It is forcing us to reconsider and re-evaluate practically every thought, every action, and every institution formerly taken for granted. Your education, your government, your family, your neighborhood, your job, your relation to "the others." And they're changing dramatically."[3]

---

1. Because of lack of space, I am not going into detailed definition of ICT here. But for a better understanding of the argument of this article, it will suffice to give what I may call a "general definition" of ICT in the words of Hamelink: "ICT encompass all those technologies that enable the handling of information and facilitate different forms of communication among human actors, between human beings and electronic systems, and among electronic systems." See Hamelink, "New Information," 3.

2. Kappelman, "McLuhan," 3.

3. McLuhan, *Medium*, 8.

Understanding the effects of technology as it relates to human beings and their relations with one another in communities was McLuhan's priority. After writing twelve books and hundreds of articles, this "prophet of the electronic age"[4] was the first to sound the alarm of the negative effect of these innovations. This has forced many scholars to come up with the thesis that adopting ICT is not necessarily a good thing.

For instance, in *Technopoly*, Postman suggests that we would be better off without such technologies.[5] But such debates are outside the scope of this article, as we are proceeding on the assumption that the digital divide, inequality and sexual exploitation (fruits of the former) are problems that need to be solved, especially as they affect African women.

Globalization, ICT, and Women

No matter the field of study, volumes can be found on globalization and its effects—positive and negative. Whether globalization is anathema to social justice or not, it is a given in the twenty-first century.[6] Bhasin defined it poetically when she said that globalization means:

> profit is paramount. For profit, anything will be made and sold: armaments, pornography, junk drinks and food, violence, just anything. Globalization means consumerism of the worst kind and plunder of nature. Globalization means centralization of control over resources and decision-making. Globalization also means lack of popular participation. Globalization means an attack on diversity whether it is agricultural . . . or cultural diversity . . . Globalization means the culture of the rich . . . Globalization means increase in violence and militarization . . . Globalization also means patriarchy becoming more powerful, more entrenched. In this global village control over knowledge and information is an important source of power.[7]

This is why Janovicek affirmed that "globalization, new technologies, and deregulation have created new challenges, and that more and more women live in poverty as a result of international trade agreements that

---

4. Kappelman, "McLuhan," 1.
5. Postman, *Technopoly*, 119–20.
6. Robins, "African Women?" 235–49.
7. Bhasin, "Women and alternatives," 4–7.

put profit before human rights."[8] The same point is made by Bolles when she said: "globalization builds on the tension that exists between two conflicting or interacting forces, elements, or ideas"[9] which I see to be capitalism and development. No wonder

On a positive note, Tiongson argues, "Globalization and the convergence of various forms of new information technologies have fuelled the widespread and rapid promotion of ideas and values at the local, national and global levels in a scale and intensity never before experienced."[10]

As a result, women are now seriously examining how these developments have "engendered or hindered the advancement of the status of women and the attainment of equality between women and men."[11] By so doing, women are diagnosing the ambiguities of globalization. These obscurities, inflamed by ICTs, are the areas under examination in Africa (my own part of the world), with particular attention to the degree they affect Nigerian women.

This exposition will be done by answering many questions:

- Are Nigerian women "being sold a bill of goods"?
- Can the new ICTs really help them take their rightful place in the decision-making that governs their existence?[12]
- The vast majority of African women especially those in rural areas are struggling daily to meet life's basic needs. Under those conditions, are ICTs relevant?

This is why the "fast-paced growth of cyberspace and the technology behind it makes research by feminists all the more important."[13] Therefore, this essay is not just an attempt to provide a "woman-centered vantage point for the examination of communication technologies" but also an evaluation of the ways these innovations affect and marginalize the African women—although socially and politically, women are excluded and are negatively impaired by these technologies.

8. **Nancy Janovicek**, "Women's Rights," 336.
9. Bolles, "Forever Indebted," 15.
10. Tiongson, "Women and Media," 6.
11. Ibid.
12. Robins, "African Women?" 240.
13. King and Hyman, "Women's Studies," 1–7.

However, in the last decade, women have benefited in the use of these "machines." At the same time, women have been studying and questioning exploitation through and by electronic media. They have been urging governments to regulate the use of ICTs, known as Computer Mediated Communication (CMC),[14] though with little result. But the challenge is to battle on—and we will examine that battle briefly here.

Who is the African Woman?

For decades, the underprivileged situation of women especially in the developing world has been object of concern not only for scholars but also for governments and philanthropists. In African societies, for instance, women are characterised as "minors" for most of their lives, falling under the guardianship first of their fathers and then their husbands.[15] Girls right from birth are perceived in the light of their future roles as prospective wives and mothers.[16]

Among the Igbo tribe of Nigeria, for example, at birth a baby girl is referred to as *akpa-ego* (bag of money), *unoaku* (house of money), or *obute aku* (source of wealth), *Ada-aku* (daughter of wealth) or *ezi-aku* (good wealth or place of wealth—with slight change in the ascent). These names are allusions to bride wealth, which would accrue when the girls get married, and other benefits that would be derived through interaction with prospective in-laws.[17] In this sense, a girl or a woman is seen as "an appendage of the husband, her father, the family, the village or the ethnic group."[18] She is never a free person. An African woman is *someone* because she is married and she *is nobody* outside marriage. A woman acquires an identity through marriage to a man. The number one ID of any African woman is *M.R.S.* (Man's Reserved Slave) in my own interpretation.

Even with this economic tag placed on the girl child from birth, most African families prefer having baby boys to girls. It is believed that a

---

14. For the purpose of this essay, the words *Internet, cell phone,* and *the CMC* are synonymous to ICTs and will be used interchangeably.

15. Sudarkasa, "Status of Women," 25–31.

16. See Nnoromele, "African Woman," 178–90, and Oyewumi, *Invention of Women*.

17. Amadiume, *Male Daughters, Female Husbands*, 77. Also see Ndukaeze Nwabueze, "From 'ori akwu' to 'odozi akwu': Impact of changing status of Nigerian women on family welfare," in Olurode, *Women and Social Change*, 93–107.

18. See Osinulu, "Contribution of Women."

boy child guarantees the continuity of the family lineage while a girl will be married away to become the "property" of another man and thus her identity is not tied to her parent's family. This is also the reason why women do not have right of inheritance like land in most African countries (even though in few matrilineal regions of the continent, women inherit land and their right to resources is not mediated through their husbands). Also there are some parts of Africa like in Edo State of Nigeria, "women's access to land depends on marriage and they retain access to land as long as they remain in their husband's household."[19] In addition, there exist volumes on other cultural and social torture African women are subject to like widowhood practices,[20] discrimination[21] at all levels, etc.

This notion, according to Olurode, has lowered the position of women. For centuries, this idea has become gradually embellished and, in part, clothed in a milder form, but by no means abolished. In her opinion, this is one of the most absurd notions that have come down to us from the period of enlightenment of the eighteenth century.[22] As we shall see later, this is exactly why women are regarded as the opposite of men. As Oduaran affirmed: "In Nigeria, women are often treated as second-class citizens, mostly relegated to the background of society."[23]

This, of course, is because the Nigerian society is essentially male-dominated. Usually, according to Akpa, "There is a popular myth at the base of the status of women in traditional Nigerian society ... the sense of inferiority."[24] Summarizing it all, Levitin and others stated that "the best of woman was a lesser man."[25]

However, we wouldn't deny that this feeling of inferiority is changing with the growth of ICT, which gives many "Sub-Sahara African women access to computers, the Internet, and other related technologies,"[26] and therefore leading to some change in the perception of their role. On the other hand, as we shall see below, we must also admit that these

19. Tunde, "Women's land rights," 2603.
20. See Akujobi, "Yesterday," 2457.
21. See Mangatu, "Glass Ceiling."
22. Olurode, Women and Social Change, 3.
23. Oduaran, "Women's Capacity," 60–70.
24. Akpa, "Gender Inequality," 6.
25. Levitin et al., "58% of a Man," 89–92.
26. Mbarika et al., "IT education," 1.

innovations perpetuate the age-long situation of women mainly because of the "macho" image attached to modern technology.

The Homo-techno Myth

Since the dot-com boom of the late 1990s,[27] the household word is new-technology this, and high-tech that, which in the Western language connotes new discoveries in the area of science and technology. In the contemporary society, new technologies implicitly or explicitly depict power, and power is usually associated with masculine. Linn observed that even a cursory review of the scholarly literature on technology reveals that the terms "woman" and "technology" are not separate; they are related terms in a vocabulary of power-relations that defines the objects men make and manipulate as "technical" and those of women as "nontechnical"—as "natural," sometimes even "nurturing," "humane," or "humanistic."[28] Kramarae argued: "Technological processes have been studied from the (usually implicit) vantage point of men's experiences. When one puts women at the center of analysis, male biases and masculine ideologies become clearer, and one discovers new questions as well as fresh approaches to old questions."[29]

On the same note, Hillman asserted: "The specific consciousness we call Scientific, Western and Modern is the long sharpened tool of the masculine mind that has discarded parts of its own substance, calling it 'Eve,' 'female' and 'inferior.'"[30]

Accordingly, Armstrong observed that when histories of technology mention women (and they do so rarely), women are usually conceived as "consumers" of technology—as users of telephones, typewriters, and similar machines.[31] This is why in Nigeria, for instance, women consider the word "technology" to have male connotations.[32] Today, other usages like "virtual world," "cyberspace," "cybermarts," "cyberoffice," "e-business"—however you name them—put women who are almost igno-

---

27. Shannon, "IT shortage," 10–11.
28. Linn, "Stereotypes," 106.
29. Kramarae, *Technology*, 7.
30. Hillman, *Myth*, 250.
31. Armstrong. "Gender Bind," 106.
32. Elijah and Ogunlade, "Uses of ICT," 1–14.

rant of these "digital vocabularies" in their so-called "natural place," the "other world of silence." This is the "andric-techno image" or "masculistic techno mystification" we are talking about. Lawley referred to this as "deterministic view of a computer ideology imposed from above"[33] that makes women "losers" because it confers power and knowledge on only a few—mostly men.

As a result, in 2006 for instance, the U.S. Department of Labor statistics indicated a marked decline—more than 10 percent—in the number of women in the IT workforce.[34] This, indeed, is troubling from a woman's perspective; it is clear that a significant number of women are excluded from the above "techno-discourse," especially in Africa. Only time will tell when women will become part of the so-called "Digital Generation"[35] to be able to understand what's going on.

From the look of things, it is not only the ICT critical analysts who are bothered about the issue of "dehumanization through technology";[36] authors in the fields of literature and literary criticism[37] are voicing their concern. This is why Davenport sees technology not as "a tool *for* change" but as "*the* change agent."[38]

The "Boom" and "Doom"[39] of ICT for Women

As the wave of ICT continues to blow stronger and stronger every day, women of all classes, ethnicities, and nationalities are encountering the monumental changes produced by its global impact. Studies on the effect of ICT on society have shown that there is a range of issues, which make it clear that the ICT have winners and losers, beneficial consequences and harmful applications.[40] Also, Winner is of the opinion that the digitization of society is not without consequences—a process he described as "a vast,

---

33. Lane, *Communication of Gender*, 3.
34. Smith, "Tech Gender Gap," 1–2.
35. Rossetto, "Why *Wired*?" 10.
36. Lane, *Communication of Gender*, 2.
37. Ibid.
38. Davenport, "Agee's *Death in the Family*," 227–39. Emphasis on *for* and *the* mine.
39. It was Hamelink who used the expression "boom versus doom" of ICTs. See Cees J. Hamelink, *The Ethics of Cyberspace* (London: Sage, 2000).
40. Elijah and Ogunlade, "Uses of ICT," 2.

ongoing experiment whose ramifications no one fully comprehends."[41] On the same note, Ellul argues, "All technical progress has three kinds of effects: the desired, the foreseen, and the unforeseen."[42] Hence, ICT is failing people in many ways, especially women in Africa.

However, any discussion of the effect of ICT on women in this part of the world must take into account the gendered nature of the social, economic, policy, and technological systems which frame opportunities for women.[43] If—as "cyber-high priests" claim—the new ICTs can help women transcend obstacles of culture, education, and poverty to take more equitable places in their countries' economic and political sectors, studies have proved that they also can "deepen the digital divide between haves and have-nots and reproduce colonial power relations."[44]

The Boom

ICT ENCOURAGES AND FACILITATES NETWORKING

Despite the problems caused by ICTs—as we shall see later—the online sharing of information and the creation of new cyber-communities are touted as crucial to women's education and political organization. The emergence of ICT is seen as an opportunity for African women to overcome some of the systemic and traditional disadvantages that they have faced.[45]

For instance, in Senegal, Robins found that the Progressive Communication's WomensNet connects organizations in the international women's movement, working with community stations and women's organizations to generate educational programs[46] for women. Also, the African Women's Media Centre (AWMC) in Senegal conducts a yearly cyber-forum to network women journalists from French-speaking African countries on a topic of importance. In 2001, for instance, 140 women journalists from fifteen countries of Africa went online to learn more about HIV/AIDS and how to use the Internet to do research and access

---

41. Winner, "Citizen Virtues," 1–8.
42. Ellul, Technological Bluff, 61.
43. Robins, "African Women?" 235.
44. Ibid., 238.
45. Ibid., 237.
46. Ibid.

Globalization and the African Woman

reliable and timely information. Also, Uganda's Healthnet is one of many organizations across the continent that monitors and promotes women's use of, and access to, health information.[47]

Again, the African Women Global Network links institutions to improve the living standards of African women and their families. In addition, the African Women's Media Centre does training and helps to establish partnerships among women journalists and women's groups.[48] These communication systems, according to Lawley, help women to escape boundaries and categories that have in the past constrained their activities and identities. By providing women with an opportunity to express their ideas in a way that transcends the biological body, ICT gives them the power to redefine themselves outside of the historical categories of "woman," "other," or "object."[49]

Helps to Empower Women

As already mentioned, information technology has been useful especially in showing women the way out of the cultural "cul-de-sac" in which they so often find themselves.[50] For instance, the study of Elija and Ogunlade found that Nigerian women's access to ICT-based economic and educational activities increases their contributions in both business and home-based activities.[51] These in turn, improve women's socio-economic status, providing access to information, communication, freedom of expression, and formal and informal associations. ICT also provide options for women, including overcoming illiteracy through distance education and creating opportunities for entrepreneurship, allowing women to work from home and care for their families. Accessing ICT from rural locations enhances and enriches their quality of life.[52] This is because ICTs can influence poverty alleviation within several aspects of work structures: creating marketable skills among poor young workers; making it possible to impart literacy and innumeracy to children of poor parents; and fighting against child malnutrition by ensuring information is avail-

47. Ibid.
48. Ibid., 238.
49. Lane, *Communication of Gender*, 4.
50. Sylvestre, "Development," 1–2.
51. Elijah and Ogunlade, "Uses of ICT," 6.
52. Ibid.

able to the household, especially the mothers. ICTs will ideally be reducing the information gap among various stakeholders so that knowledge and skills enable appropriate action for poverty reduction.[53] Furthermore, the anti-poverty measures introduced through the use of ICT have been able to generate a substantial amount of employment through the use of mobile phones by many Nigerians to earn a living.[54] Young women in particular do this by opening small call centres, usually along major roads, in squares and market places. Also, Ndukwe found that in Nigeria over 2,000 persons are directly employed by GSM operators, and about 40,000 Nigerians are benefiting from indirect employment generated by GSM operators.[55]

In Kenya, Janet Malika owes her success to the "little gadget"—her cell phone. Formerly a struggling food hawker in the Kenyan capital of Nairobi, she has become a cafeteria owner since acquiring the device about five years ago, and using it to conduct business. When asked she explained:

> Before, I would waste a lot of time trying to get ingredients from the market. By the time I got ready to start preparing food for sale, it would be so late and I ended up losing a lot of customers. With a cell phone, all I have to do is call my suppliers, who will deliver the ingredients within no time. Because of the phone, I am always on time in preparing meals for customers. My business has expanded to the point that I have opened a cafeteria. All I know now is profit.[56]

Not only in Kenya but also in Zambia Mwanja found "Zambian women often use their phones in business operations."[57] Even in India and Ghana, female entrepreneurial force revealed that using e-commerce and Internet technologies to reach global markets increases their independence and wealth. They do this by earning privatized loans from specialized female oriented institutions as well as government regulations expanding their socio and economic status.[58]

---

53. Urquhart et al., "ICTs," 203.
54. Elijah and Ogunlade, "Uses of ICT," 9.
55. See Ndukwe, "Roles of Telecommunications."
56. Mulama, "Africa," 1.
57. Kayamba, "Phone habits."
58. Ackerman, "Female entrepreneurs."

Similarly, according to a report by *M2 Presswire*, in 2005, the International Telecommunication Union (ITU) launched the establishment of a network of at least 100 Multipurpose Community Telecentres (MCTs) in twenty African countries. These centres are meant to "provide an enabling environment where women can actively participate in the economy and expand their role in communities through the use of ICTs."[59] Not only through access, but ICT can be used to empower women to have control over the kind of information they access, receive, obtain, and collect. More importantly, women can use ICT to adapt and innovate collected information into new or localized knowledge for further sharing with others in the community, thus contributing to their self-empowerment, self-determination, and well-being.[60]

Also on the social level, ICT is seen as a useful tool of empowerment for women in national peace building in Africa. Njeru is of this same opinion because she believes that marginalizing women is retrogressive in the peace building process, and that information and communication technology (ICT) can be used to mitigate the problem conflict and war in Africa. According to this author, "Peace building processes could be strengthened if organizations, people, and regions connect in effective multi-sectoral and peace building networks, and are provided with active and open knowledge banks. The inter-operability and use of ICT can provide such connections, bridging communication gaps between peace process stakeholders. ICT can be used to facilitate women's participation in this process, from the grassroots upwards."[61] But despite all these efforts and opportunities, African women still feel the ache of the "amputation caused by new technologies."[62]

The Doom

ICT Strengthens the "Old Boys' Network"[63]

As already mentioned, the potential of the Internet for African women is linked to the issues surrounding other political, economic, and cultural

---

59. M2, "ITU," 1–2.
60. Ojokoh, "Empowering Nigerian Women," 58.
61. Njeru, "ICT, Gender, and Peacebuilding," 32–40.
62. Kappelman, "Macluhan."
63. Pitt, "Masculinities@work," 379–82.

aspects of globalization.[64] A careful analysis of the points presented above will show that the African woman has "little place" in the ICT world. The great promise of the ICT instead results in familiar, oppressive patterns. Women in the information economy—because of their low level of ICT literacy—are typically found in the less prestigious and low-paid jobs, especially those that require little technological competence. In Nigeria, for instance, women make up 30 percent of all technical and related workers. However, only 1 percent of engineers are women.[65]

African women are the less educated and are the majority of the poor. Robins, quoting a South African journalist, noted: "The typical profile of an Internet user in Africa—educated, wealthy and male—has not changed since the continent went online in the early 1990s."[66]

In their study, Dutton and Peltu explain how new ICTs are developed and implemented to reinforce existing power structures. Since African women are at the bottom of the various power hierarchies, there are vast implications to current efforts to wire Africa into the global cyberspace network.[67] In the "wired Africa," the familiar and still formidable constraints are again rearing their ugly heads: poverty, illiteracy, insufficient skills—and male-dominated corporate control of technology added to the list.[68] Furthermore, Robins argues: "High-level discussions of the global marketplace almost exclusively omit women's particular problems . . . Women are lagging when it comes to the gains from globalization. Gender inequalities in the labor market and the workplace are not new. The changes in the information age favour skilled and well-educated workers, a category in which women are underrepresented."[69]

Encourages Pornography

Although we are talking about *new* information and communication technologies, many concerns regarding them are not new. Communication scholars of critical tradition mainly study ICTs in their role of

---

64. Robins, "African Women?" 235.
65. Chinye, "Gender Issues."
66. Robins, "African Women?" 237.
67. Dutton and Peltu, *Visions and Realities*, 5.
68. Robins, "African Women?" 238.
69. Ibid., 242.

"dehumanizing" interaction and individuals,[70] especially the Internet. For instance, Agger expressed concern that sexual violence will be systematically reproduced in a technocratically-controlled environment.[71] Little wonder Roberts affirms that "pornography is an old friend of technology."[72]

The Internet, in the opinion of Robinson, has made pornography (which has found a natural home online) more widely available.[73] If sex sells, then the Internet has become the primary place to purchase it.[74] "Online sex,"[75] or what Turkle referred to as "TinySex,"[76] erotica, or the expression of sexuality dominate the web. An online survey of Internet users conducted by Stern and Handel found that sexual pursuits, ranging from visiting web sites with sexual themes to intense online sexual interactions, may be the most common use of the Internet.[77] Also, Dodd affirms that sixty percent of the Internet (about 300 million Web sites) contains sexually oriented material;[78] Weiss added that these Web pages increased from 14 million in 1998 to 260 million in 2003.[79] Probably one of the most unexpected uses surrounding the growth of the Internet concerns the development of online relationships and their potentially addictive nature.[80] Pornography has moved out of the sleazy dives into the homes through 24-hour-a-day, easy Internet access. Porn has taken over much of the world's entertainment; it is addictive, it's pervasive, and it's harmful.[81] Griffiths observed that pornographers have always been the

---

70. Lane, *Communication of Gender*, 2.
71. Agger, "Dialectic," 3–21.
72. Roberts, "Dirty Little Secret," 30.
73. Robinson, "Girlie Mags," 8.
74. Ibid.
75. Lane, *Communication of Gender*, 6.
76. Turkle, *Life on the Screen*, 4. The author explains that "TinySex" is a kind of program that has to do with the transmission of sexual material and information over the Internet. The popularization of this type of program in the Internet has aroused the concern of many psychologists.
77. Stern and Handel, "Sexuality and Mass Media," 283–94.
78. Dodd, "Internet Pornography," J-3.
79. Weiss, "Human Trafficking," B-07.
80. See Kuipers, "Digital Danger," 379–401.
81. CWA, "CWA helps."

first to exploit new publishing technologies.[82] According to the study by Sprenger, it was estimated that the online pornography industry would reach $366 million by 2001,[83] although other estimates (e.g., Blue Money) around the same period affirmed that it was already $1 billion.[84] Six years later, the Bangkok *Post* declared the pornography industry worth billions of dollars a year.[85] After another six years, Peter Kleponis affirmed that it "is a $97 billion industry"[86] and long time anti-pornography crusader and Wheelock professor Gail Dines said it is a "near trillion dollar industry."[87]

Hughes, in her study, has traced this argument back to the mid-1990s, when the hottest place for commercial development was the Internet with sex-related adverts: "In early September 1995 there were 101,908 commercial domains on the Web, which was 26,055 more than at the end of July and 72,706 more than at the end of 1994. The sex industry was leading the way."[88]

In another study, the author remarked, "Web pornographers are the most innovative entrepreneurs on the Internet,"[89] with their transactions principally dealing in images of women. According to Oldenkamp, the majority of pornography viewed on the Internet depicts women as sexual objects—and thus reminds women of their unequal status within the society, since the majority of the viewers of pornography on the Internet are men.[90]

Again, Hughes noted that the largest pimps on the web—the buyers for live strip shows—are 90 percent male, 70 percent are between the ages of eighteen and forty. The buyers are young men in college and businessmen and professionals who log on from work.[91]

Even where Internet services have been meant for good, men still use them for pornographic reasons. For instance, according to a 2000 report in the *New York Times*, in the remote Cotopoxi region of Ecuador,

82. Griffiths, "Sex on the Internet," 331–40.
83. Sprenger, "Porn Pioneers," 2–3.
84. "Blue Money," 5.
85. "Agency Warns of Online Abuse," 1.
86. Pollock, "Pornography."
87. Eagan. "Porn in the USA," 10.
88. Hughes, "Internet and Prostitution," 1–5.
89. Hughes, "Trafficking and Exploitation," 3–5.
90. Oldenkamp, "Pornography, Internet and Harassment," 159–69.
91. Hughes, "Internet and Prostitution," 2.

Globalization and the African Woman

the Internet was introduced under the tutelage of aid workers. The peasants planned to gather crop information and sell their crafts over the Web. However, it was soon discovered that some of the men were using the computer to visit pornographic sites.[92] The porn industry produces 11,000 new porn movies annually—far more than Hollywood's annual output of 400 mainstream movies.[93] No doubt then that the pornography industry ruled by men with a lust for money perpetuates a misogynistic worldview, encourages prostitution and human trafficking and is the lubricant for many crimes against women.[94]

Encourages International Prostitution and Trafficking in Women

In recent years, many countries and NGOs have been battling to control the explosive spread of prostitution and the trafficking of women across international borders. The unprecedented growth of sophisticated global networks that control the sex trade has allowed the traffic to become a massive transcontinental industry.[95] We may say that these are old social problems that have been digitized, hence making things more difficult for women. According to Hughes, when those with power introduce a new technology into a system of oppression and exploitation, it enables the powerful to intensify the harm and expand the exploitation.[96] This characterizes what is happening as predators and pimps—who stalk, buy, and exploit women—have moved to Internet sites. It is true that the natures of sexual abuse and exploitation are not the same in all cultures and nations, but the recent rapid economic and political restructuring in many regions of the world, aided by globalization through ICT, has escalated this problem.

Within this milieu, women are increasingly becoming commodities to be bought, sold, and consumed by tourists, military personnel, organized traffickers, pimps, and men seeking sexual entertainment or non-threatening marriage partners.[97] The computer-based telecommunications

92. Romero, "Villages Go Global."
93. CWA, "CWA helps."
94. Hasiuk, "Porn awards," 7.
95. Ray, "Sex Trade," 62–65.
96. Hughes, "Internet and Prostitution," 1.
97. Ibid.

systems—the Internet and cell phones, for instance—can send texts, images, and audio and video files around the world in milliseconds. Cyberspace has been appropriated to accelerate and deepen the marketing of women and children for the purposes of sexual exploitation.[98] This, in my opinion, is a human rights disaster.

The 1999 UN report *Against Trafficking in Women* tells us that there are approximately 200 million people around the world being forced to live as sexual or economic slaves—of which women are the majority.[99] (Xinhua News Agency reported that in recent years, 10,000 Nigerian women have been trafficked into Italy alone.[100]) Another 1999 report of the United Nations stated that between 700,000 and 2 million women and children worldwide are trafficked every year.[101] This particular report singled out Nigeria, averring that about 50,000 Nigerian women engaging in sexual business have been stranded in the streets of Europe and Asia.[102] Nigeria is known as the African country that provides most victims of the global sex industry, with 70 percent of the 70,000 trafficked victims from Africa; this percentage of young Nigerian victims to traffickers often end up primarily in Italy.[103]

On the same note, coinciding with the start of the World Cup in South Africa, the U.S. Department of State released its 2010 Report—The 10th annual Trafficking in Persons Report. Some of the main findings of the 2010 report are

- 12.3 million adults and children are in forced labor, bonded labor, and forced prostitution around the world, with 56% of these victims being women and girls.
- The value for traffickers of this trade is estimated at $32 billion annually.
- There were 4,166 successful trafficking prosecutions in 2009, a 40% increase over 2008.

---

98. Harrison, "Cyperspace and Child Abuse," 365.
99. Coalition Against Trafficking in Women, "Pimps and Predators," 1–4.
100. Xinhua News Agency, "Nigerian Women," 1–2.
101. United Nations Fourth World Conference on Women, 3.
102. Ibid., 4.
103. Capdevila, "Right," 1.

- There are still 62 countries that have yet to convict a trafficker under laws in compliance with the Palermo Protocol (a document adopted by the United Nations on human trafficking).
- No less than 104 countries are without laws, policies, or regulations to prevent victims' deportation.[104]

This is why women in both government and at the grassroots are now coordinating their efforts to attack human trafficking together. In an unprecedented move in 2008, over sixty women leaders from different backgrounds and countries participated in the launch of a Women Leaders' Council in India that aimed at tackling what they described as the "hidden crime of globalisation."[105]

We must not forget that if a woman's life is limited by lack of education and employment opportunities, by racism, by illegal immigration or migration, by economic or political crisis, by childhood sexual, physical, or emotional violence, or by poverty, then sexual exploitation will aggravate and intensify the inequalities, disadvantage, and harm she suffers.[106] Prostitution and trafficking are not victimless crimes, or just another form of work, as profiteers of these trades would have us believe. Even when women voluntarily enter into these situations in the hope of making money or finding a better life, the dynamics of the brutal, often illegal sex industry quickly leave them with few other options and make them powerless to quit the dirty job.[107] Because there is little regulation of the Internet, the traffickers and promoters of sexual exploitation have rapidly utilized it for their purposes.[108]

Encourages Social Alienation and Isolation of, and Discrimination against, Women

The above "presumption" has been the hard truth about the negative effects of ICT on women. Carried away by the excitement of this new technology or that, debates and studies often concentrate on its positive effects. But in fact, underneath these "technological glories" also lies their

104. U.S. Department of State, "Report 2010."
105. Jaffer, "Service," 1.
106. Hughes, "Internet and Prostitution," 1.
107. Ibid., 2.
108. Ibid.

venom. Addressing this problem, Golding and Murdock advised, "The important issues posed by the new communications technologies are best addressed by revisiting the basic questions about social inequality and patterns of social access and exclusion caused by these innovations."[109]

On the other hand, Frissen asserts: "We work on the premise that technology is not neutral but made up of the ideas and values of those who own and control them."[110]

In effect, women do not have the same access to technology as men do because technology is socially and culturally constructed as a male practice, carried out in male-dominated society.[111] This is why Warnick evinced, "In the real sense of the word, the Internet excludes and marginalizes women even while it attempts to invite them online."[112]

Also, Sinclair argues, the sheer size and seeming complexity of the Internet seemed to have a chilling effect on women's interest in venturing online.[113] No wonder she described the Internet as a "vast realm," a "trackless forest," a "seemingly borderless world," a "digital jungle," and a "bizarre universe."[114] Sherman saw this "huge and unknown space" as having "dark alleys and odd characters to avoid"—like "virtual adultery,"[115] which affects women in one way or the other. For instance, the study of Grover found that virtual adultery causes divorce mostly in the West.[116]

Accordingly, Spencer described the Internet as a "toxic environment for women."[117] If control and power are the Internet's grammar, sexual harassment, she claims, is its subtext. Furthermore, she affirmed that Internet "discourse is male; the style is adversarial."[118] Chat Garcia has observed that the new ICTs also have created contradictory realities for women—from new work opportunities (particularly in production of electronics and computer hardware and computer encoding) to increased unemployment (bank tellers, telephone operators), or from greater in-

---

109. Golding and Murdock, "Unequal Information," 83–91.
110. Frissen, "Trapped?" 31–49.
111. Siew and Kim, "Status of Women?" 74–78.
112. Warnick, "Masculinizing the Feminine," 1–19.
113. Sinclair, *Net Chick*, 6.
114. Ibid.
115. Sherman, "Claiming Cyberspace," 26–28.
116. Grover, "Muddy Waters," 1–4.
117. Spencer, *Nattering*, 84.
118. Ibid., 86.

teraction and intercultural exchange and activism to deeper exclusion.[119] This is the point Webster made when she said, "In the information society, the position of women in the labor market is in no way contributing to greater gender equity."[120] This is because, as she says, "Work remains one of the key areas in which women are currently excluded from full social and economic enfranchisement and from the opportunity to develop to their full potential as members of society."[121]

On her part, Tiongson observed, "Science and technology education continues to be biased against girls and women, which explains why they are underrepresented in the technical aspects of the information and communication sectors. Women are mostly concentrated in clerical work while only a few are engaged in computer systems administration and technical development. Women in low grade technical and service jobs also make up the largest group of computer users."[122]

Accordingly, Menzies warned of new technology becoming, literally the extension of man, and by extension, the retraction of women.[123] In her opinion, the new technology also has meant "elimination of many service-related jobs traditionally held by women, such as telephone reception and banking services, or the transfer of such work into the home where workers are employed on contract, constantly monitored through their telephone or computer. Women who work in these conditions find out that they have little reason to go out during the day."[124]

In their study, Gillard et al. highlighted a systemic paradox: "that ICT skills development initiatives designed to support lone women parents . . . ironically serve to reproduce the participants' classification as socially excluded"[125] which, according to Menzies, may lead to the "disappearance of women as social beings."[126] In short globally, there is a significant "under-representation of women in computing, information technology (IT) and information systems"[127] in general.

119. Garcia, *Empowering Women*, 1–6.
120. Webster, "Second Sex," 119–40.
121. Ibid.
122. Tiongson, "Women and Media," 6.
123. Menzies, "Janus."
124. Ibid.
125. Gillard et al., "ICT," 19.
126. Menzies, "Janus," 3.
127. Elli et al., "Women's ICT," 279.

To avoid this, something has to be done. Webster asks, "What are the factors promoting the improved social inclusion of women in a future information society? What exclusionary factors operate and how persistent are they? How may women of different ethnic groups fare in the emerging information society? And are the improvements in girls' educational performance sufficient to secure them all a more equal place in the workplace and in other areas of social life? Finally, what policy initiatives—in addition to those already under way—would contribute to greater gender equity?"[128]

These are some of the questions we have so far tried to answer; they form part of our recommendations.

The Way Forward

Educating Girls and Women to Cultivate Interest in Study, Use, and Pursuit of Careers in ICT

Here, we would like to talk about the two forms of education and training—informal and formal. The first is what we may call "early childhood socialization"[129]—the "preschool period" during which children's ideologies, orientations, and behaviors are formed with the help of parents, other family members, and caregivers. As we shall see subsequently, what happens to a child at this stage affects him/her later in life. For instance, their early exposure[130] to the knowledge and use of ICTs will eventually be carried on to adulthood.

Be that as it may, however, in Africa, there are still differentiated early childhood socialization processes between girls and boys, not only in regards to ICTs but also in all spheres. In Nigeria, for example, daughters are socialized to be soft, meek, and subservient and sons to be hard, aggressive, and domineering.[131] Boys are called "sissies" if they cry, while girls are admonished if they exhibit aggression or competitiveness.[132]

---

128. Webster, "Second Sex," 119–40.

129. Amakwe and Ebere, "Mobility of Women," 22–23.

130. Ibid., 69–72. Here, I talked about what happens when children are exposed early in life to the use of mass media. Also in this essay I argue that the same identical thing could happen with ICTs.

131. Effah-Chukwuma and Osarenren, *Beyond Boundaries*, 24.

132. Northern, *Gender Issues*, 1–55.

Globalization and the African Woman

As in other areas, the learning about the so-called "hard and scientific things" is usually meant for boys and the reverse is the case for girls. In this era, boys at the early stages of their lives are often socialized to feel more at ease with the "magic machines" of ICTs than are girls (although a recent research from South Africa questions this assumption).[133]

This brings us to the concept of formal education and training—the second stage in a child's development process. The importance of what happens to a child here is as eminent as in the first stage. But unfortunately, in Africa, where families have traditionally put boys' education first,[134] the fact that a low percentage of girls and women attend formal education cannot be overemphasized.

In Nigeria, for instance, as at 2003, the total primary school enrolment is 80 percent; girls make up 44 percent of this number, boys 56 percent.[135] Again in Ethiopia, LaFraniere found that an estimated 24 million girls are without elementary school education.[136] Even the government of this country at a point acknowledged that "access to . . . education for women and girls falls short of what is required to achieve parity with men and boys."[137] This is why the dual campaigns of Education for All (EFA) and the Millennium Development Goals (MDG) made universal primary school enrolment for boys and girls a priority for developing countries in 2005. Even with these initiatives, Smalls—quoting UNESCO—noted that South Africa, for instance, "is one of the 54 countries in sub-Saharan Africa . . . that are not expected to educate girls as well as boys by 2015."[138]

It is important to note that even when girls and women attend school, they are not receiving the same quality or even quantity of education as their male classmates[139] in the "hard subjects." Confirming this, the study of Der on female education in math and sciences in Senegal found

---

133. Bovee *et al.*, "Computer Attitudes," 1762–76. The research question of the study was whether differences in computer attitude could be found between boys and girls, and to what extent these differences could be explained by student, school, and environment characteristics. In contrast to most studies on gender differences and computer attitudes, no gender differences in computer attitudes were found.

134. Dickson, "Good Cause," 2.

135. Ebigbo, "Child Abuse," 95–106.

136. LaFraniere, "For Girls," 1.

137. Taylor, "Fewer Opportunities," 8.

138. Smalls, "Unequal Access," 4–7.

139. Asimeng-Boabene, "Gender Inequity," 711–29.

that women make up 15 percent in science and technology disciplines.[140] These discoveries confirmed the report given by The Federation of African Women Educationists (FAWE), which stated that African women have the lowest participation rates in the world in science and technology education, at all levels.[141]

Similarly, Olurode remarked that in Nigeria, a majority of women are still not being trained . . . in areas that will enhance their chances at competing for positions in public life, one of which is in technology.[142] Again, Oyelaran-Oyeyinka and Adeyinka also found that in Nigeria, women's participation in modern science and technology-based occupations has been remarkably limited,[143] even though economists and policy makers from around the world have argued that given the nature of the modern capitalist economy, a workforce well trained in science and technology is essential for economic development[144] because knowledge empowers people, while information technology integrates such knowledge for purposeful action and reaction.[145] Since women are unacquainted with ICT and usually less active in learning new technologies, they need more initial encouragement and training. They need support in learning to work with, and to feel confident of their ability to use these technologies productively. Every ICT user including women should also create interest in manipulating it, although it may not seem convenient to understand its use initially.[146]

---

140. Der, "Female Education."

141. Federation for African Women Educationalists, "Girls Locked Out."

142. Olurode, *Women and Change*, 11. Also see Oolajire Bosede Ajayi and Dolly Ighoroje Ahbor, "Female Enrollment for Information Technology Training in Nigeria," presented at the 8th International Conference of the Gender and Science and Technology Association (Ahmedabad, India, 1996); and Shafika Isaacs, "It's Hot for Girls! ICT as an Instrument in Advancing Girls' and Women's Capabilities in School Education in South Africa," presented at the United Nations Division for the Advancement of Women Expert Group's meeting on information and communication technologies and their impact on and use as an instrument for the advancement and empowerment of women (Seoul, Korea, November 11–14, 2002).

143. Oyelaran-Oyeyinka and Adeyinka, "Technology and Women," 164–78.

144. McEneaney, "Cachet of Literacy," 221–37.

145. Urquhart et al., "ICTs," 203.

146. Ojokoh, "Empowering Women," 67.

Globalization and the African Woman

Hence, it is imperative that women from all walks of life are made ICT savvy.[147] Huyer summarized this beautifully when she argued, "The single most important factor in improving the ability of girls and women in developing countries to take full advantage of the opportunities offered by information technology is more education, at all levels from literacy through scientific and technological education."[148]

To help in achieving this, several women and professional associations exist in Nigeria: the Nigerian Association of Women Scientist (NAWS); Nigerian Association of Women in Science, Technology and Mathematics (NAWSTEM); Forum of African Women Educationists (FAWE) Nigerian chapter; and others. These bodies, with the help of funds from the government, help in granting scholarships to girls and women in science and technology education, organize vocational remedial courses for girls opting for science subjects, and sponsor career talks featuring different women in science and technology education[149] and career areas. And, in 2003, Suzane Bomback launched a program to give ICT training to women in Cameroon, which she called "Operation 100,000 women by 2012," in collaboration with the Yaounde-based African Institute for Computer Science.[150]

Initiatives such as these should be welcomed in Africa—though even with these projects, one finds out that African women themselves do have ambivalent attitudes toward ICTs.[151]

Globalizing the Needs and Dignity of African Women through ICT

It is a known fact that in the Western media, whenever we hear about projects for Africa either by governments or NGOs, we see sick and wretched African women sitting under huts, their long dry breasts flowing, with dirty and sick babies around them. These scenes have become clichéd for decades, usually accompanied by the announcement of millions of dollars donated to help these women. But still, every year statistics from that part of the world show a high percentage of uneducated, unemployed,

---

147. Anuja, "ICT Training," 1–2.
148. Huyer, "Gender, ICT, and Education," 1–47.
149. Imhanlahimi and Eloebhose, "Women's Access," 583–88.
150. Sylvestre, "Development," 1.
151. Anoush, "Women's Perceptions," 476.

poor, sick, and abused girls and women. None of these reports will ever conclude without yet another high percentage of women and girls with HIV/AIDS. The questions then pose themselves:

- Are these broadcast projects real, and with the right intention?
- How are they carried out?
- Who are the coordinators to make sure that the aims are achieved?
- Are the beneficiaries (the supposed African women) even aware of such projects?

Mottin-Sylla brought up these issues when she affirmed that, despite her organization's work to use the Internet to network women and to lobby against their discrimination in Africa, sometimes the local African women's groups that should have their voice heard were not even aware of any campaign happening.[152] This is why Gillard *et al.* suggested that ICT initiatives should be accompanied by changes in pedagogic practice that accommodate the more wide-ranging needs of those targeted for inclusion, as well as changes in employment settings.[153] Gender mainstreaming and the needs of women need to be taken into account in ensuring that IT contributes to women's development in Africa.

Women Should be Made Part of the ICT System

As we have seen so far, women as labor force are hit strongly by the digital divide, especially in developing countries. As a growing part of labor force and economy, women need training, access to information and financial resources so that they can enhance and benefit from the use of new technologies. The cost of ICT access especially affects women. They are generally paid less than men and often do not have control over their income. Women also have less professional access to ICT than men.

Another reason why women are isolated from ICT system is women's scarce time resources. It means then that ICTs need to be incorporated into other activities and projects destined for women's empowerment and must be sufficiently specific and active that women can see a tangible benefit from their use. ICTs should improve women's abilities more

---

152. Mottin-Sylla, "Women's Rights."
153. Gillard *et al.*, "ICT," 19.

effectively to fulfill their existing productive and reproductive obligations. Also the use of ICTs will need to be flexibly integrated into women's daily schedules. Ongoing advocacy, networking, support, and empowerment activities and projects should be facilitated through access to and active contributions of ICT. Physically, this means that ICTs should be located in contexts and organizations that support the activities that women have indicated as their priorities. For example, women's NGOs, health centers, educational institutions, self-employment and entrepreneurial centers, and perhaps even churches. Conceptually, this means that information needs to be tailored and targeted to women's specific concerns.[154]

Unfortunately, as already explained, technological systems and their effects can be a form of ideology, shaped by the designers and managers of technology.[155] Therefore, only when women become part of this process of designing and creating can they gain control of these tools—exerting substantial influence in the larger spheres of design and implementation.[156]

How can this be achieved? Only through training and educational programs,[157] as mentioned before. This is crucial for women because, according to Zimmerman: "Without political and financial control over new technologies, women will find themselves replaying a familiar scenario in which new technologies serve to reinforce old values."[158]

On the other hand, Lawley argues, "The goal of including more women in the economic and political control of technological change is a worthy one, but should not be seen as the only part for feminist action vis-à-vis that technology."[159]

This is why in this essay I advocate that women should be part and parcel of the technological system not only from the financial and political point of view, as Zimmerman suggested, but also from the "theoretical" standpoint. This will mean the active participation of women in deconstructing, reconstructing and contextualizing the discourse of ICT.[160] Thus, women will be aware of the wider social context where ICT

154. Ojokoh, "Empowering Women," 69.
155. Hubbard, Foreword, vii–viii.
156. Lane, *Communication of Gender*, 4.
157. Ibid.
158. Zimmerman, "Technology and Women," 355–67.
159. Lane, *Communication of Gender*, 4.
160. Cheung, "Global Discourse?" 1–11.

is deployed, as well as the marginalization and negative effects brought about by its development and the capitalist and globalization force intertwined with it.[161] This in turn, will help women to awaken the so-far "subjugated knowledge"[162] of ICT that affects them. The task for women is not to denounce technoscience, but to raise situated knowledge to the same status as it deemed appropriate in the social context where the knowledge/technology/practice/medium is used.[163]

Therefore, women in all spheres, especially those in academia, should engage in continuous and constant research and study on the evolution of ICTs and their effect on women. Through this process, women themselves will become the "gatekeepers" or "watchdogs" of these systems in regards to women. In order for this to be meaningful for women of every race, class, and age, it is important for women to be doing what Cheung referred to as "contextualization"—in a way appropriate to the local context,[164] restructuring the "importance of cultural changes in the consciousness level."[165] Such changes should concern not only the women directly involved in the making of power, but also ordinary women in their daily encounter with information and communication systems.[166]

For instance, I was excited to read from the *Nigerian Daily Sun* online that the new Microsoft Vista will be available in more than 70 countries, with 99 languages anticipated by the end of the year, including Hausa, Igbo, and Yoruba,[167] the three major languages spoken in Nigeria. If this works out, it will facilitate the use of the Internet by the majority of Nigerian women who are illiterate but can read and write these local languages.

Need for Regulatory Policy on the Part of Governments and States

Given the importance of communication and the speed with which ICT evolves, it is important that governments in the African regions adopt

---

161. Ribeiro, "Cybercultural Politics," 325–52.
162. Ibid., 325.
163. Cheung, "Global Discourse?" 2.
164. Ibid., 1.
165. Ibid., 9.
166. Ibid.
167. "Microsoft Vista in Hausa, Igbo, Yoruba," 1–2.

Globalization and the African Woman

and implement gender-aware ICT policies.[168] There is the urgent need to review, amend, and enforce existing laws, or enact new laws, to prevent the misuse of the Internet for trafficking, prostitution, and the sexual exploitation of girls and women.[169]

For instance, following the The Protocol to the United Nations Convention against Transnational Organized Crime, aimed to eliminate trafficking in persons, especially women and children, in July 2003, the African Union adopted a Protocol to the African Charter on the Rights of Women in Africa and called on States to take measures to ensure the prevention, punishment, and eradication of all forms of human trafficking.[170] In the same year, a nongovernmental organization—Women Trafficking and Child Labor Eradication Foundation (WOTCLEF)—was founded in Nigeria by the wife of the then-vice president, Mrs. Titi Abubaka. The work of this body yielded positive results, such as the deportation of 142 girls and young men from Italy, 160 from Spain, fifty-nine from the Netherlands, four from the United States, thirteen from South Africa, and six each from Ireland, Cote d'Ivoire, and Niger Republic.[171] Also in Gabon (May 9 2006), representatives from twenty-six countries of the Economic Community of West African States (ECOWAS) and of the Economic Community of Central African States (ECCAS) met to ratify the Palermo Protocol, aimed at preventing, curbing, and punishing the trafficking of persons, especially women.[172]

In addition, there should be support for a rating system on the Internet, so that pornography can be rated and software programs enabled to screen it out. Support for international judicial and police cooperation in the investigation of the misuse of the Internet for the purpose of promoting and/or carrying out trafficking, prostitution, and sexual exploitation of women and girls should be intensified. Countries that send men on "sex" tours and receive mail-order brides should also ban the operation of such agencies and prohibit the advertisement of these services from computer servers in their countries.[173] Governments and states should inves-

168. "Ethiopia: Affirmative Action," 1.
169. Coalition Against Trafficking in Women, "Pimps and Predators," 4.
170. M2, "UN," 1.
171. Olori, "Rights-Nigeria," 1.
172. "African Experts Meet in Gabon to Discuss Trafficking of Children, Women," *BBC Monitoring Africa*, London, May 9, 2006, 1.
173. Hughes, "Trafficking," 5.

tigate and use as evidence of crimes, acts of discrimination, advertising, correspondence, and other communications over the Internet to promote sex trafficking, prostitution, sex tourism, bride trafficking, and rape.

Also needing enforcement: maximum cooperation among governments, national, and regional law enforcement bodies in order to combat the escalating trafficking and prostitution of women and the globalization of this industry (Coalition Against Trafficking in Women.[174] For instance, the formation of International Regulatory bodies such as:

- Independent Tiplines and Vigilantes Anti-pornography Association, formed in the United States and Western Europe in 1997.

- Ethical Hackers Against Pedophilia (EHAP): A seventeen-member secret organization of skilled computer technicians that surfs around the Internet looking for sex offenders who abuse children and women.

- Morkhoven: A Belgian anti-pornography vigilante group which—despite not operating on the Net itself—was instrumental in exposing an international Internet child pornography ring in July 1998.[175]

If Bill Gates himself restricts his own daughter's Internet use to forty-five minutes a day—just for homework, and with him and his wife keeping constant watch over their daughter's browsing,[176] that says a lot. It means that this computer metaphysician knows that the situation of the new ICTs is more complex than we have so far discussed.

Conclusion

African women are coming of age. In many parts of the continent, a new generation of African women is rising up through grassroots social movements to challenge the assumptions of the established patriarchal and cultural practices in that society.[177] We think that the role of globalization, especially through ICTs, is very important in this struggle. But in recent

---

174. Coalition Against Trafficking in Women, "Pimps and Predators," 4.
175. Ibid.
176. Olycom, "Gates limita il computer a sua figlia," *24 Minuti*, 1 and 10 (Mercoledì, 21 February 2007). Also broadcast during the 8:30 pm national News on Italian Rai Due channel the same day.
177. Ilo, *African Women*, 1–13.

years, the fact that the actual processes of globalization leave emerging cultures vulnerable to ideas and beliefs which may otherwise be "alien"[178] to them is worrisome.

As we have seen so far, technology is a crucial part of this process and, of course, a process, which is male-dominated. Can this be changed by women becoming more involved in this techno-trend—not only as users, but also as technological inventors, makers, and repairers?[179] This is a revolutionary agenda for today; very few people—women or men—control these tools at these levels.[180]

Women, however, should not be discouraged by this. They should hop on the "technological train" and not look back. This is the only way to tackle the problems discussed above, and African women should become part of this system. It is worthy of note that even as Africa taps into the global information grid, she produces neither hardware nor software, and relies on foreign experts to set up and run systems for her.[181]

From our analysis so far, it is apparent that the impact of ICT in the developing world, and Africa in particular, can only be understood within a web of contingencies. Neither a naïve celebration of ICT potentials nor its condemnation as a new digital colonialism adequately captures the situation.[182] Good a thing, The African Union has placed the 2010–20 decade under the motto "Decade of African Women," to evaluate programs designed to improve women's conditions since the Beijing Summit and endeavor to reach the goals of the Millennium,[183] particularly with regard to gender equality and consolidation of women's participation in the economic, development and technological process.

For further studies and debate, we would like to conclude by asking the same questions buzzed by Davenport: "Does mechanization affect human values, and if so, how? To what extent and under what conditions should we allow technology to shape our definition of ourselves as a civilization or a species?"[184]

---

178. "World information summit," 1–2.
179. Hubbard, Foreword, vii.
180. Robins, "African Women?" 239.
181. Ibid.
182. Ibid., 236.
183. Bawaba, "African Appreciation."
184. Davenport, "Agee's *Death in the Family*," 227–39.

Pastoral Recommendations

1. The Church in Africa at all levels should sanitize, Christianize, and evangelize the dignity, image, right, and role of African women through gender awareness programs—workshops, seminars, conferences, campaigns and rallies, as well as through catechism classes and homilies. For instance, in May, Women religious from various countries joined in a campaign to "kick out" human trafficking from South Africa, in particular during the 2010 FIFA World Cup. The network publicized a message for visitors and athletes attending the World Cup: "We invite you to be careful if you receive offers of sexual services or drugs, which might be offered by victims of trafficking."[185]

Again, the Federation of Asian Bishops' Conferences and Taiwan's Episcopal Conference organized a conference in June 2010 attended by over 100 participants from about seven Asian countries highlighting the need for more help for victims of sexual harassment and human trafficking, as well as creating more awareness of how society exploits woman's sexuality.[186]

Similarly, in the same month, the New York Archdiocese in collaboration with a Catholic psychotherapist—Peter Kleponis held a mandatory conference addressing pornography during which all people worldwide were invited to participate in this Internet seminar from their own homes, to learn more about addressing the growing pornography problem in society and their personal lives.[187]

A similar thing could be organized in Africa on women issues by Church bodies like SECAM (Symposium Episcopal Conference for Africa and Madagascar), not necessarily online because of poor Internet connection, but normally that will draw participants from all over Africa. Thanks to four Southern African Episcopal Conferences—Lesotho, Namibia, South Africa and Zimbabwe, who shortly before the 2010 world cup competition in collaboration with the group Planet Waves, organized a meeting to bring global attention to the problem of human trafficking in their region.[188]

185. UISG, "2010 World Cup."

186. Federation of Asian Bishops' Conferences and Taiwan's Episcopal Conference, "Conference Laments."

187. Pollock, "Pornography."

188. Bishops of Southern Africa, "World Cup."

2. On the continental and national levels, the Church should establish more schools, institutes, and centers for the study of communication, and encourage girls and women to study in these schools. Qualified African women should be helped and encouraged to teach in these institutions.

3. On the national, diocesan, and parish levels, qualified women should form part of the administration of the communication centers, departments, and offices.

4. Just as is done with HIV/AIDS, on the national and diocesan levels, let there be centers and rehabilitation programs for the deported young girls and women from Europe who are victims of International Prostitution and Trafficking. The Nigerian Conference of Women Religious is doing something in this regard with the collaboration of their Italian counterparts. But the Nigerian Church as a whole should be more involved in this project.

6

New Evangelization in Africa: Learning from the Culture of Love in the Early Church

Bekeh Ukelina Utietiang

Introduction

FROM ITS VERY FOUNDATION, EVANGELIZATION has been the central part of the Church's mission. The call of the disciples by Jesus Christ was a call for them to be witnesses of his life and preaching and, in turn, witness this to others. Christian evangelization is the witnessing of Jesus' life of love through our words and deeds. The witness of Christ's love was at the heart of Christian evangelization in both the New Testament and the early Church before the conversion of Constantine. With the conversion of Constantine, the Church became the official religion of the empire, and to a great extent, became complacent to its central mission. It was post-Constantine Christianity that was exported to the shores of Africa. It was sometimes difficult to differentiate between the slave merchants and the missionaries, as well as between the colonial masters and the missionaries.

The future of the Church in Africa depends on a solid work of evangelization today. While the Church in Africa is growing tremendously, it is my position in this essay that this growth is not sustainable unless the Church in Africa develops a solid ministry of evangelization that takes into account the cultural heritage of Africa and the culture of love taught

New Evangelization in Africa

by Jesus Christ in the New Testament. This essay looks at the weaknesses of the current work of evangelization in Africa and proposes four concrete ways in which the Church can become the salt and light in Africa.

Jesus' Mission to His Disciples: Love One Another

> I give you a new commandment: Love one another. As I have loved you, so you also should love one another. This is how all will know that you are my disciples, if you have love for one another.
>
> John 13:34–35

The text used above is the primary mission Jesus gives to his disciples during his farewell discourse. John's Gospel is divided by scholars into two books: The Book of Signs (John 1–12) and The Book of Glory (John 13–21). Though the Book of Glory focuses on the events leading to Jesus' death on the cross, for John, the hour of Jesus' death is the hour of his glorification and the beginning of his return to the Father; and the glory Jesus had before the beginning of the world.[1] Central in the first chapter of this book is Jesus' washing of his disciples' feet. This action sets the stage for his final discourse and the mission that he gives to his disciples. This event "models for the Church the command to love one another as Jesus has loved us. It provides the only way in which we can walk through the pain of the passion and not find ourselves totally lost and abandoned at the foot of the cross, whether the cross of Jesus or one of our fellow disciples."[2]

The washing of the feet is both an example in love and a mission for the disciples of Jesus Christ to follow (John 13:12–16). This action culminates with Jesus Christ giving a "new" commandment to the disciples. This new command is symbolized by the washing of the feet; it is soteriological, as it points toward the cross, the perfect and ultimate sign of love. The commandment to love that Jesus describes as new is already found in the Old Testament. It is new because "it is grounded not in the love commands of the Jewish traditions (e.g., Lev 19:18; 1QS 1:9–11) but in the self-offering of Jesus."[3] The self-offering love of Jesus Christ is demonstrated in Jesus' dying on the cross and in his rising. The disciples must

---

1. Achtemeier *et al.*, *New Testament*, 195.
2. Howard-Brook, *John's Gospel*, 91.
3. Perkins, "John," 974.

make this kind of love the base of their relationships with others. The only way disciples can have the courage to live this kind of love is by living in "the kind of intimacy that footwashing anticipates."[4]

Love as the Model of Evangelization in the New Testament

The commandment to love was taken seriously by both the Christians of the New Testament and those of the early Church. They understood that the only way in which the message of the risen Lord was going to be effective was in their actions. Although the *kerygma* remained important to them, the emphasis was on their radical living of the law of love. This was precisely because it was through this love that other people would come to know that they were truly the disciples of Jesus Christ.

The love Jesus Christ calls them to embrace is evangelical love. It is not love for those who love them; it isn't love for family members and friends; even though this is not excluded, it is also love for enemies. Jesus Christ puts it aptly to his disciples, "For if you love those who love you, what credit is that to you? Even sinners do the same" (Luke 6:32). Their love must distinguish them from the pagans. They do this by loving those who do not love them and without expecting them to return the love. This love is unconditional because it does not expect anything in return. It mirrors Jesus' love for them. He loved them and died for them even when they were still living in sin. This kind of love is in action in Acts of the Apostles and in the epistles of the New Testament.

St. Luke's description of the communal life of Christians of the first century is a life that was marked by deep love for the other. This new Church held everything in common, sharing their possessions amongst each other according to their need and they ate their meals with exaltation praising God (Acts 2:42–47). This was a happy community, not a selfish community. This unique way of living in love characterized them as truly the disciples of Jesus. Because of that, "[And] every day the Lord added to their number those who were being saved" (Acts 2:47). There are strong signs here already how evangelical their love was. People were attracted to their characteristic way of living and they chose to be saved.

It would be a mistake, however, to think that every member of this community was perfect. There are two incidents reported by Luke in Acts which seem to undercut selfless living in this community: the story of

---

4. Howard-Brook, *John's Gospel*, 98.

Ananias and Sapphira; and the complaint of the widows. The story of Ananias and Sapphira illustrates divine punishment of those violating the purity of the early community.[5] This couple's failure to return all of their money to the community and their lying about it undercuts the oneness of heart and the culture of love that existed in this nascent Christian family. Their continuous presence in the community would do more damage to this Christian community because their actions have sown a seed of deception and lying. As harsh as the punishment for this offense might seem to be, it helped to strengthen the early Church in its life and kept it focus on its mission of love.

The complaints of the Hellenists in Acts 6:1–7 are very significant in understanding how the early Christians took the covenant of love with one another. The Hellenists complained that their widows were being neglected in the daily distribution. Luke tells us that the Twelve called together the community of the disciples and said, "It is not right for us to neglect the word of God to serve at table." The call to serve the members of the community and beyond wasn't an initiative of the twelve apostles but a command of the Lord. The apostles appointed seven reputable men to this ministry so they could devote themselves to prayer and to the ministry of the Word.

They did not see the ministry to the needy as that of the secular society and the ministry of prayer and word as that of the Church; they understood that the Church has an important ministry to the needy. What was the result of this resolution? The number of the disciples in Jerusalem increased greatly; even a large group of priests were becoming obedient to the faith.

What led to the growth of the Church here was the covenant of love that the Christians had with one another. The power of love is that it cannot be hidden. Love is attractive and possesses anyone who sees and experiences it.

St. Stephen, the first martyr of the Christian Church, lived this challenge to love. He loved and prayed for those who persecuted him and stoned him to death. The Acts of the Apostles tells us, "As they were stoning Stephen, he called out, 'Lord Jesus, receive my spirit.' Then he fell to his knees and cried out in a loud voice, 'Lord, do not hold this sin against them,' and when he said this, he fell asleep" (Acts 8:59–60).

---

5. Brown, *New Testament*, 291.

Paul devotes a lot of time preaching on *agapao* (love). He regards love for others as the single most important characteristic of the Christian life and the heart of Christian living. Everything one does is to be an expression of love.[6] He considers love to be the greatest gift any Christian can receive and it should be pursued. (1 Cor 14:1). For Paul, the only gift absolutely necessary for Christian living is love. Every other gift, such as preaching, prophesying, and speaking in tongues, might fail, but love never fails.

Why is love necessary for Christian living? St. Paul says it is because love is patient, kind, not jealous; not pompous or inflated; not selfish or quick-tempered; doesn't brood over injury or rejoice over wrongdoing. He concludes, "So faith, hope, love remain, these three; but the greatest of these is love" (1 Cor 13:1–13). This is the reason Paul constantly prays for Christians to remain steadfast in love until the coming of Christ. To the people of Philippi, he writes, "And this is my prayer: that your love may increase ever more and more . . . blameless for the day of Christ" (Phil 1:9–10). St. Paul considers love for each other as a preparation for the coming of Christ.

Love for neighbor will not only strengthen the hearts of those who love, but it will also make them holy and blameless before God (1 Thess 3:12–13). It is the barometer by which we gauge our readiness for the coming of Christ. For St. Paul, the teaching of Jesus Christ is clear that authentic Christian virtue is achieved not only in keeping to the "thou shall not" commandments but in reaching out in love to the needy. Jesus Christ said to the rich young man, "If you wish to be perfect, go, sell what you have and give to the poor, and you will have treasure in heaven" (Matt 19:21)

The author of the book of Hebrews concludes his letter, "Let mutual love continue. Do not neglect hospitality, for through it some have unknowingly entertained angels. Be mindful of prisoners as if sharing their imprisonment, and of the ill-treated as of yourselves, for you also are in the body" (Heb 13:1–3). This is a doctrine that African people know well. The teaching to serve those who are in need because you might be serving God (gods) is well enshrined in most African cultures and societies. There are myths of god(s) coming in the form of haggardly-dressed men or women to ask for help. The person who provides help is blessed and the

---

6. Mohrlang, "Love," 576.

New Evangelization in Africa

person who refuses to help might receive a curse. The culture invites its people to think of the "other" not as an independent entity but as "one" in some sense. The "I" is not lost in its independent entity but it is only fully realized in the "thou." While individual existence is a reality, the emphasis is on communal existence. The "I" must die to the "thou" that the "we" must live.

This means that the problem of one member of the society is the problem of all the members of the community. Every member of the society must be treated fairly and justly, then, because the ill-treatment of one member of the society affects other members of the society. This is the basic relational structure of any African society.

Given the analysis of the New Testament we have presented above, this is also the basic structure of the Christian message—and so, even before the first missionary stepped his or her foot in Africa, the culture was disposed to receive Christianity. The message of Jesus Christ was already in the hearts and culture of the people. What was needed was a good evangelist who would fully reveal the message to them. The question which remains much debated even to this day is how successful missionary work is in Africa.

Missionaries to Africa and the Failed Method of Evangelization

Given that Africa was a fertilized field for Christian evangelization when the missionaries came, one would have expected outstanding success in Africa. Unfortunately, the missionaries did not evangelize Africa but, rather, "missionized" her. The missionization of Africa started after Henry the Navigator (1394–1460), the sponsor of most Spanish expeditions to West Africa, visited its shores for the first time. It was after these expeditions by Henry that a priest from Lisbon by the name of Fr. Polonos de Lagos celebrated the first Mass at Cape Verde in the present West of Africa in 1445. And after his return, the Pope gave Portugal the *Padro Ado* to missionize Africa.[7]

It is important to note that Henry the Navigator (Dom Henrique) was the fourth son of the king of Portugal, King Joao I. The success of every mission is judged based on the mandate. In the case of African evangelization, the mandate given by Pope Nicholas V in 1452 to the king of

---

7. Utietiang, *Afridentity*, 38.

Portugal carried no intention of evangelization. What was necessary for the Pope was missionization. The Papal Bull read: "In the name of our apostolic authority, we grant to you the full and entire faculty of invading, conquering, expelling and reigning over all the kingdoms . . . of pagans and of all infidels . . . of reducing their inhabitants to perpetual slavery, of appropriating to yourself those kingdoms and all their possessions, for your own use and that of your successors."

It's questionable whether the Pope had any intentions of giving Africans the gift of Jesus Christ or if he was merely giving Africa to King Joao I as a gift. In this, the Pope failed to recognize that Africans were also created in the image and likeness of God and had a sense of the divine.

This stands completely in contrast with Jesus' commission of his disciples. The Gospel of Luke tells us that when Jesus sent out the seventy-two on mission, he gave them simple and precise instructions: "Into whatever house you enter, first say, 'Peace to this household. If a peaceful person lives there, your peace will rest on him; but if not, it will return to you. Stay in the same house and eat and drink what is offered to you." Even though Jesus Christ recognizes that he is sending his disciples to hostile territories and they like lambs may be consumed by wolves, he commands them to bring peace. The most striking point Jesus makes to them is to engage the culture: live with them, eat and drink with them. Food is one of the most important aspects of a culture. Symbolically, Jesus Christ is asking his disciples to embrace fully the culture of the people to whom they bring the Gospel. It is in their acceptance of the people's culture that the Word will take roots in the hearts and lives of the people.

By contrast, the missionaries that went to Africa worked hard to do away with the rich "Christian" culture the Africans had prior to their arrival. The culture was looked upon as being bad and thus not good for Christianity. Africa was to be made a "mission" of Europe; thus the Church in Africa would not have its own unique African identity, as the Church in Europe did. African culture would have been the portal through which the Christian missionaries to Africa could have evangelized Africans; yet what they committed was not the evangelization but the westernization of Africans.[8] This approach wasn't just unwise; it ran contrary to the message of love given by Jesus in the gospel and lived through the early Church.

---

8. Ibid., 39.

Long before this, in the fourth century, Pope Gregory sent a letter through Abbot Mellitus to St. Augustine in Canterbury: "Tell Augustine that he should by no means destroy the temples of the gods but rather the idols within those temples. Let him, after he has purified them with holy water, place altars and relics of saints in them . . . Thus seeing that their places of worship are not destroyed, the people will banish error from their hearts and come to places familiar and dear to them in acknowledgement and worship of God."[9] One can only wonder where this wisdom of the fourth century was in the fifteenth century.

One may argue that many baptisms were made by these missionaries and as a result, their work can be considered successful. An argument like this does not really hold because baptism as a Christian does not really make one Christlike. It is doubtful if many of the persons who accepted baptism had genuine intentions to be baptized into this "hostile Christian faith." While Christianity by its own nature is a peaceful religion, the version of Christianity that was marketed in Africa was hostile.

You may ask, what is the evidence for such a claim? The Pope's letter gave that mandate to the Portuguese. Keep in mind that the missionaries worked hand in hand with the merchants who, in most cases, traded in slaves. The King of the Congo, Don Affonso, wrote in 1526 to King John III of Portugal thus, "The merchants daily seize our subjects, sons of the land and sons of our noblemen and vassals and our relatives . . . They grab them and cause them to be sold: so great, sir is their corruption and licentiousness that our country is being depopulated . . . [We] need from your kingdom no other than priests and people to teach in schools, and no other good but wine and flour for the Holy sacrament."[10]

This brand of Christianity did not stand distinctively as a community of love. Even in the early parts of the twentieth century, the model of evangelization in most Sub-Saharan Africa was to baptize all those who came through Catholic schools. This is definitely a failed strategy: these baptized people continued to secretly sacrifice to their traditional African gods—or, when they did not have their requests granted by the "Christian God," abandoned the Christian faith and returned to their traditional African gods. There are still some who continue to hang onto the Christian faith merely to avoid the shame of returning to the traditional religion or

9. Gregory the Great, "Letter," 1102.
10. Chinweizu, *West and Rest*, 8.

out of fear of a God who would be unforgiving. It poses the question if any of these people are truly convinced and convicted Christians.

To add insult to injury, now the high cost of Catholic private education today in Africa means that fewer and fewer Africans can afford to send their children to Catholic schools. This means that even this failed strategy of evangelization—which for over 500 years has been able to bring millions of "converts"—is disappearing. A new method of evangelization in Africa must take its place.

Evangelization in the Early Church: The Method of Our Lord Jesus Christ

Jesus Christ has given Christians a tried and successful way of evangelizing: the evangelization of love. This worked for the Christians of the New Testament and in the early Church prior to the conversion of Constantine. In his thoroughly researched work, *The Rise of Christianity*, Rodney Stark advances three major theses for the rapid growth of Christianity in the Roman Empire before Constantine became Christian: epidemics, love, and social networks.

The Plague of Galen, in the second century, wiped out between a quarter and a third of the empire. This was a crisis of faith to the Romans, who could not explain why this disaster happened. Christianity had reasonable explanations for it, however, and invited the people to hope for a better future. Both Cyprian, bishop of Carthage, and Bishop Dionysius wrote comforting words to the people and encouraged them to have no fear. According to Stark, "At a time when all other faiths were called to question, Christianity offered explanation and comfort. Even more important, Christian doctrine provided a *prescription for action*. That is, the Christian way appeared to work."[11]

Evidence from the letters of Dionysius suggests that the survival rate of Christians during these epidemics was much higher than that of the pagans: "The heathen behaved in the very opposite way. At the first onset of the disease, they pushed the sufferers away and fled from their dearest, throwing them into the roads before they were dead and treated unburied corpses as dirt, hoping thereby to avert the spread and contagion of the fatal disease; but do what they might, they found it difficult to escape."[12]

11. Stark, *Rise of Christianity*, 82.
12. Ibid., 83

The higher mortality rate of pagans, compared with the lower mortality rate of Christians, was due to the Christians' response of love to their sick ones. Providing food and water helps to avert huge numbers of fatalities. This was the practical "miracle" of healing the Christians performed that led others to join them.[13] Stark reports that in A.D. 362, the emperor Julian complained in a letter to the high priest of Galatia that the pagans "needed to equal the virtues of Christians, for recent Christian growth was caused by their 'moral character, even if pretended,' and by their 'benevolence toward strangers and care for the graves of the dead.'"[14] The basic care Christians provided, not only to their members but also pagans, helped to save many lives.

For most of these people, all they needed for survival was food, water, and shelter. Christians provided these services even when doing so would put their own lives in danger. They heeded the command of Jesus Christ to care for the sick and "whatever you do to the least of my brothers and sisters, you do it to me." Like Jesus Christ, the Christians were ready and willing to give of their lives out of love for others to live.

Paul Johnson argues that Christians' response to the needs of other members of the society was so active that it was almost "a miniature welfare state in an empire which for the most part lacked social services."[15] Stark further asserts that the lower mortality rate of Christians would have provided pagans with a much greater probability of replacing their lost attachments with new ones to Christians. In these ways, very substantial numbers of pagans would have been shifted from mainly pagan to mainly Christian social networks.[16] Shifts in social networks like these often result in conversions.

Stark disagrees with those who have argued that it is the conversion of Constantine that led to a Christian majority. He writes, "Constantine's conversion would better be seen as a response to the massive exponential wave in progress, not as its cause." In an empire that was becoming more and more Christian despite the persecutions, Constantine had no other option than to become a Christian. His decision to convert to Christianity was more political than spiritual. He had to become Christian to maintain

---

13. Stark, *Discovering God*, 320.
14. Ibid., 83–84.
15. Johnson, *History of Christianity*, 75.
16. Stark, *Discovering God*, 75.

his popularity among the masses in the empire. Some authors have placed the growth rate of Christianity in the empire at 40 percent a decade; by the time Constantine was converted, about half of the empire would have been Christian.[17]

After the conversion of Constantine, Christianity took a different turn. Given that it was now the official religion of the state, Christians could worship freely and evangelize freely. But rather than the Faith remaining strong, it became weak. Corruption, sloth, power struggles, and enforced conformity worked their way into the Christian faith. Bishops became civil servants and house churches were now replaced by splendid public buildings. Rather than being an advantage to the Church, the conversion of Constantine became a cog in the large wheel of the Church, blurring the Church's vision and slowing down its growth and work of evangelization.[18]

The Church's approach to evangelization also radically changed. Evangelization was no longer based in service and social networks. According to Stark and Finke, "The Christianity that subsequently left most of Europe only nominally converted, at best, was an established, subsidized state church that sought to extend itself, not through missionizing the population, but by baptizing kings and then canonizing them as national saints."[19] The erroneous idea here was that once the king is baptized, he will shove Christianity onto the shoulders of all his subjects. The problem with this approach is that subjects do not have the free will to reject Christianity. This is not only a problem to the traditional Catholic understanding of freedom but also undercuts the very essence of the Christian religion—a personal relationship with Jesus Christ.

This was the brand of Christianity, post-Constantine's conversion, which was taken to Africa. When missionaries tried to convert the king of Benin (Nigeria), with the intention of having him and all his subjects baptized, he thwarted them immediately; he wasn't interested in Christianity. And, although he did allow his son Orhogba and some of his officials to be baptized, by the middle of the sixteenth century there was no contact between the Benin and the Portuguese any longer.[20] Given the unwilling-

---

17. Ibid., 10.
18. Stark and Finke, *Acts of Faith*, 69.
19. Ibid.
20. Sandmorsky, "Benin Empire," 134.

ness of many African kings to accept Christianity and force it on their subjects, this initial mode of evangelization failed—mainly because the missionaries did not understand the religious culture of Africans.

As powerful as African kings were, they could not insist that their subjects become Christians. Generally, the African culture is religiously pluralistic, with religious beliefs and rituals tied to ancestral heritage. While there are few rituals that a community can practice as a whole, the majority of rituals and regular sacrifices are made within one's family. Therefore, imposing religion on a people from above would have been difficult, if not impossible; the way for a religion to grow is to engage the culture, become part of it, and grow dynamically from within it.

Later missionaries to Sub-Saharan Africa, in the eighteenth century and beyond, did not learn from the mistakes of their predecessors. Certainly, their strategy was different: these missionaries, mostly from Ireland and France, used education as the primary tool for evangelization. But, like their predecessors who worked closely with the slave merchants, these missionaries were close to the colonial masters. Many missionary groups in Africa—the Society of African Missions, the Holy Ghost Fathers and Brothers, the Kiltegan Fathers (St. Patrick's Missionaries), and Missionaries of Africa (White Fathers), built numerous schools throughout Africa, with almost everyone coming through the school then becoming "Catholic." My father was a prime example of this: the first Christian in his family, he became Catholic only because he was sent to Catholic school by his parents.

Ironically enough, because many African societies were skeptical of European education, the children sent to school were the physically lazy ones who could not till the soil and work the fields. Most of these students were successful academically, for good reason—the promise of a better life through European education by the missionaries was their best and only hope. Those I tried to interview for this article could not remember what they were taught prior to baptism. What is clear, however, is that these baptisms were not done when the young student had understood and fully appropriated the new "faith."

These young "Christians," then, found themselves wandering between two worlds: their Christian world and their African traditional world. They found themselves betwixt and between. This has remained a fundamental problem to African Christianity; for the Faith to take strong roots in Africa, this problem must be seriously addressed. The Church cannot become salt and light in Africa if the members of the Church do not incarnate in their cultural life the central message of the Christian faith. Although it should be inconceivable that an active Christian will resort to fortunetelling, wear talismans for protection, or make sacrifices to traditional African deities for protection, it's not uncommon to find active Christians who go to church every Sunday, pray daily to Jesus Christ—and secretly consult traditional African ritualists for spiritual help. There is a blurred line between the two faiths in personal lives of Africans. This happened because missionaries were more concerned with the number of baptisms than they were with making sure "converts" were strongly rooted in faith. A story is told of an Irish missionary in one of the parishes in Southern Nigeria who baptized people while they were on their way to farms and work; he didn't even bother to keep records of the baptisms he performed.

One fundamental fact this priest, and many others, got wrong: Christianity is not a game of numbers. It is not how many people you baptize, but how many people are truly Christlike.

Thus, the majority of the people in the continent have not truly received the message of Christianity. The Church in Africa still has a lot of work to do. To move forward, the Church needs a new strategy for evangelization. In the next paragraphs, I will propose four concrete ways for a new evangelization of love in Africa:

1) Family Churches, Not Megachurches

The churches in the New Testament were small family churches. Paul's letter to the Corinthians, for example, was not read in one big assembly; it went to the family churches. Pockets of Christians gathered in different homes throughout Corinth for the breaking of the bread.

In the early Church, before the conversion of Constantine and the building of the "megachurches" all across the empire, this is how all churches operated. The people gathered in catacombs or homes to break the bread. A church with 5,000 parishioners worshipping every Sunday was inconceivable.

But today, Catholic churches throughout Africa are getting bigger and bigger. In situations like this, the Church loses its meaning as a family. In a family, people know each other and understand the problems every member faces. When you have a congregation of 5,000, however, it is difficult for the *pater familias* (the father of the family—the parish priest or Pastor) to even know his entire congregation. Not only does the size pose a problem to the pastor; it also causes a disconnect among the members of the church. It is a problem when you do not know anyone in the same pew with you at church.

The Church in most of Africa is blessed with numerous vocations. Thousands of young men are being ordained priests every year in Nigeria, Kenya, Ghana, Tanzania, and other countries. The temptation for the bishops is to continue to send them for missionary work to the West. But it's erroneous to think that America or Europe is in greater need of priests today than Nigeria or the whole continent of Africa. With the exception of densely populated Catholic (Arch)dioceses like Boston, Philadelphia, Los Angeles, Miami, or the like in the United States, the average parish size in the United States is about 600 families. Compare this with an average parish size of 1000 families in Nigeria. So—while thousands of Catholic parishes in the United States have less than 300 families, yet still have a priest working full-time in the parish—in Nigeria, you will rarely find a 300-family church designated as a "parish" or having a full-time priest. Churches considered big in the United States in terms of the number of parishioners are considered normal sizes in Nigeria. In those big parishes in the United States, there are often two or more priests in full-time ministry at the parish, together with some part-time help from student priests or retired priests. The argument here is not against the Church in Africa being generous enough to send missionaries to other parts of the world where the Church is in need; the argument is that the Church in Africa should not pretend it is not in need, at the same time overworking the priests left in the continent and relieving Western priests of their own responsibilities to their people. African priests leaving the continent to work in the West should only be as a response to a serious need. As the proverb goes, you do not leave your house on fire to quench the fire in your neighbor's house.

For effective evangelization in the continent, bishops must move away from creating mega parishes. The argument often made for bigger parishes is cost. But, while cost is an important factor, this is one area where the Church in Africa should never imitate the Church in the West. In North America, for example, the Church has become bureaucratic from the Catholic bishops' conferences down to the parishes. It is not strange to find a 1200-family parish with over ten full-time paid staff. But with 1200 families, what business does the church have hiring a full-time staff to mow the lawn or clean the building? Are the church's own members incapable of doing these things?

Presently, many parishes in Africa still have Mass centers (outstations) where the priest goes to celebrate Mass every Sunday. More and more of these outstations are turned into parishes as the Church has grown. But having numerous small parishes could pose a problem in the future if vocations decline or Mass attendance decreases. So, instead of changing these outstations to parishes, they would be better turned to Christian communities affiliated with a parish. One central parish with accommodations for about six priests could be used as an outreach center to these communities. This arrangement has many advantages: it will help the priests avoid the problem of loneliness—one of the major reasons priest fail in celibacy or abandon their priestly vocations—and help to make these communities truly "family churches."

2) Social Service

At the beginning of his public ministry, Jesus Christ proclaimed, "The Spirit of the Lord is upon me, because he has anointed me to bring glad tidings to the poor. He has sent me to proclaim liberty to captives and recovery of sight to the blind, to let the oppressed go free, and to proclaim a year acceptable to the Lord" (Luke 4:18–19). This is at the heart of the public ministry of Jesus Christ, who spent his three active years of ministry doing this. Whether it was the 5,000 he fed, or the blind whose eyes he opened, or the woman caught in adultery that he liberated, Jesus had the intention to free them from what held them back to enable them live the freedom of God's children.

Jesus Christ always intended that his followers continue this ministry. The liberation preached by Jesus Christ was not only attainable in heaven; it started here on earth. The temptation for the Church is to do nothing while promising the people a better life in heaven, but Jesus did not limit the blessings of this ministry to an afterlife: people experienced the healings right here on earth. Jesus' promise to his followers is that all these signs will accompany those that believe in him.

The Church does not have a responsibility only to bring liberation to her people; the people have the right to demand that the Church liberate them. This is the most profound way the Church would remain relevant in a continent in dire need of liberation. The Church works a miracle of healing when she provides healthcare to someone in need; a miracle of educating when she gives a young person an opportunity to learn; a miracle of liberation when she stands out against injustice in society.

But there is no doubt that the Church in Africa has become complacent to social evil. She is blessed with an opportunity for evangelization in a continent devastated by poverty, disease, war, corruption, and dictatorship. It is not enough for bishops' conferences to write communiqués or put out statements. The Church must rise and take active roles in society to change the lives of the people. Jesus Christ did not sit on the sidelines when his people were sick, dying, or imprisoned. At each point, he stepped in to set them free. In this way, the Church in Africa has an opportunity not only to be prophetic in word but in action. The clergy and leaders of the Church must be on the side of their people, not politicians and dictators. The Church cannot wait for the government to solve all the problems of her people, but she must step in to give her people a helping hand to solve their own problems.

Many times, however, Catholic social institutions are the exclusive province of the wealthy, a majority of whom have impoverished the masses through corruption or exploitation. When the institutions of the Church cater solely to the needs of these people, the Church has failed in its social ministry. Parishes must begin active social ministries that help not only Catholics or Christians; they should reach out to everyone in society, because Christians believe everyone is created in the image and likeness of God. Catholic schools should be directly funded by the dioceses, and a percentage of parish income should be paid to the diocese for the funding of Catholic schools. While the schools will still charge tuition, this should be based on family income, and no child who academically qualifies to enter into a school should be turned away because they cannot afford the tuition. Not only should the homebound or the aged be provided with food and medication if they cannot afford them; parishioners should visit them, helping them with laundry and housekeeping.

Further, it is unchristian for a Catholic health facility to turn away a sick person for lack of money. The Church must find avenues in which she can work with the government in responding to the social needs of the people. Like the early Christians reached out in love to the pagans of Rome, the Church in Africa must reach out in love to traditional religionists and Muslims. Christians must differentiate themselves from others by the way they love not just each other, but those who do not love them as well. This love would be visible through their active participation in society. This kind of love makes Jesus Christ visible to the people and will definitely draw many other people to come and learn about the life of Jesus Christ and the Church.

3) Lay Participation in Ministry.

The Vatican II decree on the apostolate of lay people, *Apostolicam Actuositatem*, acknowledges that the laity has a special role in the Church's works of evangelization. The laity, the Council Fathers say, is called to share in the threefold office of Christ: the priestly, the prophetic, and the kingly. The Fathers write, "In the concrete, their apostolate is exercised when they work at the evangelization and sanctification of men [and women]."[21]

Contrary to generally held beliefs in Africa—that it is the priest's ministry to evangelize and sanctify the people—lay people are also called to this special ministry of the Church. Irrespective of the number of priests we have, the laity is needed to assist the priest in the work of evangelizing and sanctifying. Relegating this responsibility to priests and religious does not help the evangelization work of the Church.

Two areas of evangelization that have been successfully carried out by the laity in Africa are serving as catechists and belonging to pious societies of the faithful, such as the Legion of Mary. Without the glamorous title of "permanent deacons," and without a place in the hierarchy of the Church, African men and women have taken on the responsibility of conducting prayers and church services in areas where there is no priest. They have also worked with priests in both urban and rural areas to prepare people for the sacraments. The Fathers of Vatican II allude to the work of the catechists when they write, "In many regions where priests are very scarce or (as is sometimes the case) deprived of the freedom they need for their ministry, it is hard to see how the Church could make her presence and action felt without the help of the laity."[22]

---

21. *Apostolicam Actuositatem*, no.2.
22. Ibid., no. 1.

In line with the call of Vatican II, that the lay apostolate should be "infinitely broader and more intense,"[23] it is necessary that the Church in Africa work with the Church in Rome to review and revise the role of catechists. Catechists have made the Church felt in many rural communities where, sometimes, a priest comes by only once a month for Mass. Like permanent deacons, their role should be formalized and placed within the hierarchy of the Church. Possibly, they could be elevated to the ranks of elders or un-ordained deacons and deaconesses. Given the nature of their work, the Church should provide adequate training in doctrine and ministry to them and officially assign them roles similar to those exercised by deacons and acolytes—such as preaching at Sunday liturgy, performing baptisms and weddings, burying the dead, and conducting Eucharistic services in the absence of the priest. This will help to strengthen the wonderful ministry they are already doing and will give tremendous support and care to rural churches where they already minister.

The Legion of Mary—through its apostolic work of visiting the sick, those in prison, and the homebound, as well as home-to-home visits, has helped to bring the love of Jesus Christ and Mary to many. Other pious associations in the Church in Africa must be reformed to include active apostolic ministry. Lay people can also take other responsibilities in ministry, such as bringing the Eucharist to the sick or those shut-in or invalidated or incapacitated by old age.

In a continent where millions of people have yet to receive the gospel of Jesus Christ, the Church cannot run as a "service station" where people come on Sunday to refill, and the Church's ministry is restricted to those who walk in through the doors of the church. The Church in Africa is called to be aggressive in its work of evangelization, not in screaming the word of God at nonbelievers but in living out the gospel principle of love as it engages the culture. Priests need to realize that engaging lay people in ministry does not usurp their power but enables them to further the work of the Kingdom here on earth.

4) Adult Education

The majority of catechisms used in Africa are still based in part on the questions and answers of the Baltimore Catechism. The Faith is still

---

23. Ibid., no.1.

learned through memorization of answers to key questions that every Catholic is expected to know. But the knowledge of the Faith that most adults have is the one they learnt in the parish school of religion as children; the New Catholic Catechism is not promoted in the parishes. Both the Code of Canon Law and the documents of Vatican II are almost the exclusives of priests.

While there is nothing wrong with a basic catechism format when one is a child, as children become adult, they must learn the Faith in ways that they can better appropriate and make part of their lives. If parents do not concretely understand the Faith beyond the memorizations, how can they live it out concretely and pass it on to their children? Pope John Paul II reminds families that they are the "domestic church." But how can they be an effective church if they have not learned about the Faith beyond their childhood catechism?

Bishops should insist that parish priests have some form of continuing education in their parishes for adults where they can learn more about the Faith. While Sunday homilies help to explain some aspects of the Faith, they are not enough. The theology of priests also needs to be updated beyond seminary theology. Continuous education opportunities must be provided to priests by their bishops to keep them updated on the development of Catholic theology. Both priests and lay people need to be properly educated on inculturation. Given the rich culture of Africa, the Church must not make a mistake of ignoring it.

Conclusion

The challenge for the Church in Africa is great; the graces are abundant. But the status quo will not lead to victory. What will lead to victory is a radical reassessment of where the Church is and how it has got here. The bishops need serious discernment on what has worked and what has not worked. They must be humble enough to accept both the successes and the failures of the Church and courageous enough to make radical changes as they move into the future. The changes may not necessarily be what the Church in Rome wants, but they must make a forceful case to Rome for their people. At the end of the day, tradition must always begin somewhere and at some time. Perhaps, for once in a lifetime, a Sub-Saharan African tradition will be part of the tradition of the universal (Catholic) church. This will make the Church truly Catholic.

Conclusion

Stan Chu Ilo

OUR GOAL IN THIS VOLUME has been to present the conviction that the Church in Africa is a blessing to the continent, and that we need to recover the riches of the Church to bring about communion, love, solidarity, and abundant life for our people. The Church in Africa has come of age. The latest edition of Church statistics published by the Vatican shows that the number of Catholics increased from 1.131 billion to 1.151 billion between 2005 and 2006, representing an increase of 1.4 percent.

These statistics confirmed what many people already know: the Church in Africa is witnessing a new wave, a resurgence of not only the Catholic faith but also in the Protestant churches, the evangelical and Pentecostal movements, and the blossoming African independent churches. Africa, for instance, has the a larger Anglican community than Europe. Indeed, according to the BBC, "In Nigeria there are more Anglicans than in England, America, and Canada put together."[1] Within the Catholic Church, while seminaries and parishes are being closed in many dioceses in Canada and the USA, seminaries are being expanded in many African countries—and still, many prospective seminarians and aspirants are being turned down for lack of facilities to accommodate them. Seminaries and convents are bursting at the seams. Many bishops can no longer meet the ever-growing demands for new parishes and new dioceses in many parts of Africa. The churches in Africa are witnessing a new harvest and a new Pentecost with an exponential rise in attendance. Churches are packed full every Sunday and hold robust, dynamic liturgies, testifying to the fact that the apprehension of Christianity in Africa is at the level

---

1. http://news.bbc.co.uk/1/hi/world/africa/3074969.stm.

of cultural identity; hence, the new cultural imagination being created by the presence of the Christian faith in the continent.

The number of seminarians in Africa has grown from a little over 580 in 1968—when Pope Paul VI made his first visit to Africa—to an astonishing 23,580 in 2007. African priests and religious are now providing services in many North American and European churches, in what appears to be a reverse mission from the global South to the North. Many people are convinced that we are at a turning point in the Christian movement, as global Christianity grapples with what is obviously a post-Western Christianity being influenced by a post-Christian West. There is thus a need for a realignment of forces and charisms in Catholicism, as well as a re-evaluation of the relationship between the heartland Christianity of the West and the frontier Christianity of the global South, where the future of Christianity is presently being determined.

In his 1994 Exhortation *Ecclesia in Africa,* released in Yaoundé, Cameroon, Pope John Paul II wrote this about Africa: "Indeed, this continent is today experiencing what we call a sign of the times, an acceptable time, a day of salvation. It seems that the 'hour of Africa' has come, a favourable time."[2] The Pope's expressions—"historical moment of grace," "a sign of the times," "an acceptable time," and "hour of Africa"—indicate his conviction that the Church in Africa has come of age. The time has come for African Christians not only to celebrate the Christian faith as a gift but to use the liberating force and transformative grace of the Gospel to bring about a new Africa and a new way of "being Church." It is true that, if allowed to take root in people's hearts, the Good News of Jesus Christ will set them free from poverty, hunger, illiteracy, sickness, and other debilitating conditions that have plagued this beautiful continent. This is, therefore, the favored time to reconstruct the disfigured image of Africa by interpreting the signs of the times and listening to what the Spirit is communicating through this historic moment.

There are three challenges, among many African Christianity faces, that contributors to this volume identify:

- The question of identity, concerned with the inner dynamics of being Church and the problem of the autonomy of local churches within the universal Catholic family.

---

2. Ecclesia in Africa, 6.

- The question of accountability, broadly conceived.
- The challenge of religious freedom and inter-religious dialogue with African Traditional Religions and Islamic religion.

The other concern here is the apparent state of Catholicism within global Christianity: Is being Catholic perceived today, within societies where the Roman Catholic Church has a strong footing, as a positive force for change and religious and spiritual regeneration?

The question of the autonomy and identity of the Church in Africa is not a specific challenge but a common concern, as many local churches struggle to maintain a balance between contextualization and communion in a Catholic faith still weighed down by a very synchronizing Church authority at the center. This debate was very prominent ten years ago between Cardinal Walter Kasper and then-Cardinal Ratzinger. The debate led to the publication of two books by both prelates (*Leadership in the Church: How Traditional Roles can Serve the Christian Community Today* by Kasper; and *Called to Communion: Understanding the Church Today* by Ratzinger) defending their opposing positions on whether the center has priority over the local. While this volume does not wish to get into the debate, it is obvious that a centralizing tendency or a universalizing theology, so often the case in the Catholic family, is not a healthy means of promoting autonomy and identity of local churches to meet the specific challenges facing them. This is particularly true in liturgical and moral issues, along with administrative and pastoral policies that have to deal with specific local challenges and problems. Does being Catholic mean being the same, having a monolithic culture, and a common curriculum for clergy and religious? Is a universalizing tendency not a tidal wave that will sweep away creativity and dynamism in local churches; extinguishing local customs and ancient traditions' ability to meet the challenges they face? Is it not true that the context is the place where the universal is potentially present, and that Catholicism is universal to the extent it makes the particular part of the validating claim of any universality?

There is a serious concern among African Catholics, especially the laity, about greater autonomy and participation in shaping the direction and policy of the churches. This is particularly important with regard to the structure of the Church, which will bring about a servant leadership among local clergy; they need to balance their double loyalties to the Pope as the Vicar of Christ with the needs and faith context of the faithful, which demand their attention and utmost commitment. One has the impression that African bishops are legates of Rome, more concerned with how they please papal nuncios and improve their chances of climbing higher on the ecclesiastical ladder than how they can improve the practice of the Faith in Africa relative to the social context. We, as young theologians and servants of God's people, are concerned about the future of the Christian enterprise in Africa. The silent cries of many African Catholics for greater freedom to live their faiths as Africans and not on European terms and conditions continue to touch our hearts.

The Catholic Church in Africa has been blessed with the vibrancy of womenfolk. Effective evangelization in Africa calls for greater involvement of African women in African churches, where women are treated as second-class citizens, holding any position at the mercy of a male-dominated hierarchy and leadership across the board. Such treatment of women in the Catholic churches in Africa parallels the patriarchal cultural frameworks that furnish and legitimize the ongoing marginalization of women through various uncritical cultural assumptions. There is also the need for greater involvement of the lay faithful and local priests in the selection of bishops, as well as an ongoing evaluation of the ministries of bishops in the light of how they promote the practice of the Faith and its relevance to the concrete life situation of the people. This is the challenge of accountability.

We believe that the Church in Africa is being called at this moment of grace to account to the Lord for how she has used her gifts, her growing number of faithful, and the riches of the gospel to transform both the Church in Africa and the wider African society. This accountability extends also to the use of the temporal goods of the Church. Many lay people in Africa complain that they never get from their bishops or priests annual financial statements showing clearly how their offertory and donations have been used. This "don't ask, don't tell" policy does not make the Church credible in challenging the growing high-handedness and lack of accountability in many countries in Africa.

Catholicism in Africa is in dire need of an inner renewal of the clergy and religious, who sometimes live above the levels of the people they serve, and whose lifestyles contradict the call of the church in Africa to live simply and to identify with the social conditions of the African faithful. While many priests and religious continue to render heroic services and making majestic sacrifices in many dark alleys and hidden corners, as the voice of many voiceless poor in Africa, this has become in many parts of Africa the exception instead of the norm. Church officials today in some African countries receive donations of SUVs, huge financial gift from public officials which only continues to erode their authority and undermine the simplicity and poverty of spirit required to arrest the moral and spiritual decline in a continent that is awash in religious sentiments, but sill far from concretely reflecting these sentiments in the public and ecclesial contexts.

Many people in the West are calling for a paradigm shift in Western theologies to meet the new challenges of Western Christianity since the boundaries are shifting in a very fundamental way. If these Western theologies are no longer meeting the challenges of today's Western Church, or if the challenges of the Churches in the West are no longer being met by a recycling of the same theological frameworks, are there valid grounds to propose those theologies to the global South? It is still surprising to many Catholic theologians that the curriculum for the training of priests in African Catholicism is made in Rome, thus making it difficult for local churches in Africa to train their priests and religious to understand the cultural and social context of the practice of the Faith.

Is Africa today a mission territory, especially Sub-Saharan Africa? We believe that most churches in Africa are no longer mission churches since they are self-perpetuating, and can be self-sustaining if they shed themselves of the very expensive replication of Western churches' administrative bureaucracy, the use of imported expensive Western vestments, liturgical vessels, sacramentals, tabernacles, altars, and expensive church architecture, chanceries and rectories. A vulnerable church in Africa which uses the things discoverable in the African world, to build African faith communities, sensitive to the economic limitations of the faithful will be a sustainable church. If many African Independent, Pentecostal, and Orthodox churches are surviving without any support from the West, why wouldn't the Catholic churches of Africa survive without sacrificing her creativity because of her financial dependence on Rome?

Beyond the internal challenges facing African Catholicism is the external challenge of religious freedom and interreligious dialogue. Are African Catholics still operating from the worldview of African Traditional Religions, or is the Faith still superficial, a mere veneer over a deeply rooted traditional worldview? The task of inculturating the gospel in Africa is still far from being realized, whether with regard to liturgy, morals, ecclesiastical structures, the criteria for clerical life, pastoral practices, or translation of Biblical and liturgical texts and the like. It seems that the project of inculturation is a landmine for many practitioners as they struggle sometimes with abandoning the fruits of their cultural studies in order to find a way of fusing African Christianity into the norms and categories of the institutional church. The challenge of syncretism in African Catholicism remains a real one as Africans look for multiple appeals to traditional religions outside of Christianity to find answers to the questions of witchcraft, ancestral communion, sicknesses, childless marriages, personal, family and communal misfortunes, mental health issues, female genital mutilation, circumcision, demonic attacks, sorceries, sexual identities, and other limit situations which are not addressed in traditional Western Christianity.

There is also the challenge of interreligious dialogue with Islam. According to a report published by the *Aid to the Church in Need* in July 2006, the greatest challenge facing Christianity in Africa is the question of religious liberty. A sample of some of the findings of the report will reveal the extent of this challenge.

For instance, although with the ending of a number of civil wars the more intense waves of violence characterizing Angola, the Ivory Coast, and Sudan have ceased, the conflict in Uganda that caused the death of the Caritas worker Okot Stalin—and resulted in an atmosphere of persecution addressed at the Catholic Church—is by no means over. While countries like Morocco and Tunisia are looking for new ways to promote dialogue and tolerance between Christians and Muslims, in 2006, Algeria approved a law punishing conversion from Islam. The Catholic Church, the Protestant community, and the Seventh Day Adventists are currently the only non-Islamic denominations acknowledged and allowed to operate in this country.

The same could be said of a country like Egypt. In spite of a degree of openness shown by the government, the clash between Islamic extremists and Orthodox Copts—often the victims of threats—along with attempts at forced conversions and mass attacks, now seem to have become radicalized in Egypt. Although the Egyptian constitution guarantees freedom of worship, acknowledging all creeds and forms of cult, the authorities effectively impose restrictions and obstacles to freedom of worship for believers in faiths that are not Islam. Islam is the official religion in the Arab Republic of Egypt and the Shari' a is the main source of legislation, in fact, any revision of the laws and various codes is approved by the law professors in the Al-Azhar district—universities and mosques—in Cairo, linked to conservative and, in some cases, extremist Islam. Even if belonging to Islam, every religious and civil practice conflicting with the Shari'a is forbidden and is subject to the imams' and the sheikhs' rigid and binding control. Although Orthodox Copts represent about 15 percent of the population, in the parliamentary assembly their presence is reduced to less than 1 percent. They are in practice excluded from even secondary-level appointments within the state administration and public education. Income from taxation is used for building and restoring mosques, while other Christian places of worship do not receive public funding.

Radical Islam is not simply a North African problem, where African Christians are still nostalgic about the ancient Christian civilizations that were wiped away, beginning in the sixth century. Radical Islam is also spreading in sub-Saharan Africa. Radical Islamic advance is also perceived in Kenya, Eritrea, Ethiopia, Chad, Cameroun, Uganda, Sudan, and above all in Nigeria, where the enforcement of Shari'a Islamic laws are imposed on non-Muslims and have caused continuous tension, often resulting in attacks on the Christian communities, with dozens of victims on both sides. The recent violence between Muslims and Christians in the Northern Nigerian city of Jos, in October 2008, and still ongoing in 2010 is a good example of the tinderbox which the religious tension in Northern Nigeria has become.

In Angola, one of the two countries visited by Pope Benedict in March 2009, the conflict between the Catholic Radio Ecclesia and the government has not been solved. This radio station—which has been broadcasting since 1954 and is the most listened-to independent radio station—has for years hosted programs that criticize the government, addressing issues often ignored by other national media: for example, the clashes in the Cabinda region, the conflicts for control over diamond trafficking, and the opposition's policies. This radio station can only broadcast in the Luanda region (that is, the capital of Angola), and for years has unsuccessfully requested authorization to cover the entire national territory. Since the month of November, a number of its programs have been broadcast by Vatican Radio so as to also be heard outside Luanda.

What is obvious is that the Church in Africa has the large membership, a very passionate following, and the inner resilience that comes from the gospel to meet these challenges. Unleashing the inner strength of Catholicism in Africa, and the enthusiasm of African Christians for Christianity, will demand finding a balance between innovation and tradition; contextualization and centralization; and the dynamic cultural creativity in African Christianity, compared to the continuity of the rich history of the Christian faith beyond Africa. This volume aims to help articulate in a systematic way the hopes, dreams, and pathos of many suffering Africans who still continue to hold on to the Christian faith as the only thing that will never fail them, even as many other things around them continue to display signs of instability and decay.

Bibliography

Achtemeier, Paul J., et al. *Introducing the New Testament: Its Literature and Theology.* Grand Rapids: Eerdmans, 2001.
Ackerman, Stephen D. "How information and communication technologies impact female entrepreneurs in India and Ghana." Master's thesis, Long Island University, The Brooklyn Center, 2008. ProQuest (AAT 1449013).
Adebowale, Akande. "Nigeria Latest." *OneWorld.Net* (12 Nov 2006) 6.
"African Experts Meet in Gabon to Discuss Trafficking of Children, Women." *BBC Monitoring Africa* (9 May 2006) 1.
"Agency Warns of Online Abuse." *The Bangkok Post* (7 Dec 2005) 1.
Agger, B. "The Dialectic of Deindustrialization: An Essay on Advanced Capitalism." In *Critical Theory and Public Life*, edited by J. Forester, 3–21. Cambridge: MIT, 1985.
Akpa, C. S. "Gender Inequality and Fundamental Rights of Women Among the Nenwe People of Igboland." BA thesis, University of Calabar, 2001.
Akujobi, Remi. "Yesterday You Were Divorced. Today I Am a Widow: An Appraisal of Widowhood Practices and the Effects on the Psyche of Widows in Africa." *Gender & Behaviour* 7.2 (Dec 2009) 2457–68.
"An Alternative Strategy for Africa's Sustainable Economic Development: The Case for a Non-NEPAD Approach." 1–36. Online: www.macua.org/kofi.pdf.
Amadiume, Ifi. *Male Daughters, Female Husbands: Gender and Sex in an African Society.* London: Zed, 1987.
Amakwe, Mary, and John Bosco Ebere. "Factors Influencing the Mobility of Women to Leadership and Management Position in Media Industry in Nigeria." PhD diss., Faculty of Social Sciences, Pontifical Gregorian University, Rome, 2006.
Anoush, Simon. "Women's Perceptions of Technological Change in the Information Society." *Aslib Proceedings* 58 (2006) 476–87.
Armstrong, Nancy. "The Gender Bind: Women and the Disciplines." *Genders* 3 (1988) 1–23.
Arthur, Kwame Boafo. "Tackling Africa's Developmental Dilemmas: Is Globalization the Answer?" *Journal of Third World Studies* 20 (2003) 27–54.
Asimeng-Boabene, Lewis. "Gender Inequity in Science and Mathematics Education in Africa: The Causes, Consequences, and Solutions." *Education* 126 (2006) 711–29.
Augustine of Hippo. *St. Augustine: Homilies on the Gospel of John; Homilies on the First Epistle of John; Soliloquies by St. Augustine.* Nicene and Post-Nicene Fathers of the Christian Church. Edited by Philip Schaff. Grand Rapids: Christian Classics Ethereal Library. Online: http://www.ccel.org/ccel/schaff/npnf107.
Ball, David Mark. *"I Am" in John's Gospel: Literary Function, Background and Theological Implications.* Sheffield, UK: Sheffield Academic, 1996.

Bibliography

Barclay, William. *Gospel of Matthew*. Vol. 1. Edinburgh: Saint Andrew, 1956.
Barth, Fredrik, ed. *Ethnic Groups and Boundaries*. Boston: Little, Brown, 1969.
Bauckham, Richard. *God Crucified: Monotheism and Christology in the New Testament*. Grand Rapids, MI: Eerdmans, 1998.
Baum, Gregory. "From Solidarity to Resistance." In *Intersecting Voices: Critical Theologies in a Land of Diversity*, edited by Don Schweitzer and Derek Simon, 49–66. Ottawa: Novalis, 2006.
———. "The Meaning of Hope in Evil Times." *ARC* 20 (1992) 79–83.
Bawaba, Al. "African Appreciation for Tunisian Experience in the Areas of Women and Youth." *Tunis Afrique Presse* (23 January 2010) 1.
Beasley-Murray, G. R. *Gospel of Life: Theology in the Fourth Gospel*. Peabody, MA: Hendrickson, 1991.
Bediako, Kwame. *Jesus and the Gospel in Africa*. Maryknoll, NY: Orbis, 2004.
Benedict XVI. "Discourse to the Clergy of the Diocese of Rome, 2 March 2006." *L'Osservatore Romano* (English edition), 15 March 2006, 7. Rome: Vatican Press.
———. *Jesus of Nazareth*. New York: Doubleday, 2007.
Beutler, J., and R. T. Fortuna, eds. *The Shepherd Discourse of John 10 and its Context: Studies by Members of the Johannine Writings Seminar*. Cambridge: Cambridge University Press, 1991.
Bhasin, Kamla. "Women and Communication Alternatives: Hope for the Next Century." *Media Development* 41.2 (1994) 4–7.
Bishops of Southern Africa. "World Cup Cloaks Human Trafficking." 28 May 2010. No pages. Online: http://www.zenit.org/article-29399?l=english.
"Blue Money." *Guardian* (27 May 1999) 5.
Bock, Darrell L. *Luke 1:1—9:50*. Baker Exegetical Commentary on the New Testament. Grand Rapids: Baker, 1994.
Bovee, Chantal, et al. "Computer Attitudes of Primary and Secondary Students in South Africa." *Computers in Human Behaviour* 23 (2007) 1762–76.
Brackley, Dean. *The Call for Discernment*. New York: Crossroad, 2004.
Brown, Raymond. *An Introduction to the New Testament*. New York: Doubleday, 1997.
———. *The Gospel according to John I–XII*. The Anchor Bible. Garden City, NY: Doubleday, 1966.
Browne, Maura, et al., eds. *The African Synod: Documents, Reflections and Perspectives*. Maryknoll, NY: Orbis, 1996.
Bujo, Benezet. *African Theology in its Social Context*. Eugene, OR: Wipf & Stock, 2006.
———. *Christmas: God Becomes Man in Africa*. Nairobi: Paulines Africa, 1998.
Cahill, Lisa Sowle. *Family: A Christian Social Perspective*. Minneapolis: Fortress, 2000.
Capdevila, Gustavo. "Right: Nigeria Cited as Major Source of Trafficked Girls." *Global Information Network* (27 May 2002) 1.
Chazan, Naomi, et al. *Politics and Society in Contemporary Africa*. 2nd ed. Colorado: Rienner, 1992.
Cheung, Denise M.Y. "An Empowering Global Discourse? Information Communication Technology (ICT), Media and Women's Empowerment in the Beijing Platform for Action and its Review." 18 January 2001, 1–11. Online: http://www.antenna.nl/viio/paper-denise-2001.html.
Chinweizu. *The West and the Rest of Us*. London: Nok, 1978.

Bibliography

Chinye, Stella Chiemeka. "Gender Issues and Information Technology in Nigeria." Paper presented at the International Conference on Women in Engineering and Sciences (ICWES), Ottawa, Canada, 2002.
Coalition Against Trafficking in Women. "Pimps and Predators on the Internet—Globalizing the Sexual Exploitation of Women and Children." 1999, 1–4. Online: http://blue-fox.com/nepal.
Concerned Women for America (CWA). "CWA Helps Sponsor Briefing on the Harms of Pornography." *Targeted News Service* (7 June 2010) 1.
Costello, John E. *John Macmurray: A Biography*. Edinburgh: Floris, 2002.
Cromwell, David. Review of *The Compassionate Revolution: Radical Politics and Buddhism*, by David Edwards. *medialens* (7 Feb 2000). No pages. Online: http://www.medialens.org/articles/book_reviews/dc_de_compassionate_revolution.html.
Curry Jansen, Susan. "Gender and the Information Society: A Socially Structured Silence." *Journal of Communication* 39 (1989) 196–215.
Davenport, F. Garvin. "Machines and Sexual Ambience in James Agee's *A Death in the Family*." In *Beyond the Two Cultures: Essays on Science, Technology, and Literature*, edited by J. W. Slade and J. Y Lee, 227–39. Ames, IA: Iowa State University Press, 1990.
Davies, Desmond. "Whither African Renaissance?" *West Africa* (Dec 1999) 13–19.
Davies, W. D. "The Johannine 'Signs' of Jesus." In *A Companion to John: Readings in Johannine Theology*, edited by Michael J. Taylor, 91–115. New York: Alba, 1977.
De la Potterie, Ignace. *The Hour of Jesus: The Passion and the Resurrection of Jesus according to John: Text and Spirit*. Translated by Dom Gregory Murray. Slough, UK: St. Paul, 1989.
Der, Ngoya. "Female Education in Mathematics and Sciences." Paper presented at the International Conference on Women in Engineering and Sciences (ICWES), Ottawa, Canada, 2002.
Dickson, Martin. "All in a Good Cause—CAMFED INTERNATIONAL: FT Readers Have Donated 529,000 Pounds to a Charity that Tackles Poverty in Africa." *Financial Times* (27 Jan 2007) 2.
Dodd, A. Aileen. "Forum on Internet Pornography." *The Atlanta Journal-Constitution* (14 April 2006) 1–3.
Dube, Musa. *Postcolonial Feminist Interpretation of the Bible*. St. Louis: Chalice, 2000.
Dunn, James D. G., and John W. Rogerson, eds. *Eerdmans Commentary on the Bible*. Grand Rapids: Eerdmans, 2003.
Dutton, W. H., and M. Peltu. *Information and Communication Technologies: Visions and Realities*. Oxford and New York: Oxford University Press, 1996.
Eagan, Margery. "Porn in the USA: Women's Groups Take Sides." *Boston Herald* (10 June 2010) 10.
Ebigbo, P. O. "Child Abuse in Africa: Nigeria as Focus." *International Journal of Early Childhood* 35 (2003) 95–106.
Effah-Chukwuma, Josephine, and Ngozi Osarenren. *Beyond Boundaries: Violence Against Women in Nigeria*. Lagos: Mbeyi, 2001.
Ela, Jean-Marc. *African Cry*. Translated by Robert R. Barr. Maryknoll, NY: Orbis, 1986.
Elijah, Obayelu A., and I. Ogunlade. "Analysis of the Uses of Information and Communication Technology for Gender Empowerment and Sustainable Poverty Alleviation in Nigeria." *International Journal of Education and Development using Information and Communication Technology* 2 (2006) 1–14.

Elli, Georgiadou, et al. "Women's ICT Career Choices: Four Cross-cultural Case Studies." *Multicultural Education & Technology Journal* 3 (2009) 279.

Elliot, Larry. "A Cure that is Worse than the Disease." *Guardian Weekly* (24–30 Jan 2002) 14.

Ellul, Jacques. *The Technological Bluff.* Translated by Geoffrey W. Bromiley. Grand Rapids: Eerdmans, 1990.

"Ethiopia: African Women Urge Strengthening of Affirmative Action." *BBC Monitoring Africa* (15 Oct 2004) 1.

Federation for African Women Educationalists. "Girls Locked out of Science Course." 2000. No pages. Online: http://www.allafrica.com.

Federation of Asian Bishops' Conferences and Taiwan's Episcopal Conference. "Asian Conference Laments Exploitation of Women." 17 June 2010. No pages. Online: http://www.xt3.com/library/view.php?id=3031&categoryId=38.

Fitzgerald, Valpy. "The Economics of Liberation Theology." In *The Cambridge Companion to Liberation Theology,* edited by Christopher Rowland. Cambridge: Cambridge University Press, 1999.

Fitzmyer, Joseph A. "The Composition of Luke, Chapter 9." In *Perspectives on Luke—Acts,* edited by Charles H. Talbert, 139–52. Edinburgh: T. & T. Clark, 1978.

Flannery, Austin, ed. *Vatican Council II.* Bandra, Mumbai: St. Paul's, 1975.

Friedman, Thomas. *The Lexus and the Olive Tree.* New York: Anchor, 2000.

Frissen, V. "Trapped in Electronic Cages? Gender and New Information Technologies in the Public and Private Domain: An Overview of Research." *Mass Culture and Society* 14 (1992) 31–49.

Garcia, Ramilo Chat. "Empowering Women in the Global Information Era." Paper Presented at the Conference on Vision for Asia-Pacific Women in the Information of the 21st Century—Women's Status and Communication Technology Information Era, Seoul, Korea, November 1998. Online: http://www.isiswomen.org/womenet/indes.html.

Getui, Mary. "The Place and Role of Women in African Theology." *African Christian Studies* 19.3 (2003) 19.

Gibellini, Rosino, ed. *Paths of African Theology.* New York: Orbis, 1994.

Gillard, Hazel, et al. "ICT Inclusion and Gender: Tensions in Narratives of Network Engineer Training." *Information Society* 23 (2007) 19.

Goar, Carol. "Protectionism's Fresh Appeal." *Toronto Star* (5 June 2006) A. 16.

Goergen, Donald J. "The Quest for the Christ of Africa." *African Christian Studies* 17 (2001) 1.

Golding, P., and G. Murdock. "Unequal Information: Access and Exclusion in the New Communication Market Place." In *New Communication Technologies and the Public Interest: Comparative Perspectives on Policy Change,* edited by M. Ferguson, 83–91. London: Sage, 1986.

Gonzalez, Justo L. *The Changing Shape of Church History.* St Louis: Chalice, 2002.

Grant, Brian W. *The Social Structure of Christian Families.* St. Louis: Chalice, 2000.

Gregory the Great. "Letter to Abbot Mellitus." In *The Christian Faith,* edited by J. Neuner and J. Depuis, n.1102. New York: Alba, 1982.

Gremillion, Joseph. *The Gospel of Peace and Justice.* Maryknoll, NY: Orbis, 1976.

Griffiths, Mark. "Sex on the Internet: Observations and Implications for Internet Sex Addiction." *The Journal of Sex Research* 38 (2001) 331–40.

Grover, J. Z. "Muddy Waters." *Women's Review of Books* 13.8 (May 1996) 1–4.

Haffajee, Ferial. "Midwives Behind African Renaissance Incorporated." *Electronic Mail and Guardian* (7 Oct 1998) 10.
Hamelink, Cees J. "New Information and Communication Technologies, Social Development and Cultural Change." Discussion paper DP86, UNRISD, Geneva, 1997.
Harrison, Christine. "Cyperspace and Child Abuse Images: A Feminist Perspective." *Affilia* 21 (2006) 365.
Hasiuk, Mark. "Porn Awards Show Fuels Misogyny, Adds to Death Culture; Former Porn Actress Helps Women Exit Pornography Industry." *Vancouver Courier* (9 June 2010) 7.
Hay, Charles, J. "The Bible and the Outsider." Toronto: Inter-Church Committee for Refugees, 1996.
Hick, Douglas. *Inequality and Christian Ethics*. Cambridge: Cambridge University Press, 2000.
Hillman, James. *The Myth of Analysis*. New York: Harper & Row, 1972.
Howard-Brook, Wes. *John's Gospel and the Renewal of the Church*. Maryknoll, NY: Orbis, 1997.
Hubbard, Ruth. Foreword to *Machina ex Dea: Feminist Perspectives on Technology*, by J. Rothschild, vii–viii. New York: Pergamon, 1983.
Hughes, Donna M. "The Internet and the Global Prostitution Industry." *Women in Action* 72 (1999) 1–5.
———. "Trafficking and Sexual Exploitation on the Internet." *Women in Action* 70 (1997) 3–5.
Huyer, Sophia. "Gender, ICT, and Education." 2003, 1–47. Online: http://www.wigsat.org/engenderedICT.pdf.
Ihonovbere, Julius O. *Africa and the New World Order*. New York: Lang, 2000.
Ikenga-Metuh, Emefie. *Comparative Studies of African Traditional Religions*. Onitsha, Nigeria: Imico, 1987.
Ilesanmi, Simeon O. "Leave No Poor Behind: Globalization and the Imperative of Socio-Economic and Development Rights from an African Perspective." *Journal of Religious Studies* 32 (2004) 71–92.
Ilo, Stan Chu. "The Condition of African Women: A Religio-Anthropological Critique." *The Face of Africa with Stan Chu Ilo*. 2006. Online: http//www.civilizationoflove.org.
———. *The Face of Africa: Looking Beyond the Shadows*. Ibadan, Nigeria: Spectrum, 2008.
Imhanlahimi, E. O., and F. E. Eloebhose. "Problems and Prospects of Women's Access to Science and Technology Education in Nigeria." *College Student Journal* 40 (2006) 583–88.
International Finance Corporation. *The Business of Health in Africa*. Online: http://www.ifc.org/ifcext/healthinafrica.nsf/Content/FullReport.
Jaffer, Mehru. "Europe's Bollywood Mania: Swooning Over Shah Rukh." *Women's Feature Service* (New Delhi) (3 March 2008). http://www.wfsnews.org/.
Janovicek, Nancy. "Women's Rights," *Labour* 63 (Spring 2009) 336.
John Paul II. *Ecclesia in Africa*. Vatican City: Libreria Editrice Vaticana, 1995.
———. "Homily at the Opening Liturgy of the Special Assembly for Africa of the Synod of Bishops." 10 April 1994.
Johnson, Paul. *A History of Christianity*. New York: Atheneum, 1976.
Kanyandago, Peter, ed. *Marginalised Africa: An International Perspective*. Nairobi: Paulines, 2002.

Bibliography

Kappelman, Todd. "Marshall McLuhan: 'The Medium is the Message.'" Plano: Probe Ministries, 2001. No pages. Online: http://www.leaderu.com/orgs/probe/docs/mcluhan.html.

Kayamba, Mwanja. "Female Entrepreneurs' Cellular Phone Habits in Zambia and South Africa." Master's thesis, University of South Africa, 2008. ProQuest (AAT 0669086).

Kerr, Fergus, ed. *Contemplating Aquinas: On the Varieties of Interpretation*. Notre Dame: University of Notre Dame Press, 2003.

King, Alyson, and Avi Hyman. "Women's Studies and the Internet: A Future with a History." *Resources for Feminist Studies* 27 (1999) 1–7.

Kirkpatrick, Frank. *Community: A Trinity of Models*. Washington, DC: Georgetown University Press, 1986.

Klie, Shannon. "IT Shortage Provides Opportunity for Women" *Canadian HR Reporter* 19 (18 Dec 2006) 10.

Kombe, Gilbert, et al. "Highly Active Anti-retroviral Treatment as a Bridge Towards Education for All in Sub-Saharan Africa." *International Social Science Journal* (Paris) 57 (Dec 2005) 609.

Kramarae, Cherry. *Technology and Women's Voices*. London: Taylor & Francis, 1988.

Kuipers, Giselinde. "The Social Construction of Digital Danger: Debating, Defusing and Inflating the Moral Dangers of Online Humor and Pornography in the Netherlands and the United States." *New Media & Society* 8 (June 2006) 379–401.

LaFraniere, Sharon. "For Girls in Africa, Education is Uphill Fight." *International Herald Tribune* (23 Dec 2005) 1.

Lane, Elizabeth Lawley. *Computers and the Communication of Gender*. 1993. No pages. Online: http://www.itcs.com/elawley/gender.html.

Legge, Marilyn. "Building Inclusive Communities of Life." In *Intersecting Voices: Critical Theologies in a Land of Diversity*, edited by Donald Schweitzer and Derek Simon, 285–304. Ottawa: Novalis, 2004.

Levitin, Teresa, et al. "A Woman is 58% of a Man." *Psychology Today* 6 (1973) 89–92.

Lewis, Arthur W. *The Theory of Economic Growth*. London: Allen & Unwin, 1954.

Linn, Pam. "Gender Stereotypes, Technology Stereotypes." *Radical Science Journal* 19 (1987) 127–51.

M2. "ITU: ITU launches Multipurpose Telecentre Initiative in Africa; 20 African Counties to be Focus of Project that will Empower Women." *M2 Presswire* (10 Jan 2005) 1–2.

M2. "UN: Secretary General Calls for Transformation in Men's Attitudes to End All Forms of Violence Against Women." *M2 Presswire* (25 Nov 2003) 1.

Macmurray, John. *Persons in Relation*. New York: Humanity, 1999.

Malherbe, Abraham J., and Wayne A. Meeks, eds. *The Future of Christology*. Minneapolis: Fortress, 1993.

Mangatu, Naomi Mawia. "Beyond the Glass Ceiling: A Phenomenological Study of Women Managers in the Kenyan Banking Industry." PhD thesis, University of Phoenix, 2010. ProQuest (AAT 3407443).

Matera, Frank J. "The Future of Catholic Biblical Scholarship: Balance and Proportion." *Nova et Vetera* 4.1 (Winter 2006) 120–32.

———. *New Testament Christology*. Louisville: Westminster John Knox, 1999.

Mbarika, Victor W. A., et al. "IT Education and Workforce Participation: A New Era for Women in Kenya?" *Information Society* 23 (2007) 1.

Mbeki, Thabo. "Thabo Mbeki Speaks at the United Nations University, Tokyo." 9 April 1998. No pages. Online: http://www.unu.edu/unupress/mbeki.html.
Mbiti, John S. *African Religions and Philosophy*. London: Heinemann Educational, 1969.
McCormick, Richard, SJ. "The Social Responsibility of the Christian." *Blueprint for Social Justice* 52.3 (Nov 1998) 1–3.
McEneaney, Elizabeth H. "The Worldwide Cachet of Scientific Literacy." *Comparative Education Review* 47 (2003) 221–37.
McLuhan, Marshall. *The Medium is the Massage*. New York: Bantam, 1967.
Menzies, Heather. "Janus Project Workshop—New Learning Technology and Women-Proceedings." Part 1 of 6. Montreal, Quebec, 21–22 March 1997.
"Microsoft Vista Available in Hausa, Igbo, Yoruba before December." Online: http://odili.net/news/source/2007/feb/14/801.html.
Mohamed, Adam Azzain. "Three Types of Conflict in the Darfur Crisis." *Horn of Africa Bulletin*, March 2007.
Mohrlang, R. "Love." In *Dictionary of Paul and His Letters*, edited by Gerald F. Hawthorne and Ralph P. Martin, 576. Leicester: InterVarsity, 1993.
Moloney Francis J. *Sacra Pagina: The Gospel of John*. Sacra Pagina Series, vol. 4. Collegeville, MN: Liturgical, 1998.
Mottin-Sylla, M. "Use of Electronic Communication for Women's Rights." 1998. Online: http://www.globalknowledge.org/english/archives/mailarchieves/gkd/home.html.
Mugambi, J. N. K., and Laurenti Magesa, eds. *Jesus in African Christianity: Experimentation and Diversity in African Christology*. Nairobi: Acton, 1998.
Mulama, Joyce. "Africa: A Rural-urban Digital Divide Challenges African Women." *Global Information Network* (15 Feb 2007) 1.
Ndukaeze, Nwabueze. "From 'Ori Akwu' to 'Odozi Akwu': Impact of Changing Status of Nigerian Women on Family Welfare." In *Women and Social Change in Nigeria*, edited by Olurode Lai, 93–107. Lagos: Unity, 1990.
Ndukwe, E. "The Roles of Telecommunications in National Development." Paper presented at the nineteenth annual Omolayole management lecture at the Chartered Institute of Bankers' Auditorium, Victoria Island, Lagos, December, 5, 2003.
Njeru, Shastry. "Information and Communication Technology (ICT), Gender, and Peacebuilding in Africa: A Case of Missed Connections." *Peace and Conflict Review* 3.2 (2009) 32–40.
Nnoromele, S. C. "Representing the African Woman: Subjectivity and Self in the Joys of Motherhood." *Critique* 43 (2002) 178–90.
Northern, Deborah. *Gender Issues* (2002) 1–55. Online: http://www.fiuc.org/esap/MWANZ/MWANZ8/General/Northern.
Nyamiti, Charles. *Jesus Christ, the Ancestor of Humankind: Methodological and Trinitarian Foundations*. Nairobi: Catholic University of Eastern Africa, 2005.
Nyerere, Julius. "The Church's Role in Society." In *A Reader in African Christian Theology*, edited by John Parrat, 109–19. London: SPCK, 1987.
Oduaran, A. B. "Building Women's Capacity for National Development in Nigeria." *Convergence* 30 (1997) 60–70.
Ogbonnaya, Joseph. *The Contemporary Nigerian Church and the Search for Social Justice in Nigeria*. ThM thesis, Toronto School of Theology, 2005.
Ojakaminor, Efeturi. *Nigeria's Ghana-Must-Go Republic Happenings*. Iperu-Remo, Nigeria: Ambassador, 2004.

Bibliography

Ojokoh, B. A. "Empowering Nigerian Women Using Information Technology: Practical Strategies." *EAF Journal* 20.1 (2009) 58.

Okumu, Victor, OSB. "A Christo-Pastoral Response to Suffering and Evil in Africa: Aylward Shorter's 'Jesus and Witch Doctors.'" *African Christian Studies* 21.2 (2005) 5–47.

Oldenkamp, Evelyn. "Pornography, the Internet and Student-to-Student Sexual Harassment—a Dilemma Resolved with Title VII and Title IX." *Duke Journal of Gender Law and Policy* 4.1 (1997) 159–69.

Olori, Toye. "Rights-Nigeria: Life Sentence for Human Traffickers." *Global Information Network* (28 July 2003) 1.

Olupona, Jacob, ed. *African Traditional Religions in Contemporary Society*. New York: Paragon, 1991.

Olurode, Lai, ed. *Women and Social Change in Nigeria*. Lagos: Unity, 1990.

Onyeneke, A. African Traditional Institutions and the Christian Church: A Sociological Prologue to Christian Inculturation. Enugu: Snaap, 1993.

Osinulu, C. "The Social Contribution of Women to National Development: An Anthropological Approach." Paper presented at the NAUW (National Association of University Women) Conference on the Contribution of Women to National Development, Lagos, June 1990.

Ott, Craig, and Harod A. Netland, ed. *Globalizing Theology: Belief and Practice in an Era of World Christianity*. Grand Rapids: Baker Academic, 2006.

Oyelaran-Oyeyinka, Banji, and Foluso Adeyinka. "Technology and Women in Nigeria." In *Nigerian Women in Society and Development*, edited by Amadu Sesay and Adetanwa Odebiyi, 164–78. Ibadan: Dokun, 1998.

Oyewumi, O. *The Invention of Women: Making an African Sense of Western Gender Discourses*. Minneapolis: University of Minnesota Press, 1997.

Parrinder, Geoffery. *African Traditional Religion*. Connecticut: Greenwood, 1976.

Perkins, Pheme. "The Gospel according to John." In *The New Jerome Biblical Commentary*, edited by Raymond E. Brown *et al*, 942–85. Upper Saddle River, NJ: Prentice-Hall, 1990.

Philpot, Catherine. "Intergroup Apologies and Forgiveness." PhD diss., University of Queensland, 2006.

Pierli, Francesco, *et al.*, "Ethnicity and Human Development: The Missing Link." In *Ethnicity: Blessing or Curse*, edited by Albert de Jong, 32–45. Nairobi: Paulines, 1999.

Pitt, Lisa. "Masculinities@work: Gender Inequality and the New Media Industries." *Feminist Media Studies* 3 (2003) 379–82.

Pobee, John Samuel, ed. *Exploring Afro-Christology*. Frankfurt: Lang, 1992.

Pollock, Genevieve. "What to do about Pornography (Part 1)." 24 June 2010. No pages. Online: http://www.zenit.org.

Postman, Neil. *Technopoly: The Surrender of Culture to Technology*. New York: Vintage, 1993.

Prebisch, Raul. *The Economic Development of Latin America and Its Principal Problems*. New York: United Nations, 1950.

Rahner, Karl. *The Church After the Council*. Montreal: Palm, 1966.

Ravendran, Anuja. "ICT Training for Women." *Computimes Malaysia* (New York) (16 Sept 2002) 1–2.

Ray, Carina. "The Sex Trade in Colonial West Africa." *New African* (Nov 2006) 62–65.

Bibliography

Ribeiro, G. L. "Cybercultural Politics: Political Activism at a Distance in a Transnational World." In *Cultures of Politics, Politics of Cultures*, edited by S. E. Alvarez et al., 325-52. Boulder: Westview, 1998.

Roberts, Bill. "Dirty Little Secret." *Electronic Business, Highlands Ranch* 32.7 (July 2006) 7-30.

Robins, Melinda B. "Are African Women Online Just ICT Consumers?" *Gazette* 64 (2002) 235-49.

Robinson, James. "Business & Media: Girlie Mags Must Stay Abreast of the Net." *The Observer* (London) (11 Sept 2005), 8.

Rolheiser, Ronald. *Against an Infinite Horizon: The Finger of God in Our Everyday Lives*. New York: Crossroad, 2001.

Romero, Simon. "When Villages Go Global: How a Byte of Knowledge Can Be Dangerous Too." *New York Times* (4 May 2000).

Rossetto, L. "Why *Wired*?" *Wired* Premiere Issue (1993) 10.

Rowland, Christopher, ed. *The Cambridge Companion to Liberation Theology*. Cambridge: Cambridge University Press, 1999.

SABC. Office of the Executive Deputy President. "The African Renaissance Statement of Deputy President Thabo Mbeki." Gallagher Estate, 13 August 1998. No pages. Online: http://www.africanrevolution.org/

Sandomirsky, Natalie. "Benin Empire: Oba Ewuare, Trade with the Portuguese." In *Encyclopedia of African History*, vol. 1, edited by Kevin Shillington, 134-42. New York: Taylor & Francis, 2005.

Sanks, T. Howland. *Salt, Leaven and Light: The Community Called Church*. New York: Crossroad, 2007

Schillebeeckx, Edward. *Church: The Human Story of God*. New York: Crossroad, 1990.

Schineller, Peter. "Inculturation and the Issue of Syncretism: What is the Real Issue?" In *Evangelization in Africa in the Third Millenium: Challenges and Prospects*, edited by Justin Ukpong et al. Port Harcourt: CIWA, 1992.

Schokel, Luis Alonso. *The Inspired Word: Scripture in the Light of Language and Literature*. Translated by Francis Martin. Montreal: Palm, 1965.

Schreiter, Robert J., ed. *Faces of Jesus in Africa*. New York: Orbis, 1996.

Second Committee on Human Development and Civil Society. "Countries Emerging from Conflict: Lessons on Partnership in Post-Conflict Reconstruction, Rehabilitation and Reintegration." Addis Ababa, Ethiopia, 2003.

Sherman, A. "Claiming Cyberspace: Five Myths that are Keeping Women Offline." *M2* 6 (1997) 26-28

Shorter, Alyward. *Christianity and the African Imagination*. Nairobi: Paulines, 1996.

———. *Jesus and the Witchdoctor: An Approach to Healing and Wholeness*. London: Chapman, 1985.

Siew, Susan, and Wang Lay Kim. "Do New Communication Technologies Improve the Status of Women?" *Media Asia* 23.2 (1996) 74-78.

Sinclair, C. *Net Chick*. New York: Holt, 1996.

Smalls, F. Romall. "Unequal Access." *Scholastic News* 75 (5 March 2007) 4-7.

Smith, Mark. "Tackling the Tech Gender Gap." *Technology & Learning* 26 (Jan 2006) 1-2.

Spencer, Dale. *Nattering on the Net: Women, Power and Cyberspace*. Canada: Garamond, 1997.

Sprenger, P. "The Porn Pioneers." *Guardian* (30 Sept 1999) 2-3.

Bibliography

Stark, Rodney. *Discovering God: The Origins of the Great Religions and the Evolution of Belief.* New York: HarperOne, 2007.

———. *The Rise of Christianity: How the Obscure, Marginal Jesus Movement Became the Dominant Religious Force.* Princeton: Princeton University Press, 1997.

Stark, Rodney, and Roger Finke. *Acts of Faith: Explaining the Human Side of Religion.* Los Angeles: University of California Press, 2000.

Stern, Steven E., and Alysia D. Handel. "Sexuality and Mass Media: The Historical Context of Psychology's Reaction to Sexuality on the Internet (Part 1 of 2)." *The Journal of Sex Research* 38.4 (2001) 283–94.

Sternberg, Meir. *The Poetics of Biblical Narrative: Ideological Literature and the Drama of Reading.* Bloomington: Indiana University Press, 1985.

Stinton, Diane B. *Jesus of Africa: Voices of Contemporary African Christology.* Maryknoll, NY: Orbis, 2004.

Stoeber, Michael. *Reclaiming Theodicy: Reflections on Suffering, Compassion and Spiritual Transformation.* New York: Palgrave Macmillan, 2005.

Sudarkasa, Niara. "The 'Status of Women' in Indigenous African Societies." In *Reading Gender in Africa*, edited by Andrea Cornwall, 25–31. Indiana: Currey, 2005.

Sylvestre, Tetchiada. "Development: Cameroon Women Seek Freedom through Technology." *Global Information Network* (1 Feb 2005) 2.

Synod of Bishops. General Secretariat. Second Special Assembly for Africa. *The Church in Africa in Service to Reconciliation, Justice and Peace.* Lineamenta, Vatican City: Libreria Editrice Vaticana, 2006.

Talbert, Charles H. *Reading Luke, A Literary and Theological Commentary on the Third Gospel.* New York: Crossroad, 1982.

———, ed. *Perspectives on Luke–Acts.* Edinburgh: T. & T. Clark, 1978.

Taylor, Diane. "Look Into the Future: Half the World: Women Almost Everywhere Have Fewer Opportunities in Comparison with Those of Men." *Guardian* (3 Sept 2005) 8.

Taylor, Michael, ed. *A Companion to John: Readings in Johannine Theology.* New York: Alba, 1977.

Tetchiada, Sylvestre. "Development: Cameroon Women Seek Freedom through Technology." *Global Information Network* (1 Feb 2005) 1–3.

Thlagale, Buti. "Religion and Renaissance." *Worldwide* (Feb 2000) 16–22.

Tiongson, Mari Luz Quesada. "The State of Women and Media in Asia: An Overview." *Isis International Manila* (Sept 1999) 1–15. Online: http://www.isiswomen.org/womenet/indes.html.

Tunde, Charles Iruonagbe. "Women's Land Rights and the Challenge of Patriarchy: Lessons from Ozalla Community, Edo State, Nigeria." *Gender & Behaviour* 18.1 (2010) 26.

Turkle, Sherry. *Life on the Screen: Identity in the Age of the Internet.* New York: Simon and Schuster, 1995.

Uchem, Rose. *Overcoming Women's Subordination: An Igbo African Christian Perspective—Envisioning an Inclusive Theology with Reference to Women.* Enugu, Nigeria: Snaap, 2002.

UISG (International Union of Superiors General). "Women Religious Mobilize for 2010 World Cup." 2 June 2010. No pages. Online: http://www.religiousindia.org/2010/06/02/women-religious-mobilize-for-2010-world-cup/.

Ukachukwu, Chris Manus. *Christ, the African King.* Frankfurt: Lang, 1993.

Bibliography

UNDP. "Human Development Report (2003)." In *Perspectives on Governance in West Africa: Recommendations and Plan of Action*, by Economic Commission for Africa, 1–33. Accra, Ghana, 2003.

United Nations Fourth World Conference on Women. 1999. Online: http://www.undp.org/fwcw/dawfwcw.html.

Urquhart, Cathy, et al. "ICTs and poverty reduction: A Social Capital and Knowledge Perspective." *Journal of Information Technology* 23.3 (Sept 2008) 203–13.

U.S. Department of State. "Trafficking in Persons Report 2010." No pages. Online: http://www.state.gov/g/tip/rls/tiprpt/2010/.

Utietiang, Bekeh. *Afridentity: Essays on Africa*. Silver Spring: Africa Reads, 2007.

Uzukwu, Elochukwu. "The Birth and Development of A Local Church." In *The African Synod: Documents, Reflections and Perspectives*, edited by Maura Browne et al., 3–8. Maryknoll, NY: Orbis, 1996.

———, ed. *Religion and African Culture*. Enugu, Nigerian: Snaap, 1988.

Walls, Andrew. *Cross-Cultural Process in Christian History*. Maryknoll, NY: Orbis, 2005.

Warnick, Barbara. "Masculinizing the Feminine: Inviting Women On Line Ca. 1997." *Critical Studies in Mass Communication* 16.1 (1999) 1–19.

Webster, Juliet. "Today's Second Sex and Tomorrow's First? Women and Work in the European Information Society." In *The Information Society in Europe: Work and Life in an Age of Globalization*, edited by Ken Ducatel et al., 119–40. Oxford: Rowman & Littlefield, 2000.

Weiss, Daniel. "Porn Feeds Human Trafficking." *Denver Post* (27 Jan 2006) B–07.

Westcott, Brooke Foss. *The Gospel according to St John: The Greek Text with Introduction and Notes*. Vol. 2. Grand Rapids: Eerdmans, 1954.

Winner, Langdon. "Citizen Virtues in a Technological Order." In *The Politics of Knowledge*, edited by Andrew Feenberg and Alastair Hannay, 1–8. Bloomington: University of Indiana Press, 1995.

Witherington, Ben, III. *What Have They Done with Jesus: Beyond Strange Theories and Bad History—Why We Can Trust the Bible*. New York: HarperSanFrancisco, 2006.

"World Information Summit: Forum Calls for 'Cultural Respect.'" *BBC Monitoring Media* (17 Nov 2005) 1–2.

Xinhua News Agency. "10,000 Nigerian Women Trafficked into Italy." 11 January 2002, 1–2. Online: http://quotes.freerealtime.com/dl/frt/N?SA.

Zalot, Josef D. *The Roman Catholic Church and Economic Development in Sub-Saharan Africa*. Maryland: University Press of America, 2002.

Zerwick, Max, and Mary Grosvenor. *A Grammatical Analysis of the Greek New Testament*. Rome: Editrice Pontificio Istituto Biblico, 1996.

Zimmerman, J. "Technology and the Future of Women: Haven't We Met Somewhere Before?" In *Women, Technology and Innovation*, edited by J. Rothschild, 355–67. Oxford: Pergamon, 1982.

Contributors

Alex Ojacor, PhD, is Professor of Religion and Research Method in Religious Studies at Makerere University, Kampala, Uganda. He is also a professor of theology in the Faculty of Theology, National Seminary, Kampala, Uganda. He is the founder and Director of the Children's Educational and Welfare Foundation (Uganda), and a member of the Ugandan Joint Christian Council and the Doctrinal Commission of Uganda Episcopal Conference and the National Spiritual Director of the Uganda Catholic Charismatic Renewal.

Bekeh Ukelina Utietiang is a native of Nigeria. He is a priest of the Diocese of Wheeling-Charleston, West Virginia. Bekeh has a bachelor's degree in Philosophy from the University of Ibadan, Nigeria and a graduate degree in Religion and Culture from The Catholic University of America, Washington DC. He is the author of three books including, *Afridentity: Essays on Africa*; he writes regularly on Religion, politics, and culture for different news media in the United States. Rev. Bekeh is currently the President of Africa Reads Books Inc. and the associate Pastor of St. Margaret Mary Church, Parkersburg, West Virginia.

Ebere Bosco Amakwe, HFSN, is a Nigerian nun and an expert in gender studies. She earned her doctorate on social communication from the Pontifical Gregorian University, Rome. Until recently, she worked as webmaster of www.vidimusdominum.org—a site belonging to the International Union of Superiors General (UISG–women) and Union of Superiors General (USG–men), Rome. Also she was an assistant manager and network administrator of Greenstone website at the Salesian International News Agency, Rome. Sister Amakwe is the author of *The Factors Influencing the Mobility of Women to Leadership and Management Positions in Media Industries in Nigeria*, and has published many articles on women and the media in Africa. She is an assistant professor in the Department of Communication at Seton Hall University, New Jersey, USA.

Emeka Xris Obiezu, OSA, who holds a PhD from University of St Michael's College, Toronto, after studying political theology at Regis College, University of Toronto, is the Permanent Representative of the Order of St. Augustine's NGO at the United Nations. He is a researcher on the intersection of theology and social sciences; the Roman Catholic Church's relations with International Organizations especially the UN; social justice; current dynamics of globalization; religion and violence; and international development discourse. He is the author of *Towards a Politics of Compassion: Socio-political Dimensions of Christian Responses to Suffering.*

Joseph Ogbonnaya, a Nigerian priest, holds three masters degrees in theology, philosophy, and philosophical theology. He earned his doctorate in theology from St. Michael's College in the University of Toronto. He is a scholar at the Lonergan Research Institute, Toronto. He is a member of the Association of Christian Therapists and Canadian Association for the Study of International Development. Pastorally, he serves the Igbo (Nigerian) Catholic community in Toronto and also works as a hospital chaplain at Sunnybrook Health Sciences Centre, Toronto, Canada. He is widely published and is a highly sought after speaker on African development, spiritual wholeness and health among others.

Stan Chu Ilo, PhD, E.ED (cand) is Assistant Professor of Religion and Education, University of St. Michael's College in the University of Toronto, Canada. He is the founder and director of Canadian Samaritans for Africa, and the publisher of the online journal of African theology and social justice *theologyinafrica.com*. He is the author of *The Face of Africa: Looking Beyond the Shadows*, and *Aid and Development in Africa and the Role of Churches and Christian Charities in Africa's Social Context: A Creative Appropriation of Catholic Social Ethics.*

www.ingramcontent.com/pod-product-compliance
Lightning Source LLC
Chambersburg PA
CBHW062045220426
43662CB00010B/1666